T0146486

A HOTELIER'S MIND

SETTING STRATEGY FOR THE FUTURE

JEROEN GULICKX

authorHOUSE®

AuthorHouse™
1663 Liberty Drive
Bloomington, IN 47403
www.authorhouse.com
Phone: 1 (800) 839-8640

Published by AuthorHouse   06/03/2016

ISBN: 978-1-5246-1185-9 (sc)
ISBN: 978-1-5246-1184-2 (e)

Library of Congress Control Number: 2016908791

Print information available on the last page.

Any people depicted in stock imagery provided by Thinkstock are models,
and such images are being used for illustrative purposes only.
Certain stock imagery © Thinkstock.

This book is printed on acid-free paper.

About the Author

Jeroen Gulickx is a well-traveled hospitality professional with two business degrees and extensive experience within the hotel-and-spa segment.

The main capabilities vary from streamlining cost and operational models to strategy yielding, business development, and marketing and digital marketing.

In 2006, he started Mocinno International, a hospitality consulting company that now has offices and representation in seven countries in Europe, USA, Middle East, Asia, and Russia. The team is focused on delivering incremental revenues for hotels and spas and also develops and strategizes hotel suppliers, using mainly the Six Sigma methodology.

Mocinno International works with a network of highly experienced, energetic, and innovative people based in key locations. The team also leads client or Mocinno-originated projects or concepts.

Jeroen shares his over twenty years of industry knowledge through his blog, or other social media, and speaks in travel, marketing, innovation, or strategy related forums.

Contents

"Don't make a change, make a difference"
Jeroen Gulickx

Introduction

There are many publications and articles that are published these days on what a Hotel General Manager or Operator should and should not do in order to have a successful business. My goal with this book is to share my firsthand experience and the insights I have gained in a way that will make the take-aways easy to make sense out of and implement.

I have passion to protect and educate those who put their heart and soul into running their hotel, whether they own it, manage it or work in it. I want people who read the pages to understand that, we are all in the people business whether that be our employees, our suppliers, our owners and of course our customers and guests. Let's create strong cultures – let's make our workplaces a place to enjoy – let's deliver the best possible customer experience that we can!

I have been fortunate to meet some great people in this industry and as part of the sharing philosophy that this book is based upon, I am sharing some of my favourite published articles and interviews which I hope will bring the insights more to life for the reader.

Whether you are an Operator, a Manager, a Restaurant Manager or someone aspiring to work in a hotel one day, I hope you will not only enjoy reading this book but it is my goal that there will be some insights that I have shared which will help you to deliver a better experience for your customer whether that be internal or external! It is fine to have a strategy but when it is all said and done it all comes down to the final guest experience – whether that be internal or external.

One recent article I wrote for YFS Magazine in the USA, describes the way of thinking that can get anyone inspired to be a part of this fabulous industry and to start something for yourself, enter or continue in an industry that you are passionate about, because passionate people is what this industry needs and is looking for!

Consider this scenario ...

You've got an amazing business idea, and you know it will be a total hit! Now you just need to put it into place and put some cash and time behind it, right?

Not so fast! I want to share my thoughts and personal lessons learned about startup motivation — what it really takes to make it through the early startup stage.

For me, it all began with a passion for travelling, leading to research, teamwork and a recently launched venture (which led to a lot of lessons along the way).

Chasing Inspiration

I founded Mocinno International, a consultancy within the hospitality industry, in 2006. I started my company with an understanding and depth of experience related to the economic difficulties within the travel industry as a result of terrorism, flawed corporate governance and more.

Hotels were suffering, so hotelier's resulted to filling vacancies by dropping room rates, signing large accounts at low rates and signing up aircrews to cover the basic costs of running hotels. This prompted a clear and radical change in operations; cutting down on staffing costs mainly and streamlining guest's offerings.

Fast forward to 2015 and the hotel industry is fighting to hire the skill, knowledge and experience back to adequate levels. Some are succeeding while others focus on shareholder value and financial performance (i.e., EBITDA delivery, which remains a high priority concern). Lessons to be learned, best practices, and all kinds of contingency plans were put into place. A huge learning curve (painful for many, within the industry) followed, but it was certainly useful.

My experiences running Mocinno have solidified three essential startup lessons that you, too, may find useful.

1.   Know (and relate to) your customer:

Knowing your customer is at the core of every successful venture and directly influences the future value of your company. Data, readily available from the Internet, is a great resource to help you decide whether your product or service has market potential.

A great example of actionable data is competitive. Competitors often (unknowingly) give away valuable data, so sign up for their newsletters and subscribe to their feeds. Learn to look beyond the data for clues.

These clues could lead you to a new way of selling or branding or even creating an entirely new market. Can that be done still? Absolutely! It happens every day, and a good marketer will know how to address this kind of opportunity.

Objectively, why would a customer buy your product or service? What can you learn about consumer behavior (in your industry) on the Internet?

The other part, is creating loyalty. Ensure customers feel comfortable with the way you communicate with them. This can often compel them to make another purchase based on an emotional connection, alone. The good old 4 p's of marketing (i.e., Price, Product, Promotion and Place) are not enough. It's time to move forward to content marketing, creating stories and communicating in a compelling lifestyle.

As a travel industry inspired writer or blogger connecting with cultures, design and people worldwide, it becomes easier through these new modes of marketing; primarily storytelling. Sharing stories with customers allows them to learn (and consume your products and services) in an engaging way. Travel and product recommendations then becomes personal, relatable and believable; instead of being selected by a group of office interns with no direct experience in the field.

2. Learn what makes a 'dream team'.

Leadership expert Robin Sharma had said, "The bigger the dream the more important the team." This is true. Startup success is not just up to you. The selection of your "dream team" depends on many factors (e.g., location, availability, skills, experience, etc.). However, not only should you aim to make the best hires, but you should also hire entrepreneurial employees.

A team member with entrepreneurial hunger can make a big difference. They are generally eager to learn and adapt quickly.

Also, don't hire based on skills alone. You'll need to build a team where each member has a solid skill set that contributes to the overall vision in shaping your company. Often you'll see a bunch of friends starting a business together. That could work well, or it can turn very sour. While you may respect someone for social reasons, working with close friends is always not the best choice.

Performance is another important factor when building a startup team. As I mentioned before, only work with people who are driven to perform. There are plenty of skilled people, most of whom prefer a typical employment scenario with steady packages, working hours and a cubicle where they can hang the family photos. There's nothing wrong with that, but it won't help you along the roller coaster ride you'll face as a startup.

Finally, respect and trust your team. This can be accomplished with communication and incentives.

3. Motivate and stay in tune with yourself.

While you're focused on knowing customers and developing a team, perhaps it's time to take a very close look at yourself.

Don't be afraid to take a break, not too long though. I have a personal rule to never skip looking at my goals or making progress on a project for more than two days. This helps me avoid losing track and disrupting workflow.

I have found out that self-motivation has become harder than it was, say 10 to 15 years ago. This is often a result of information overload and the current events of society and the world around us. It's hard not to be constantly reminded of horrendous life events from wars, to natural events like floods, crashes and so forth.

I limit my news consumption to 3 news channels a day: BBC, Le Monde and NOS News (the Dutch in me, wants to stay connected to Holland, even though I have not resided there for a very long time). They are rather neutral and give me a good overview of what's going on in the world.

Recently, I decided to turn off smartphone notifiers; there is just too much negativity. When we are on information overload, bombarded by hard news, we forget that there is so much beauty in the world too.

Just before the Summer of 2015, I decided to take an objective look at how I spent my days in order to decide what I could improve on. It was refreshing, as my mental library was pretty full leading to quick email reads, short conversations, and rushed decisions. I seemed perfectly fine, however time was limited and I was pushed.

The reality is this: a startup, entering or continuing in a new or existing hospitality business requires a lot of energy from you. Start with your personal goals. These are probably pretty clear to you. Your mind and behavior is the key to daily motivation and gaining the drive you need to reach goals.

When it comes to goals, sort and compartmentalize your energy. Not everything can be completed in a very short time. Hospitality is extremely exciting, so it's easy to expend all of your energy in the beginning. Hold on to some of that energy, you will need it down the road too.

Three years ago I started rowing. Similarly, while embarking on entering the hospitality industry, I was so excited and just wanted to get going. My teacher (probably a retired marine) gave me such a hard time. I soon had blisters on my hands and could not work for days because of the muscle pain.

Then one day he said, "Pick a boat, and go solo." I spent two hours trying not to fall into the water. I forgot to focus on technique (the fundamentals I learned early on) and ended up looking like an elephant trying to dance. In contrast, today I am comfortable, focused and I take my time (and yes, I still fall in the water from time to time). But at least I control the boat, and not the other way around.

I hope this book will be an inspiration for many, within and outside the hospitality industry. I will continue to share strategy and innovation, through my blog.

Chapter 1

Hotel Brands
The rise of brand and diversity

The year 2015 and 2016, can easily be recognized as years of rebranding or branding. New hotel brands are popping up like mushrooms. Mainly with one target, to market the Millennials generation with heavy influence and propelled by the Internet. I will write more about the Millennials much later in the book.

A few examples of new brands are AC by Marriott, Virgin Hotels and Tommie Hotels. Another example is the new group of boutique hotels, Indigo Hotels by InterContinental Hotels Group. A recent example is the OE collection by Loews Hotels, a lifestyle collection with focus on original experiences. This immediately follows the new brand of Langham Hotels called Cordis Hotels & Resorts, a brand that unlike the others, is not focused on the Millennial generation.

Hotel companies are obviously feeling the need to serve a customer, whom they don't currently cater for, and who will be the deciding generation of the future.

Branding is a strategic matter; it is the core of any business. The goal of a brand is to create a differentiated and significant presence in the market place.

Creating a brand is like creating a startup company. There is an idea based on market knowledge and an expectation based on facts that there is a need that is currently not fulfilled. That also requires a process, within which the hotel business is based more on feeling than a mission or a goal. Even within the branding, goals for the hotel are not well defined, easy to get off track which allows flexibility in the design or core of the brand. Additionally, and often misunderstood is that creating a brand is not for the now, it is for the future. In short, a brand needs to reflect:

1. A solid motivation for the buyer
2. Credibility
3. An emotional connection
4. A clear message about what the product of service will deliver
5. A strong potential for loyalty
6. Recognition
7. Uniqueness

Hotels are not unique in and of themselves but can be differentiated with design, the services offered, and/or the use of technology. I have learned a lot from the Blue Ocean strategies and innovation. They preach discovered ways not to compete in an existing market but rather finding a new market. Is that even possible within the hotel industry? To answer that, we need to look at how a brand within hotels can be created that can really make a difference to travel in the future.

Creation of the brand

1. Market research and data collection

This is by far a static part of the process. Before defining what your product is really about, you need to base that on much more than gut feeling, common sense, brainstorming or workshop. Data is readily available from the Internet and a brilliant start to what is needed to lay the groundwork for either collecting additional data be it interviews or questionnaires. The main reason for collecting data is to understand the process of how consumers or guests make a decision to choose a hotel. Through this exercise, you will also find opportunity that you never know existed.

2

Collecting data is not industry driven. In fact, most of the great innovations came from learning from other industries and their consumer behavior. Getting stuck in the typical hotel selection process is not wrong, but it will make it harder to find a niche. That niche should be defined as a next step, which is all about defining the core values of your product or service.

Another advantage of collecting data is that all team members start getting involved at a very early stage. Often, team members should be responsible for the creation of the brand step once the core values of the company has been defined, or sometimes even later. Remember how many companies talk about the importance of internal communication? This process is much the same; knowledge, experience and involvement are the key to creating the right base for the creation of the hotel brand.

Without exception, you find clear answers and opportunities in the process of looking for data using online or offline research and interviewing,. The goal has to be specific. A brand should be as uncomplicated as possible and it should carry a clean message.

Another advantage of collecting data, is that once you start defining the brand, you would have identified potentials for future expansion through adding concepts, product variation or adding services at later stage that will keep your guests and customers loyal and interested in your story. This is also important for the marketer, who will be in charge of sales and strategic planning.

Naturally larger companies have the financial resources to do some serious market research. Historical data has often been used to measure behavior of spending or purchasing as well as to find structural changes in the market place over time. This can be used to identify market potentials or even analyze trends. Market research trends are another way of identifying behavior and can often be more successful when looking beyond the Hotel industry itself. For example, what makes Lufthansa successful? How is it possible for them to fly a plane, with sales campaigns to the low cost traveler as well as the first class traveler, while maintaining the same high service levels? Or how did Audi become a trendy, cool premium brand from the old rusty brand that they were years ago? Another popular method, though quite costly, is a proper trend analysis. The analysis can be split into many different elements, like intensity, individuality, affinity and should be measured over time leading up to what the brand is today. This trending analysis is a useful tool for predicting where the service or product should be in five years, for example. Note that none of this research really make sense to conduct without a very skilled team, often outsourced. The objective needs to be extremely clear and should be in line with the company's vision.

2. Define the core values of the company

In many cases, defining the core values is the starting point for a team working on hotel branding. A clear definition of the core values of the brand or company, is essentially needed. Core values are tools that in turn help to create strategy and vision, tools that have to be strictly pursued, internally as well as externally. They don't all have to be set out from the beginning, but can be fully defined and mastered at a later stage. A core value is not a guideline. It is a value that all team members should adhere to when making important decisions, to that ensure one's cohesive direction reaches the company objectives is maintained. Marketers clearly use these in communicating with their consumers as well. Some examples of core values include:

1. Guest happiness first
2. We create wealth by creating profits first
3. Do more with less
4. Pursue growth and learning
5. Build open relationships with communication

Often these core values are communicated online, in annual reports or painted on the walls in a staff lounge. They are a constant reminder of what the company really believes in and strives to promote and what the company wants its team members to further do in their work.

This part of the branding is the basis for strategic decisions and is used for communication with all stakeholders. Even more so, the entire company culture is based on the core values.

3. The Mission

The mission is another part of the creation of the brand, which reflects the purpose of the company. Missions are slightly more difficult to define, yet not of less importance. The mission statement typically has 3 key elements which include: the target customer, the product you are providing that customer and what makes your product unique. The mission statement should answer the following questions: (1) For whom do we do what we do? (2) What do we do? (3) How do we do it? and (4) What is it worth for the stakeholder? A mission statement explains the path to reach company objectives and therefore, should be one that can be fully understood by all stakeholders. It is also often used for setting targets for personnel.

4. Vision Statement

A vision statement should communicate the objective of the company. It answers the question 'what does the company want to become?'. It is in fact, part of the mission. It is long term focus and direction, not too specific and yet not too broad. It should reflect what your business does and how you would like that to affect the consumer or guest. It reflects your appearance to the world.

5. USP AKA Value Proposition

The Unique Selling Point or Value Proposition is one you create to set your hotel apart by creating an experience or product that stands out from your competitors. The hotel industry is not complicated in what it has to offer. However, each individual whose business you are trying to win is different, with different expectations, different ideas, and different backgrounds. In the UK, a 4-star hotel designation is totally meaningless when compared to a 4-star hotel in Dubai. Even though hotel brands can offer a similar size room and all of the standard amenities, it might totally miss guest expectations without offering something unique. This is not to say that all guest expectations need to be exceeded, as that may depend on an individual. Many people choose a hotel for the loyalty points rather than the room size it has to offer. What we do know is that the USP serves as a very important differentiation.

The early days of the '4 P's of marketing', (detailed later in this book) has now made space for content marketing. Content marketing is a way of creating marketing strategy which is based on creating a connection with your guest. That connection is created through differentiation, through highlighting those elements that are incredibly important for the guest. The USP has to appeal to the guest in both short as well as long term. The USP is your personality, and by all means, it should be very personal.

A hotel can have many USPs, but not too many as the message needs to remain clear. You have to first build on your promise. My team recently created a very good example of this. Many hotels are currently struggling with their gyms. Guests often choose a hotel for its gym, whether they use it or not; it is an important factor in hotel selections, particularly long stays. In a recent survey, we tested the use of the gym and found over 60% of women and men who use the gym in the hotel between 7-8 in the morning and/or 5-7 in the evening. This lends itself to machines not being readily available, refreshments out of water, queues, etc. We found that more than 70% of women don't want to use a gym when it is located in a small dirty room at the end of the corridor where they do not feel safe. As a result, we created the 1Sq Meter Gym with Casall, a Swedish fitness and clothing company. It includes a number of machines and fitness tools that fit into 1 square meter, that can be added to hotel rooms. It was created to train all muscles of the body. It even comes with an app that can be set to whatever time the guest requires. Upon check in or at time of booking, a guest who is looking for exactly that can choose this room, and you can charge a premium for that room. This is potentially amazing USP, as you can market your hotel as the cool, healthy option on the block furthering the concept of exercise and promotes good sleep and health.

6. Tagline

Not all brands have a tagline, but I strongly advise creating one. A tagline is created by combining a few words that strengthen and support the brand name. The tagline should be special or specific and serve to identify a product or service.

The tagline is often remembered by consumers and seen as fun, or particularly even weird sometimes. A tagline is extremely important in marketing as it delivers the first part of a story that the marketer needs in order to create a content. The tagline is to be short, explanatory, be about your company delivery and simple.

7. Creation of the Brand Personality

This often is one of the harder steps within the branding process. It requires deep understanding of why the brand is created, and often even by whom, and definitely, for whom. Just like humans speak, think, act and behave, a brand needs to do the same. These characteristics help to ensure that a team, marketers and all involved communicate in the same and identifiable manner. This will lead to a deeper relationship with the consumer and that leads to loyalty and sales.

Some typical examples of brand personality characteristics include: fun, exciting, creative, and trustworthy. To be more successful, make sure to create a brand personality with a unique voice - not an echo.

8. Brand Identity

Finally, an important part of branding for hotels includes the name, design, the logo or symbol, and color schemes. You guessed it, brand identity needs to reflect all of the above values and traits. It is the representation of your company. Consumers see it before you even have a chance to talk to them and certainly before you have the opportunity to show them more. Brand identity opens doors and must create interest.

This representation of your brand should show purpose, passion, strength and above all, value.

In a recent interview with Barak Hirschowitz, President of the International Luxury Hotel Association, I asked about his expectations of hotel brands, operations, and what he feels are important factors that will influence the future. Indeed, all elements that should be taken into consideration when creating a brand.

Interview: Barak Hirschowitz President of the International Luxury Hotel Association

1. Please tell us about the objectives of the International Luxury Hotel Association?

    Answer: Our vision is to become the pre-eminent association promoting, unifying and advancing the luxury hotel industry. We hope to achieve this by providing insight, opinion and research to executives and professionals in the business.

2. We will see a continued growth in the diversification of brands, what impact will that have on setting Hotel Strategies?

    Answer: No. Independent and soft brands are ranking top of online reviews in many major cities by a large margin. The trend towards diversification that was strong two years ago has reversed because of this. In the past, affluent travelers relied on the consistency that brands offer. Today they are less brand loyal use easily accessible online reviews to see which hotels are delivering. Hotels need a strategy that focus less on promoting the brand and more on ensuring the property is providing authentic experiences and personalized service that will drive its reviews higher.

3. What influence are large Corporate Brands having on actual Hotel operations?

Answer: Big hotel brands can bring enterprise level resources and trainings along with corporate culture. But they need to realize that travelers care less about the brand name and more about the hotels total experience. This is good for the industry, it puts the emphasis back on service and less on big money marketing. The brands also need to keep a close eye on those properties whose online reputation is not stellar as it will weigh on the rest of the group.

4. Which departments within Hotel Operations will see the biggest change and why?

   Answer: HR – it's now vital that hotels recruit the top talent, train them and retain them. Bad service damages online reputation quicker than any other factor and great service drives it up.

5. What does the shift to online bookings mean to Hotel Strategies?

   Answer: That online reputation and transparency will continue to be the top decision-making factor in the luxury segment.

6. How can Senior Management adapt to the quickly changing market segmentation?

   Answer: Go local. Luxury hotels that provide authentic experience based on their local or regional market will continue to do well. There was a time when the affluent traveler sought a common consistency as they traveled the world. Leading luxury brands would provide a similar food, design and décor across their properties regardless of where they were. Today a New York hotel should provide an authentic New York experience while in Manila the focus should be on that region.

7. What would you suggest is the best way to keep up to date and action change with regards to Technology?

Answer: The ILHA covers tech trends and best practices at our events and through our online resources.

8. What other industries do you feel we can learn most from and why?

    Answer: The cruise industry provides a great template for how to take ownership for your guests through technology. They provide an active engagement program that starts the day they make their reservation and continues right through their stay.

9. What can Hotel Owners expect from the future, will hotels remain a lucrative investment?

    Answer: Yes, especially in the luxury segment. According to last year's BCG report, todays affluent travelers spend almost double on luxury experience including travel over luxury goods. That is a seismic change and bodes well for the hotel industry.

10. What is your view on attracting highly qualified staff within Hospitality and what is the best way forward?

    Answer: The most successful hotels have always seen their team as the most important asset. Those that invest in their people first will see a higher retention and stronger reputation. Retention is important, people pay attention to those companies that have a high turnover than those that don't and the stars will always gravitate towards those with the best reputation.

Branding for Hotels

As a very frequent traveler, I noticed that I am potentially the most annoying person to travel with as I tend to think about every department - every service element, the brand, the site and so much more - and quietly bring some of those things to the table, only if I am asked of course. I have experienced a lot of the large hotel brands and have set my expectations accordingly. I am clearly not a good example of the typical traveler, the booker of guest.

In branding for hotels, there are a number of aspects to consider which make branding extremely important - even more important than for a product. First, travel needs planning. Before a trip is booked, the traveler primarily reviews the hotel online, spending a considerable time before the actual consumption of the product. After a booking is made there is still opportunity to cancel it, to review it on sites like Tripadvisor, or get feedback from friends and family. The stronger the connection with the brand is, the stronger the brand story, the greater the chance the guest will book, confirm and stay! Secondly, travel or hospitality cannot be tested or tried like a product. It is a service, and every experience or visit will be different. Sure the bed might be the same as it was on the first visit, the bathroom amenities and the breakfast similar, but the experience will be different. There will be a different person checking you in or serving the coffee. Lastly, it's important to know that the guest actually wants to experience something different, something local, and also feel the safety of the brand or story.

So when we go back to the 7 elements that a brand should reflect, and we understand we are selling something much more complicated than a product, how are hotels currently performing? Is the brand driving the value to the bottom line?

The team and I have seen and educated many on core values, revenue, marketing which is all to do with branding. Large corporations like Hilton, Starwood or Marriott have huge teams allocated just to branding. They understand the value and also the financial result. Much research has been done on what financial impact a solid brand has on the bottom line. The brand type is directly associated with a higher occupancy, and also a higher average rate. This is also the case for the size of the brand, take Nike or example which creates security through the availability of the brand in numerous stores and also flag ship stores. Also I have seen that hotel brands aiming for a cheaper market segment score higher in guest satisfaction than the expensive hotel brands. The reason is that the expectations are lower, and therefore the value of service has more potential to meet or exceed expectations of the guests, creating loyalty the brand.

Branding is complicated; it contains many messages and is of extreme value for any hotel. So what happens to the small hotel chains, or the independent hotels, those who have become so extremely important for the current and future travelers, the millennials and following generations?

What must be understood first is that even though large hotel chains have a large team, that really does not mean their brand is currently improving loyalty, or that the brand team will lead change. In fact, this is far from true. It is becoming harder for hotel chains to manage their brands. The online trend will continue to grow dramatically. And, coupled with the aspects mentioned before, like advanced booking, product differentiation and guest expectations, it will continue to be harder to communicate with the potential or existing guest. Control of booking is at people's fingertips, rather than in the hands of booking agents or large consortia; personal choice and locality are important.

More and more pressure will form on how the brand is communicated, first internally, and then externally. This means that all employees should be fully aware of the brand and its assets, from the accounting department to housekeeping and management. In fact, employees and guests do all the work for you - you just need to listen to ideas, understand behavior, respond, react, develop and implement. Breaking through traditions, of which there are so many in the hotel industry, is the only way to do this. We have seen the importance of guest satisfaction, but more effort needs to be devoted to this even before the guest has actually stayed. That role lies mainly with the marketer. The marketers should understand the market space best and should aim to connect on emotional levels with the potential guests over a long period of time before the stay. Since hotels have a marketing budget allocated to this, which in comparison to products or brands from other industries is extremely low, emphasis needs to focus on content to ultimately create value to the guest. Also, rather than centralizing activities, make sure a solid budget is allocated to branding and marketing is vital for success.

Interview

Stefanie Patch

Managing Director – Patch Music

Your quote on the future of hotel branding

The lines of creativity are blurring more and more these days, which means that there is more crossover between marketing materials, music, interior décor, food and everything else about the brand, achieving stronger and more consistent brands.

1. Please tell us about the objectives of your company Patch Music?

   Answer: Patch Music is about creating soundtracks. This can apply to so many different things, from visual media to spaces or objects. Pairing music to any 'thing', will alter our perception of that 'thing', so it is a very powerful tool to use in branding. We use it for good (not evil!), to spotlight the best parts of our clients, and to make the customers' experience enjoyable.

2. You have incredible experience in Music development, how has the concept of music changed over the years and how does that impact the Hospitality Industry?

   Answer: Music has always been something that everyone can relate to or have emotional connections to, and although styles of music have changed over time, everyone still likes some form of music. So I see the existence of music in society as rather consistent on the whole. What changes, is how we listen to it. Format has evolved rapidly but the point we are currently at with streaming is the most exciting! Despite sometimes feeling bombarded with too many options, there is more music available than ever and it is very accessible. In hospitality, it's very easy now to play a great variety of music and find a really unique sound for the space. As a consumer, it provides more options to dine, travel and stay in places that are more suited to personal taste.

3. What are the core principles of creating a Brand through Music?

   Answer: There are a number of elements to consider, including the visuals associated with the brand (interior and marketing materials), the brand's voice and values, geographic location and targeted demographics. Each element has its own connection to music so it's a matter of finding the right combination and balance.

4. What type of Restaurants or Hotels are currently buying into Music branding and how will that change in the future?

   Answer: I'm noticing more consistency in the music playing in bigger brands and chains (eg. McDonalds or Starbucks). This is thanks to technology that can cover all outlets for one brand. As it becomes more and more accessible, smaller chains and brands will see the benefit.

5. Your Client base varies, from shopping malls, to even parking garages, what can Hotels learn from other industries, other than Music, with regards to Branding?

   Answer: Different music influences different environments greatly, and it is an important consideration to make for brands. Brilliant examples of this are calming music in stressful environments, such as airports, or unintrusive music in cafes. This leads to a positive emotional response for patrons and often a higher rate of return visits. Guest loyalty is a key objective for most hotels and playing appropriate music is a great way to achieve this.

6. How can Hotels establish a relationship with their guests, through Music and smell?

   Answer: Both music and smell connect to very strong human senses and capture emotional response as a memory. With relation to hotels, a unique music experience or pleasant smell will capture a lasting impact for guests. The same familiar music or smell can later trigger memories of a great holiday and take them back to a place they loved. When they hear the song, it plays like a soundtrack to the 'mental movie' in their head, of their holiday.

7. How do you establish the market segment for a client, adjust the Music accordingly and keep being ahead of the game?

Answer: Music trends are often pretty clear before the masses start following so it's easy enough to keep up with new music as it is released and keep clients up to date. If it is the client that changes direction, we come back to considering the key elements (above) and working out what to change in the music. Sometimes it will mean a complete overhaul, other times it'll just be subtle flavors added or removed to the existing music.

8. You have recently been working with Spotify Enterprise to manage some of their clients' playlists, an amazing development for corporate companies. What other type of innovation can you foresee?

Answer: It is indeed a breakthrough for businesses and hospitality being able to legally play music from a huge catalogue, and artists are receiving the royalties they deserve! It will be interesting to see how Spotify Enterprise expands and hopefully the record labels embrace this as an opportunity for artist exposure.

9. Music branding has a clear association with the Generation X and Y, how is Music communicated to the for example the Baby boomers?

Answer: Music branding is a conscious effort for the brand themselves, however the consumers aren't necessarily aware how tailored the music is. People of all ages can connect with music, and if a brand has assessed their demographics correctly then the music they choose to associate with their brand, and the format of delivery, will apply appropriately. For example, a bar targeting clientele under 30 may promote music as part of their events and reputation, and even to the extent of advertising their own playlists to subscribe to on Spotify. However, a restaurant targeting an older crowd, will play less intrusive music and perhaps something more of their clientele's era, and not bother with the interactive technology promotions due to lack of interest.

10. Will the Music industry continue to develop, and how will that impact our daily lives?

Answer: We all like music, perhaps not the same music, but it is in all of our lives to some extent. This will continue until the end of time, however the industry will continue to evolve and grow in different ways. Music Branding is a relatively new concept, despite probably being utilized unintentionally for a long time, so there is a lot of potential for artists and record companies to embrace this. With stronger brand sounds developing, music will have more associations that it may have today, triggering memories and personalizing experiences more and more.

Small hotels, often with their own personalities, have an advantage if that character is communicated well. Of course, online availability and use of technology are key to that communication. Small hotels with only a generic Gmail address are suffering in average rate and occupancy, even when branding and marketing efforts are solid. I have worked with small hotels, luxury and basic, and the impact of branding is tremendous for the bottom line - not to mention the motivation from the employees and enthusiasm of guests.

Branding for the Future

Don't let this be misunderstood; branding is a strategy. The buyer or guest persona is extremely important and has to be understood and supported.

All departments in the hotel must follow the brand otherwise there will be failure. All employees must be involved under leadership of the knowledgeable marketer, who understands where the digital world and online presence is leading us.

Finally, making sure that tools that support branding and marketing efforts are made available is essential. Financial resources for great CRM, online booking tools, yielding and of course, people to make sure these tools are used correctly, are a must. There is no time for mixed messages or useless information. In the age of over-indulgence of information, these will get deleted from the email box, social media and eventually the brain. A manager from Scandinavian airlines sent me a message the other day that they have upgraded their Economy plus package to include a hot towel and that they started using a newly designed mug. Will that message to all loyalty card members actually turn heads or make people pay an additional 500 Euros more? Marketing is about finding the right message for the right consumer.

Start listening and testing the behavior of your buyer or guest persona. A business traveler has a different expectation than a wedding couple, but even though the purpose of the visit is different, they have based the decision to stay with you for a reason or a connection that needs to be understood. The way the hotel reacts to that, should be tested and analyzed. It's not hard, everybody wants to be understood, so just ask or use data to lead you.

Read, watch and learn - a source of inspiration is needed for all employees directly influencing the brand and marketing it. There are numerous blogs, newsletters and books you can read that will impact the way hotel branding is trending. Watch videos. Many companies or individuals share their knowledge online. This is an easy way to identify and showcase opportunities during a break or even morning meeting. You know, when you are at a conference what a video does to your alertness. Capturing essence is key, both in reading and watching videos, and it will deliver a guaranteed impulse in enthusiasm and knowledge.

You need conviction. Dig deeper and test what you have learned.

Lastly and by no means least important, is building relationships. Your guest is the most valuable asset in building your branding strategy. The human touch is already so incredibly important in the service industry, so ensure that your influencers get the recognition they deserve. User Generated Content (UGC), or the leveraging of guest comments and experience is becoming much more valuable than an ad.

Branding has never been so personal.

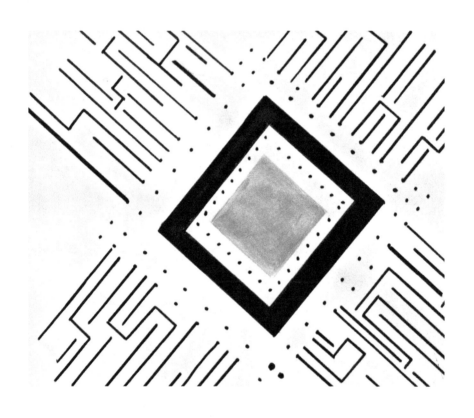

Chapter 2

I Need a Dollar
Data Collection in a New Light

The Change in Data Collection

Two years ago my mentor told me that I should publish a blog. Yes, sure I thought – like I seriously have time for that between the travel, family and fantastic clients that we have and work around the globe. And not to mention that I read too, a lot. I read those stubborn textbooks, graphs, statistics, updates on Six Sigma, marketing, strategy and of course, Time magazine and Quora.

Two years later, I've been thinking this through again and finally now, I will start a blog. It's not that I've ignored social media - don't worry, I'm actually pretty up to date!

Wondering what this has to do with hotel brands? Creativity is not only found in books and innovative ideas. Those are just concepts; and that would be too easy. People create brands through their environments, experiences, and ultimately when they understand their customer. And that's precisely when things start becoming a little tricky. Following others, learning, copying, setting examples, collecting data and opinions, creating content, piloting, understanding generations as well as booking and cleaning trends, are the paths that pave the way to the future.

Information is available. We want it. We need it. And we will start by finding it online.

In this chapter, I will challenge the ordinary and help you understand the importance of getting a hotel strategy right. In the marketing world, new jargon pops up all the time, so let's start with Big Data.

Big Data

The title more or less describes it already. Big Data is data that is large, encompasses numerous sources and pretty much needs an analyst to decipher it. Many hotels or hotel chains have employed such a person, an analyst and those guys are getting it right. When I studied Six Sigma in 2001, I learned more about data than I did in all the years of my marketing career. Not only did I learn about collecting data, but more importantly, I learned about how to use it. You have to remember that I did not grow up with Big Data, in fact, quite the opposite. Internet hadn't been born yet, hotel systems were slow and reports even slower. Companies were perhaps more open in sharing data than they are now, but getting to the right person to collect and share the data was next to impossible. Technology was also not readily available to process the data. It was mostly a manual exercise that took ages and days of queuing for the right book at the library. A library is a place where you can borrow books, for a limited time - remember those? Clearly the Internet revolution quickly replaced all that waiting time and people started sharing and learning from each other. Now, in 2016, there is a wealth of data available from internal as well as external resources. There are numerous institutions in the tourism industry that are available to pass on information. These include tourist centers, regional visitor boards, airports, and even government offices that focus on visitor's data, an important source of income for a country and its many businesses. Competitor data is available online and you can find anything from brand booking rates and occupancy levels. Naturally, data collection encompasses way more than tourist or hotel-related data. This is critical as there is so much to learn from other industries. Consumer behavior is important to discover as well as looking into the market segment for your hotel. So, if your hotel is a premium brand, make sure to look at other premium brands like Nike, BMW, or Starbucks, for example. These companies have a lot of valuable data that can be used to help set strategy for your hotel or hotel chain.

Outsourcing data collection and analysis is a good option when you don't have the knowledge or skills in-house. Though I strongly recommend an employee with this skill for large companies, especially outsourcing remains an option and there is a good selection of companies available for the role.

I recently published an article on data. I wrote it as I was shopping and found more or less the same sign in a number of retail shops. I questioned its use. In the article, I explained the three stages of data collection - pre, during and post - using that experience as an example. I also include some recommendations in choosing the right partner for outsourcing data collection and analysis solutions.

Article

Jeroen Gulickx

www.4hoteliers.com

Measuring guest satisfaction, think again!

Get your hands on data that can help you make real strategic decisions.

One of the cores of most businesses is guest or consumer satisfaction leading to loyalty. To be able to fully understand behavior of the guests, there are numerous ways of collecting data, data that should be used by management to adjust the marketing and sales strategies. Now whether the information is used in the right way is an entire different story. I would like to focus on the collection of the data.

Image 1. How did you experience our service today?

Rather than starting with the hotel industry, I would like to take an example of another industry. Recently, I walked into one of the largest if not the largest Scandinavian consumer electronics shops. On my way in there, was something that caught my eye, my mind and put an instant question mark on reliable data research.

On the way in was a machine, offering an option to rate the customer service that you received today. Interestingly right and a pretty nice way of showing that there is an interest into what we think after we shopped there.

4 Buttons, the one on the left was dark green, with one of those super smiles on it. The one next to it, light green, that green that reminds you of something natural and hygienic, still smiling, just not as much as his green brother, then there is the orange warning sign, not smiling, a little sad in fact. The red button on the far right is clearly the unhappy guy. So the machine invites you to hit one of the buttons on it. Boom, I am a generous guy, I hit the dark green button or shouldn't I?

In data collection there a 3 phases that should be recognized and followed through:

The pre data collection:
The pre data collection is the base for a good end result. This phase should start with defining goals and objectives of the data collection. Also the

means and the method of the data collection should be agreed. There are many different methods and tools that can be used; each of them can be applied to different ways. Note as well that within the hotel industry, there is incredible data available from all the internal systems, like front office or accounting systems.

Within the first phase, also ensure that data is accurate, stable and can be reproduced. In my example, how many kids do you think walk by and play with these colorful buttons, making the data collection totally inaccurate?

1. Define goals and objectives.

* Collecting data starts with a description of the project:
What is the project?
Is there a problem?
Is there something we can do different to improve a customer's experience?
Is there sudden revenue decrease?
Are there unexpected expenses or is the payroll going up following revenue increase?

* What specific data needs to be collected?
Is there data that is already available, and needs cleaning up to be understood or do we need to collect new data?
What data can be used to best reach solutions to ensure we reach our goals.

* What is the reason or purpose of collecting that exact data? There is an incredible variety of data available, which one serves us best in reaching our goals?

* Changes to be made to reach our goals are always a process and the data collected needs to make sure it reflects and provides insight to how that process can be improved. An example is luggage handling upon guest check in. The issue often is that, when the guest has checked in and has entered the room, they would like the luggage to arrive immediately, as they are ready to go out or take a shower. There are all kinds of data you can collect in this process of finding the source of the issue to ensure that it can be improved. It turns out that communication or to be more exact,

the telephone call between the bellboy and reception is often the issue, relating to the ticket that has been given to the guest.

* Besides collecting useful data, before it is actually collected, you need establish what you will actually use the data for, to avoid mistakes, confusion or unnecessary collection.

* Finally and perhaps a combination of the above, some typical stratification groups should be established:
Who: Which people, groups, departments or organizations are involved?
What: Relevant machines, equipment, technology, products, services or supplies
Where: The typical location of the defect or problem
When: What time of the day, day of the week, or step of the process is involved?

In the example of the buttons at the Electronics shop, why are the buttons there? Are we measuring staff friendliness, speed at check out, availability of products, the interior?

What do we get out of people pressing those buttons; in fact, do we want to catch all of them or just the ones who received personal service?

What insight can this data provide us about the customer who just walked out? And finally can this data be used at all and what is the objective, what are they trying to fix, what part in the process is broken?

> *2. Define the methodology and create clear operational definitions that are equally understood by all involved in the data collection as well as the interpretation of it.*

Operational definitions literally mean to define something specific, like variables or objects in terms of a process. That sounds pretty funny, but when we go back to the example of the Electronics shop, I keep talking about the machine with buttons. These buttons can be visualized in many different ways, they can be small, hardly visible or could look like a computer. I think you know what I mean with buttons, I just need to make absolutely sure that we are talking about the same machine in a data collection process.

The operational definitions tell us how we should measure something, what tool to use and how to document it. This is an important step for the improved team. Remember all of this data collection is aimed to deliver final improvement to your organization or hotel, solving a failure in the process or creating a new or additional service. This is immediately related to the guest or customer. So it might be a good way to ask what they have available. Why not ask a decent sample size of customers how they would like to give feedback on a specific service, perhaps it is an online survey or an app, perhaps they want to share comments or an evaluation with other customers.

Creating clear operational definitions are also important in reducing waste. This means that, the data needed for a change or pilot is true data, supplied by the right source. Data collection should always be cleaned from any waste of information that cannot be used. In the example, we would have to remove all the touches of the buttons by kids as that is not our target market, they are not the right source and they are most likely not informed about the purpose of the data collection in the first place.

The reliability of the data is also important for future data collection or additional data collection that is needed for a change. Often teams go back to old data and adjust the way to collect data, as part of reaching the ultimate desired input.

3. *Understanding the measurement variation*

In a weirder term, measurement variation is actually quite simple. To be able to measure and collect data, you need data that is accurate. Accurate information is needed to establish correct end values. Accuracy can slightly differ, for example, when another person collects the data or a different tool is used. That is totally fine, but the difference between the two occasions of data collection should be as small as possible.

On many occasions, the team looking for a solution needs to go back or wants to go back to collect more data in exactly the same way it was collected the first time. Sometimes however, the data needs to be collected in another way to make sure that defects are removed. An example is the color of the buttons on the machine at the Electronics shop. I am not sure if you have noticed, but they start the dark Green (positive) button on the left. That is rather unusual, as I can imagine most people would expect that on the right instead. That seems more logical and in this case can cause confusion. They could switch the buttons to make the actions repeatable, but most do it in such a way that variation is small, and is explained well.

There are clearly benefits in continuing data collection, or going back to data, tools or means of collection. Again the deviation should be as small as possible. Further data collection can show variations because of some kind of action that has happened and can be both positive and negative. The beauty of measuring data is that you can react fast and make the appropriate changes, repeating the great and the positive while removing the root cause of problems.

During data collection

Data collection is a vital step in the path to making the right decision, and creating or adjusting a company strategy. Data collection is a valuable process and to ensure that the results are 100% accurate, the data collection should be followed through totally, in an allocated time span.

The actual data collection is very often a challenge. After you have established who should be asked and how the data should be collected, the actual collection commences.

4. *Taking the path of collecting data*

What is vital in this step is to inform all members of staff, what is going to be done, why it is important to support the data collection and what will be done with the information after. The support of your staff will help the process tremendously, but also they can assist in handing out forms, explaining machines and tools. They are the ones facing the people they collect from, or are implementing the collection. They will be able to explain reasons for the data collection and answer questions about the survey, form or machine.

Within the hotel industry, data collection is a very normal and accessible activity. Every day people are checking in with a lot of their personal data, passport, email address, phone numbers, credit card details and much of such data. When you Google data collection for hotels, over 32 million search results appear. Interestingly, most large hotel chains have updated privacy policies to protect their guests and clients and also clearly indicating what the data can only be used internally.

I have been part of numerous data collections since 2001, some more challenging than others, mainly because of cultural differences. Measuring productivity for example, can be an interesting exercise when a union member follows you around or on one instant even a security guard. What is also amazing is that data collection is such a beautiful and useful exercise and yet, it is done wrongly so many times. Quite a while ago, I came across a restaurant questionnaire. The guest had to fill out ten questions, some open answers, and mostly multiple choice. Personnel handed them out at the end of a dinner. If you have followed me so far, you will start asking questions already, about the reliability of this tool. Indeed, when I looked further into this type of collection, the data was totally useless and even more so, with whatever statistical tool I tried, I could not find any correlation between any of the questions on the form. For example, the question was your dinner value for money, was totally unrelated to the scoring of the service. Again, I am not saying that every form is like that or has to be like that, but it is a warning sign for the use. Other questions you can ask are, is the guest happy to fill this out? Can every answer be read the same? Is the questionnaire only handed to happy guests? Are they also hotel guests? Where are they from? and you can continue forever.

The result of this data collection or survey was astonishingly useless. No correlation, no education, no target subject, no clear operational definitions, no solid objectives, no calculated data collection, no description of the guest or customer and much more. And I remember the boss of the hotel said in front of the executive team; this information is of extreme importance *'it gives us a good indication of how we are doing'*. Until today I am trying to understand what that meant.

Post data collection

Now here is the most interesting part of the data collection. In the many years of hotel consulting, data has been collected; solid data, from systems like Micros Fidelio, accounting systems, loyalty systems and revenue systems, mostly existing data. Follow through of results of data collection is a requirement of success.

Recently I was at a hotel, where all rooms were identical, absolutely no difference in design, look or amenities. The data on revenues and room pricing was readily available in the system. The hotel had an average occupancy of 89% on Mondays, Tuesday and Wednesday nights. The rest of the week, and weekends occupancy was quite a lot less. The data showed the same prices on all days, except the weekend. Now you can start asking questions; can they have higher rates on the high occupancy days? Should they do something to get more long stays? And what are we doing with the pricing on the weekends. How can it be booked, and made visible? When I looked at the data, I also found out that, many guests had requested specific rooms. So when I did a site inspection, I immediately found out why. Half of the rooms was facing the park, a lovely green scene in the middle of the city, on other side, a car park, great if you are a fool for cars, but I am thinking most of us want that green view. The data here showed that the hotel should pilot a different pricing level on rooms with views. A great opportunity based on data already collected on a daily basis.

5. Use it and use it well

The data has been collected with the tools established in the previous chapters. It is now time to enter this data into a collection tool and start analyzing it. There are numerous ways of doing this. In Six Sigma, the information we now have is called raw data. This now needs to be implemented into yet more tools that can ensure that the right and accurate data has been collected and that the process can be repeated without any variation.

In the many years of data collection in the hospitality industry, I have not come across a form of data collection that seems to be entirely watertight. Trustworthy data in our industry is mostly data that is already being collected with the back of house systems that are in place. Some examples are housekeeping, front desk, engineering and inventory systems to name but a few.

I strongly recommend starting there, in house. Depending on what needs to be measured, the improvement team needs to validate the data that can be captured from this data.

There are however numerous companies available to assist with new data collection. You need a professional to ensure that your data collection process is a valuable one. Most of these professional companies use online data collection. Some suggestions to look into are Cendyn or LRAworldwide.

Some of the criteria to consider for outsourcing data collection are:

- I prefer working with E-collection. Online data can be collected at the customer convenience through the web, or an app.
- Make sure that data collected also has a tool that indicates a need for immediate action. Sometimes opportunities can be spotted immediately (low hanging fruit) or in case of dissatisfaction by a customer, immediate action can be implemented to make sure the customer is retained
- Ensure that data collected is complete and that all x's, y's and z's have been crossed off.
- Make sure collection is repeatable at no considerable extra cost. As stated before, there often is a need to repeat data collection which can be a costly exercise
- Ensure the company can support your staff with training or education where needed to both read the data, but also communicate with the customer

- Make sure that data collected can be used not only to read your current guest or customer's experience but also assist in marketing efforts to gain new customers
- Ensure there is feedback possibility, this again helps retain customers and keeps them engaged in the process
- Keeping it personal creates a bond, personal welcome or thank you note from the General Manager for example
- Check and establish the reporting methods used, in some cases reports are not giving the answers you are looking for

Some final words

The example with the Consumer Electronics shop is one from another industry to show you that opportunity is everywhere. You can see these kinds of methods throughout the hospitality industry. Now you know not to just Google restaurant satisfaction questionnaire or hotel satisfaction questionnaire and blindly use any of the 143,000 or so results or images.

Create a plan, a data management plan and use the stages described before as basis of establishing means and tools that can help get to your objectives.

Collecting data is fun, it creates direct contact with your customer, it increases loyalty; your customer wants to be heard in their preferred way. Appreciate and use the information collected wisely as it can make huge difference to your customer's loyalty, personnel engagement and your bottom line improvements.

Which button will you press next time?

The Use of the Data and the Analysis

Now that I have explained some methods on how to collect data, I will go into more detail on how to actually use this data and analysis for hotels.

Revenue Management

The most common data analysis in the hotel industry is revenue management, also called yielding. The revenue manager is now a key role in the management team and is often part of the executive team. Revenue managers are using predictive analysis to manipulate the prices for the rooms. This is an extremely lucrative business, as they understand past trends, current trends, analyze city events and much more, to calculate what price to offer to guests to reach the highest Revenue Per Average Room rate (RevPar). The basis for the pricing is agreed in a so-called budget that is presented yearly to stakeholders and adjusted weekly or monthly in an outlook or forecast report. Note that the revenue forecast can and should also be used in other departments, like meeting & events. Other managers can follow trends closely as it helps them to predict their revenues or costs. For example, housekeeping will use it to predict how many people need to be available on a certain date and a chef can estimate food supply requirements to prepare breakfasts or dinners on specific dates. The sophistication of the revenue manager progressed from excel to some very advanced revenue systems that are based on historical input and human intelligence. The human element will always remain a very important factor but difficult calculations are now automated. Revenue management is an important skill and requires a person's competent in analytics. Data analysis can be applied across many industries like car rental, public transport, museums, spas and even opera houses.

In this book, I will not dive deeper into revenue management as entire books are available on how to collect and apply data analysis. One opportunity I would like to share though is that, many hotels, small as well as large, independent as well as chains, can and should use data better to control costs. I have given some examples but there are many more, like stock and inventory in food & beverage or of linen and even staffing of service department0s.

Marketing Management or CRM

In the article above, I wrote about data sourcing and outsourcing this function. The reason for outsourcing data collection and analysis is mainly that the skill and knowledge is not available in-house.

I am sure that you have signed up for newsletters. Perhaps you aren't on those lists because you actually specifically chose to sign up, or perhaps you enrolled because there is one single element of the newsletter that is important to you. Often, the main reason for travelers to elect to receive a company newsletter is to keep an eye on the loyalty points. The loyalty points are an incredibly important factor for travelers to choose one hotel or airline over the other. You can also see this trend in retail, particularly in consumer goods.

The challenge and biggest problem for a marketer is to ensure that the information sent out is actually relevant. A great example is a local supermarket chain. I believe we all have one of their cards. They are great in some cases; you get an immediate loyalty discount and in other cases you can use them for discounts on airlines tickets or presents. So, I have one of those cards too. Here is the thing though: I am bombarded by this supermarket's online newsletter. I purposely have not unsubscribed yet because I want to first understand the purpose of the newsletter and second, to see whether they are changing their approach over time. I have been subscribed for seven years and so far I have not been asked my age, my interest, my shopping behavior or any other information that would be useful for their marketer. A loyal customer is someone who has a reason to come back. In this example, that could be someone for whom the supermarket is the closest one or because they have a good selection of organic products, a delicacy counter, or employees who are welcoming and friendly. As a matter of fact, as I am writing this I am getting one of their letters. It is an offer for a discounted *Falukorv*, a weird sausage that the Swedes eat for lunch or dinner. I can buy that for 20 SEK less (about 2 Euros) elsewhere. So what is the expectation of this newsletter? Sure, there might be success in some additional sales of this sausage; there is power in suggestion. But it won't be from me. I will not jump to go buy this product. I might not like it. I might find it too expensive. I might have done my shopping for the week or I am a vegetarian. Actually, I have tasted it and will never buy it again. These are just some examples of why this newsletter is not targeted and potentially wasted on me. This newsletter is actually not creating loyalty, it is creating irritation and it has quite the opposite result of triggering loyalty or an impulse purchase. It is very clear that they have not followed or analyzed my shopping behavior at all when sending this newsletter. I, for example, buy groceries in the evenings, mostly organic and probably buy 90% of the same products regularly and mostly at the same supermarket. And that's just some of my shopping behavior that can be used just by analyzing my current account which still has no personal data other than name and address. Even more to the point, I also receive a magazine at home with all kinds of promotions and recipes. It comes with a plastic cover and is delivered in my physical mailbox irregularly. I admit I have opened it only a few times and since I don't know how to unsubscribe, it mostly ends up in the garbage.

So what has changed over the years with this supermarket card subscription? Absolutely nothing of consequence. It is more regular, the format has changed and recently the point system has been revamped. Other than that, I don't feel special and don't make use of any of their offers, unless it's by coincidence.

The term for managing loyalty is called Customer Relationship Management (CRM). CRM refers to a strategy, through the use of technology and analysis, to oversee customer interactions and data. The goal is to understand customer behavior and build a relationship with them by creating loyalty, driving sales and forging sales growth. I will not go too deep into the methodology as there are many 'how to' books written on this topic. Rather, I want to give you some examples of how this can be applied to hotels - small and large.

The data that hotels have available on guest behavior is endless. From the moment of booking, we already know a customer's address, whether they are male or female and their booking behavior (online directly on hotel site or via a third party booking site or a booking agent). Once checked in and the guest has filled in the check-in form - online with pre check-in or at reception, the hotel has even more data, including reason for stay and age. During the stay, the hotel knows when guests have breakfast, their spending behavior in the restaurant or with room service and even the wine or dish they have chosen. All this raw data can be collected and translated into useful material that is in line with the market segment the company has set for their short and long term objectives.

The data does need to be 'cleaned up' and analyzed, so that it becomes useful for the marketer. With help of this analysis, the marketer can analyze trends and predict the future. This is obviously very useful when thinking about doing special promotions, weekend deals, or upgrades. Another great opportunity is to use social media aimed at your target group; send targeted deals that make sense, offers that are interesting or/and potentially even more important, start building a connection with your market segment with stories (see also the chapter on marketing). By directing marketing efforts to the right people, you will create a true opportunity to develop relationships and make the information you communicate relevant and interesting. There is absolutely nothing worse than just being bombarded with useless property information or promotions that mean absolutely nothing to you. Feed customers with interesting information about your city or happenings in the world that match the interest of your market segment.

Let's go back to the supermarket example. I would love to read something about where the organic lamb comes from, who the farmer is and his story or get an alert on a deal I can expect on Thursday night, my most regular shopping night. How great would it be to get to test a new home delivery service at no extra cost, since I travel a lot? Making an effort to connect with my needs and expectations might even make me try that *Falukorv* again and even change my mind.

Interview
Lola Akinmade Äkerlind
Travel Writer & Photographer
Editor in Chief - Slow Travel

Your quote on the Future of Hotel and Exploration of data
Hotels need more human storytelling voices and less glossy magazine personas. Guests are savvy and aren't easily lured by perfect hotel stock photos. They want to hear human stories, to go behind the scenes, to follow

their food's journey from farm and sea to plate, and to learn what hotels are doing to stay sustainable in creative and innovative ways.

1. Please tell us about the objectives of your company?

   Answer:

   Geotraveler Media Sweden is the umbrella company for all my creative consulting services – from content marketing and generation to editorial work, photography, social media campaigns, and other digital services that help travel brands and destinations reach their target audiences.

2. You travel the world, collecting data for major Hotel chains, and being involved in the content marketing. How do you feel the Hotel industry is adjusting to follow this trend of active data collection?

   Answer:

   The hotel and its services need to seamlessly wrap around the customer. By analyzing and harnessing big data about your customer wisely, the smartest hotels have used this data to build engaging relationships with their customers. The customers do not only stay at the property and possibly review their experiences on sites like TripAdvisor, they come back and actively engage with the brands on social media. From specific hashtags which build a sense of community and belonging to participating in Twitter chats hosted by the hotel brand. It is all about engaging your customers that organically grows them into brand ambassadors. For example, Four Seasons Hotels & Resorts uses hashtags such as #FSTaste for food & drink and #FSFamily for family experiences so its customers can share and rally around those themes to create a sense of community.

3. What are the core principles of creating a Brand through content marketing?

Answer: For me, it's all about consistency, community, and creativity. You want to create and market content that is consistent in terms of quality and style so that even if it changes direction in terms of subject matter, people still recognize the brand in the messaging. Building community is important and this could involve crowdsourcing of information and data so customers feel invested in the brand, and of course, creativity in terms of staying fresh and relevant in this new digital age.

4. What can hotels do to improve the use of Data Collection?

Answer:

Hotels need to mine data in a smart way that not only connects them to their customers' preferences but actually to their customers' daily rituals and routines. They need to start getting to the level of knowing, not only if the customer wants a hotel with a gym, but actually if their customers get up early for morning jogs and how they can make that experience as seamless for the customer as possible by delivering suggested jogging routes, monitoring tools, gear, etc. even before they check in.

5. You are a busy writer, blogger and photographer. Within Hotels there is an incredible enthusiasm and need, what are the key skills for a person to be able to transfer your experiences to manageable materials?

Answer:

Hotels should continue to look to external influencers, writers, and photographers to bring a more authentic voice and unique storytelling beyond beautiful brochure pictures. Guests are savvy and aren't easily lured anymore by the perfect hotel stock photo. They want to hear human voices and stories, they want to go behind the scenes, and learn more about the journey the food takes from its source to their plates, they want to learn more about the people and staff that work at the hotel, and they want to learn more about what hotels are doing to be sustainable in creative and innovative ways. Hotels need more human storytelling voices and less glossy magazine personas.

6. How can Hotels establish a relationship with their guests through content marketing and use of photography?

Answer:

As I've mentioned above, by creating an engaging community where guests can tag and share their content as well and feel part of the tribe as it were. Hotels can crowdsource advice, run chats to directly engage, regularly feature and spotlight guests, and make it more about uplifting the guest and their experiences organically as a natural ambassador for the brand.

7. Besides the actual use and applications of the content, photography and online presence, what should hotels build into their Strategy related to this?

Answer:

Hotels should have dedicated budgets put aside for online engagement and social media outreach and amplification through campaigns and by working with travel influencers and digital storytellers.

8. As a frequent traveler yourself, what ways do you feel Hotels can be more effective within communicating directly with you, and what are the privacy challenges in that?

Answer:

As I've mentioned, hotels need to smartly analyze their guest data so they can connect on a more personal level with the guests even before they ever check in. I remember a wonderful experience with The Milestone luxury hotel in London where I was sent a simple form to fill out before I arrived at the property with a ton of preferences with questions like:

- Which of the following items may we place in your room? Feather pillows, foam pillows, neck support pillow, printer for laptop, trouser press, humidifier, etc.
- What are your hobbies/interests/favorite colors/favorite cocktails, etc.
- Asking if they could pre-book a personal trainer, English afternoon tea, make dinner reservations, etc.

All before I ever arrived and checked in at the hotel. Hotels need to form relationships with guests by learning their preferences and continually communicating with them using those preferences long after they've checked out. The goal is to have guests become your natural brand champions

9. Branding within Hospitality is highly associated with the recognition of the many generations. What part does Social Media take in that, and will market segmentation be enough?

Answer:

Social media is here to stay. It will evolve and mutate to flow with the ways we choose to discover and consume information but for the most part, it is here to stay. Brands who are not actively using any form of social media or adding it to their business strategy risk becoming isolated, obscure, and left behind. Social media can also easily hijack your brand and brand message, so hotels need to be actively involved in various social media channels to make sure they are monitoring their brand message.

10. Content marketing is often misunderstood as being a stand-alone effort within Hotels. What are some tips of how Senior Management can ensure that it is a part of the entire Strategy?

Answer:

This ties back to the fact that guests and consumers are becoming more and more savvy in their needs, requirements, and tastes. They want true and authentic stories they can connect with and so digital content marketing and storytelling should be an integral part of a hotel's marketing strategy.

The Best Source: Your Employee and Guest

Your best assets naturally, are your employee who deal with your guests' day after day. The tangible data streaming from technology from your guests is endless and extremely valuable. There is, however, still another way to get great data; through interviewing. This method is not used so often because it is time sensitive and hard to interpret and measure.

That said, the employee is such an amazing source of data. Employees experience the hotel operations daily. Ask them how they feel and what feedback they get from guests, highlight issues, listen for ideas and ask about the other departments. Note that getting responses from employees should not go unseen or unrewarded. Make sure employees receive recognition for their feedback and that at least some of the ideas are implemented so that they remain motivated. Remember the data they provide is of extreme value and should be taken seriously, even though it may require a lot of filtering.

Guests themselves can also provide similar information. I remember back then, when I worked in hotel operations and we had organized a loyalty cocktail evening once a week for our VIP guests. The goals were to show our appreciation for the business, to create a personal connection, and finally to get feedback and information. I believe it was highly appreciated by the guests but we missed an opportunity. I truly cannot remember one occasion where information was actually used to make a change or to improve a performance. Again, guests love it when you ask them what they believe should be improved, and most of your guests want their opinions heard and want follow up.

Controlling Cost

The rather boring and yet so very important data to collect is all about costs. Costs abounds; costs of linen in housekeeping, glassware breakage, energy costs, and the highest cost for all hotels personnel costs. Data collection around cost allows you to better manage costs and even create other benefits. A cost controller is a role that can often be found in hotels. There are many ways to make controlling costs fun and rewarding for employees. Often it helps to do some cross training and to make it an objective process. A very simple example of this can be found in the staff canteen, a cost that is among the most typically annoying, no matter how good the quality, people will complain about the food. One hotel decided to change this by getting all employees to better understand the cost of food by having employees rotate to work in the kitchen for the staff canteen for a week. This turned out to be extremely fun. This particular hotel had over 30 nationalities working there. So when this started, a lady from Lebanon decided she would theme the entire week with Lebanese food and even brought flags from home. She started a trend that of her country's themed weeks. It created understanding of costs, happiness, interest in cultures, and overall excitement. It resulted in a slight cost decrease, fewer complaints and added a fun element to the work environment.

Another great example can be found after analyzing data costs on the use of linen in housekeeping. In an effort to decrease cleaning cost and inventory, one hotel sent some members of the housekeeping and accounting teams to the outsourced supplier company for two days. Their mission was to better understand the delivery process and cleaning process. Within a month following their visit, they had changed the delivery process which led to better control of the stock, less waste and two fewer deliveries a week. By controlling stock, the hotel managed to work with four towel sets in the cleaning process instead of six. One set was in house, one in transport, one in the cleaning process and one in delivery back to the hotel. The cost saving was in stock and in deliveries. While not a huge cost on its face, added up over a year, it made a significant change to the bottom line.

My last example has to do with data collection and psychology. In one restaurant, a serious wine connoisseur created a wine list in a very popular hotel and focused primarily on ensuring the right and best wines were available, disregarding costs slightly. When we looked into it, we found the costs for the top five wines sold were more or less the same, but the revenue (or price to the guest) differed. We also found out that the wine that was the second least expensive on the menu was the one that was most popular. We changed the wine list slightly by adding a wine with a lower cost to the restaurant and priced it as the second least expensive on the list. Turns out guests kept choosing that one, increasing our profit margin significantly. The psychology was that the guest did not want to choose the cheapest wine, rather the next one on the list, so as not to not seem too cheap.

As you can see, cost data can be fun and managing costs can be highly effective.

Data is Sexy

There is a wealth of data available to hotels. Opportunity can be found in every department. The aim of collecting the data is primarily to understand whether there is opportunity for growth in revenue and a decrease in cost. Eventually though, the underlying goal is to bring up your guest satisfaction rating. As you have seen, guest satisfaction will create loyalty, and then opportunity in revenue and occupancy increase.

Data is sexy. Data is invigorating, it will energize your hotel and give new direction to the hotel strategy.

Chapter 3

Eat Me
Opportunities in F&B

The quest for finesse, flavors, and atmosphere continues for hotels and their many restaurants, bars and room service challenges and opportunities. The financial opportunity is to make sure that the hotel guest stays and eats at the hotel and to get people from outside to come in and eat. In this chapter I will not bother you with all the standard chatter about who should eat what, why hamburgers are still so popular with hotel guests, or why minibars will never be a profitable ancillary. I will also stay away from dwelling on the expensive water bottles in the gym or the standard and ridiculous umbrella drinks at the pool. Rather, I will tell you what trends you should be looking for and offer a bit of help for the development of your next bar or restaurant.

Fighting Corporate Standards

How successful are hotel restaurant actually? I have seen and eaten in many. I have enjoyed some, but am mostly disappointed. I often find empty tables, a corporate concept coming from a disconnected management, and prices that are almost laughable. I remember when I was young and the hotel chain I worked for offered me, as an employee, an amazing low cost opportunity to test some of the best 5-star hotels in the world. Service, table clothes, incredible silverware were the norm in the restaurants and bars. They were great to look at but a little too costly for most; perhaps appropriate for one night out of a 5-night stay. For the remainder I wanted to experience the atmosphere of the city, taste the buzz of the town, and get food that was affordable and good. So what is this race for perfection all about? Must hotels have a restaurant that matches the 5-star hotel rating, and what is the definition, look and feel of such a restaurant?

I once stayed at one particular hotel in Los Angeles, which, at the time, was one of the first to offer all of the 'advanced technical stuff' in the room. With a touch of the button you could open curtains, turn on and off lights, get in touch with the concierge, or book a ride into town in one of those oversized luxury vehicles. All fun, and trust me, I tested every button at least once if not more. I then opened the big leather folder on the desk to see what services they offered, what restaurants they had, and what bar would be great for an afternoon drink. The restaurant offered a story about the history of the hotel, and so did the bar. The information even showed which celebrities had eaten or had a drink there, which got me curious. I made a reservation at the restaurant for later that afternoon, after returning from some serious CD shopping (yes, they sold those at that time, and I am into music). The bar was gorgeous, the design was amazing, and the well-dressed traditional waiters and waitresses looked stunning. There were a few guests sipping on glasses of champagne and being served what looked like an afternoon tea. I sat down with my partner and we were welcomed with class and the menus were presented to us. The menu was old fashioned, sporting a thick and a velvet cover that matched the color decor. I opened my menu but quickly closed it again after making a mental note of the prices. I asked for a couple of glasses of Cabernet, and after a swift moment the waiter returned with the whole bottle, poured a taste into my glass, and explained the wine, the grape and origin. It was a nice experience. It was true luxury. I never looked at the price until we checked out of the hotel, and to be honest, it was irrelevant. The experience was truly one to remember.

The dinner followed in pretty much in the same classy way, with the waitress presenting herself as our host for the evening. After a 5-course tasting menu, we were not only full, but had tasted flavors and their combinations that were beyond beautiful. The piano player enticed even me to be quiet during dinner. The dinner had cost us more than the 5-night stay, but it was well worth it - every dollar. The hotel had delivered and exceeded expectations. My needs were met and fulfilled, and I strongly believe a hotel of that class and style will need to offer that experience to those who want it. The question that arises though is does it work for the hotel. Do they make money? I stayed at the hotel for five days and only went to the bar and the restaurant once. Maybe I was not the typical guest, but the atmosphere was special and unique in many ways, and even if I could have afforded it at that time, I don't think I would have been a guest twice. It was overpriced, the restaurant was not busy, and there was nothing that I could really relate to personally, at the bar or elsewhere, that would bring me back repeatedly.

This kind of experience is not rare; quite the contrary is true. Corporate structures create a concept that seemingly should drive revenues. In so doing, they forget the most important element; the guest. I have been in many meetings, workshops, research and data collection efforts, discussing what the guest wants. The result was often the same Italian cuisine, low profile atmosphere, good service (good service... I will come back to that later), and affordable. Clearly, there is not a lot of innovation in reaching these conclusions. For the most part, hotels are running restaurants primarily to serve the most profitable part of the current restaurant operation, the breakfast.

One very important element that is usually totally forgotten, but is starting to see changes in 2016, is around guest choice. The guest decides.

Typically, there is no F&B concept that is developed around the potential guest's need. The restaurant, like any other outlet in the hotel, should be run and developed as a stand-alone. It should be standing on its own feet like any other restaurant down the road. As a concept should be developed that suits a market segment naturally, one should suit the hotel guest too. Leave the bar and restaurant design and concept development to F&B professionals, as, in general, hotel management are simply not equipped with the skill and knowledge required to make the place a real success. It's often a challenge to get a property owner to invest in such a concept, but the return of investment is solid. People rate restaurants online and a mediocre review reflects on the hotel too. Furthermore, the atmosphere and price need to reflect a personality and be affordable enough to encourage a return on several occasions during one stay. A full, happening restaurant bar is more fun to return to then a stiff, standard, typical hotel bar. A hotel bar should reflect an internationally attractive meeting environment, almost like an extension of the lobby. Perhaps the amazing service and the silverware are not so relevant any longer, no matter what generation you want to attract. Guests all want to feel comfortable and feel a buzz, and even when spending is not an issue, prices still need to be fair and reflect good value to encourage return visits.

Developing the Concept

Creating a hotel restaurant or bar concept is a straightforward yet challenging exercise. Even though the steps to creation are simple, the implementation faces many challenges.

It is most important to start with market research to understand what customer your restaurant or bar needs to serve. Data is readily available from other cities, online and offline, as well as from competitors. Finding and defining unique benefits for customers and hotel guests is critical.

Based on the data collected it is vital to highlight a number of unique selling points and values that are of extreme importance to a potential guest. Retaining a hotel guest in the hotel restaurant has always been a serious challenge, and often made even more difficult because breakfast (often buffet) is served in the same space. It can seem rather unpleasant to have breakfast and dinner in the same place. That said, if you do it right and make the experience for dining unique, you will notice changes. In fact, breakfast offers great opportunity for some marketing. Nowadays, in 2016, success is often found in creating a unique selling point directly linked to a local area. It is always a pleasure for any traveler, no matter what generation, to taste something local: be it food, beverage, design, or atmosphere. And, of course, for the local guest, it is nothing but attractive to stay local and yet enjoy the international atmosphere that a hotel can offer. The same strategy can be applied to the hotel bar concept, though more focus should be on making it a round the clock meeting experience for travelers and locals who want to work and meet in an internationally inspired space.

Hotels have also started to bring other cultures or countries to their hotels, no matter where they are located. Offering cultural experiences is currently a trend that will surely continue with the Millennial generation.

The location of the hotel is also an important factor. Is it surrounded by offices? Consider offering the perfect quick lunch concept. Is it in a residential area? You might consider adding a bakery to the restaurant or serving a small breakfast in your bar or on a terrace.

Key in creating the concept and defining the Unique Selling Points (USP's) is to start thinking in advance about marketing. How is the venue different? What can the marketing effort be about now and in the future? What is the story? What value does it deliver? What is the brand name about? Many questions should be asked and answered before deciding on the final USP's.

Once the market has been analyzed and the USP's have been established, the team can move on to select, describe, and develop the theme, the design, and the final concept of the bar and restaurant in detail. The theme chosen should impact the design and selection of equipment for the kitchen and operations. Another and very important element these days are uniforms; they confirm the style and theme of the bar or restaurant. Also keep accessibility in mind. Is there a street entrance and how are the restaurant and hotel reflected? Are people able to valet park, for example (a very uncommon service in Europe but a standard inthe Middle East and many places in the US)? Naturally, the menu created by the Chef should go hand in hand withthis concept development as well.

Great views - Adelina Barphe
Vice President – International Food & Beverage Association
How do you believe a stand-alone restaurant is run differently from those within a Hotel?

Seriously, this is a fascinating question and one of my favorite research topics as well! How an independent restaurant is run differently has always been a hot controversial subject. As an entrepreneur and restaurateur, with a first-hand experience in both operating structures, I may describe both as "Phenomenally alike, yet totally different!" The stand-alone and a hotel restaurant are two different species living and operating in an entirely different ecosystem. We could analyze this forever, but let's focus only on their striking differences such as management, mindset, available resources, and their operating environment and structure.

To begin with, running a stand-alone restaurant requires different management style and skills from running a hotel restaurant. After all, hotels and restaurants are two different businesses, with different operations and visions. When it comes to management styles, of course, there is no right or wrong, it clearly depends on the circumstances and situation you have to manage. However, it seems that flexibility and adaptability in management plays a great role in the bottom line success. Especially in such challenging field as Food & Beverage, where everyone, from personnel to management team, will have to keep engaged and committed to achieving results.

Like most entrepreneurs, the successful restaurateurs have an undying passion and enthusiasm for their business, and most importantly the spirit to do whatever is required to survive and achieve sustainability. They are warriors, with a strong sense of purpose, forward thinking, creative, willing to take risks and try new things, as opposed to F&B management in a hotel who are not necessarily equipped with these entrepreneurial skills and mindset. Even if paradoxically someone would have that kind of mentality would be nearly impossible to create and influence changes within a hotel operation framework.

Specifically, hotel departments and corporate brands have a tendency to impose rigid standardized procedures and behavior. Couple this, with the reporting structure and the centralization of decision-making over just about everything, and we end up with a management style that has a slow reaction time, is inflexible, and unwilling to change. A system which is strictly based on SOP and rule enforcement tends to frustrate and disengage highly skilled and creative employees who strongly resent micromanaging. How far can you go without engagement, creativity, and motivation? Guests' expectations and employees' needs are in a fast-track change in today's environment. Without taking into account these changes, management is setting up to fail.

On the other hand, the management of a stand-alone restaurant is clearly interdependent with the mindset and vision of the entrepreneur. Communicating and sharing this vision on a daily basis keeps everyone aligned and committed. Employees' participation and contribution are much higher. Management focuses more on initiatives and adaptability, giving the team the flexibility needed to try new ways of doing things and experiment. This ability to change, or be changed means everything in grasping new trends and staying ahead of the game.

Moreover, when looking it from a resources perspective, differences are huge. Hotels have inexhaustible gifts, a real horn of plenty, for their outlets. Their restaurants have exceptional resources for marketing and public relations, their advertising and promotions reach national and international scales, the expenditures and operating cost, along with services like cleaning and maintenance, on the other hand, are shared with the hotel, making it considerably cheaper to run. They enjoy preferential pricing from suppliers and vendors; they attract a higher quality workforce, and the list could go on and on.

Despite all this, the F&B department remains the "Achilles' Heel" in most hotels. This obviously raises the question why? Where does the responsibility lie? The truth is that if a restaurant in the real world is not successful and profitable, the whole responsibility lies with the manager or in many cases the owner. That is not the case at hotels. The bad F&B results in a hotel are somehow chopped and sliced in many pieces along the management team. This tendency to feather off the bad results and accept speculations is one of most important factor why this has always been the case with F&B departments. Poor management and operational decision, waste and mishandling are overlooked under the security umbrella of the hotel property and rooms division revenue. Therefore, it actually is the mentality and the comfort zone syndrome that plays the most decisive role here.

It would not be far from reality if we resembled the ecosystem of a stand-alone and a hotel restaurant with the difference between wild animals and domestic. Just imagine their ecosystems. The wild animals running in the wild, free and independent; hunt and fight for their food every day; prepared for the worst; crazy adaptable to external conditions and resources' availability; learn to survive by themselves and cope with difficult conditions and circumstances. On the contrary, domestic animals live in a totally protected and controlled environment; entirely dependent and conformed to their ecosystem where humans provide them with their basic needs, shelter, food, medical care, and more. Altogether, such diversification in the operating environments affects management and the overall attitude of the business.

So getting back to the point, the stand-alone restaurant has to be financially sustainable by itself, or get out of business! As simple as that! It does not have the resources or the "big brother's" support. It has to establish a strong competitive advantage, get beyond conventional approaches, to adapt, adjust and be flexible, to go off mainstream and find creative ways to stay successful and profitable. So yes, this mentality is huge, and it affects everything, and not only the way of managing it. Ironically enough, most hotel brands do not even consider applicants that their experience comes from outside the hotel breeding ecosystem. That is totally absurd! An F&B manager who profitably runs a stand-alone restaurant has a lot more to offer in a hotel if he manages to tackle the system. Even more, hotel operators and F&B management still consider food and beverage outlets as hotel accessories with no particular identity, when in fact restaurateurs and most people consider restaurants as living and breathing characters with their own unique spirit. That generic feeling in hotels reflects on the guest experience and satisfaction! It also remains the primary reason why hotel guests search for that unique experience outside the hotel. Although the last decade we have seen an evolving and increasing trend in the F&B departments through the involvement of restaurateurs in managing hotel restaurants. Many brands and boutique hotels are finally treating their outlets as "stand-alone" destinations. But that is another chapter.

In conclusion, independent restaurants may lack significant resources but in the end, all comes down to the extraordinary passion and perseverance to make it happen. The restaurant industry, unlike F&B outlets within hotels, has embraced over time new and creative approaches, leading the way to an exciting and innovative dining experience. Comparatively, hotel F&Bs have a whole multidimensional mechanism, tools and resources to support them, though, not enough authority to influence changes, not enough power to move that dinosaur! As long as hotel restaurants would be like dinosaurs, nobody will ever manage to move them, at least not fast enough. Unless they change and adapt, unless they are willing to become panthers, jaguars, leopards, or antelopes, making space for these creatures to thrive, it would be unfeasible to get hands on, and stay on the cutting edge of the industry.

Interview
Hai Poh Cheong
General Manager/ Grand Park City Hall
President of International Food & Beverage Association
Chairman Hospitality Alliance Singapore

Quote on future F&B:

"The quality in a product or service is not what you put into it but it is what the customer gets out of it. As consumers become better educated and more affluent, their taste buds and expectations get more sophisticated. Therefore, keep as close as possible to your customers, understand their preferences, needs and expectations, never stop improving on what you already have, keep an open mind to changes according to trends and customers' needs to ensure continuity of your F&B business."

1. Please tell us about the objectives of the IFBA?

   Answer:

   1. To enhance the image of the industry and professionalism level;
   2. To promote educational interests relating to hospitality;
   3. To strengthen knowledge and professionalism in food and beverage (F&B) industry;
   4. To improve work environment and processes;
   5. To create career progression through skills upgrading and development programs;
   6. To increase overall job satisfaction and lifelong employability;
   7. To develop industry communication; and
   8. To create networking opportunities for our members.

2. You have been part of many concept development projects. What is the core to success in creating a concept that will attract hotel guests as well as guests from outside the hotel?

   Answer:

   - Having absolute dedication to understanding and satisfying the needs of guests in well-defined target markets by having a concept that focuses and meets the trend and needs of the market that we want to target.
   - Getting the right people onboard with proper training
   - Being innovative and creative with the ability to expand
   - Product needs to talk and service needs to speak to help our guests see and appreciate the greater value of the brand concept

     to ensure continuity of business
   - Recognition of signature dishes
   - Proper positioning and marketing strategy setting.

3. How do you believe a stand-alone restaurant is run differently from those within a Hotel?

    Answer:

    Stand-alone restaurant should be run differently as the market place of operation is different. Hotel restaurant used to be upfront with their F&B concept but in today's Asian market, independent restaurant is much more creative and innovative in their business unit with the added flexibility to making changes as compared to hotel restaurant where the latter is too much of being guided by SOPs especially those from the international chains.

4. Hotels continue to focus on customer retention. How will the Food & Beverage industry tackle this?

    Answer: We need to constantly reassess and audit current trend and needs of our targeted market especially in view of the cross exchange of generation. More importantly, it is to look at the future expectations of the Food and Beverage industry. Hence, it may even create a revolution in both products and service delivery to meet the new generation's expectations which may include the need to address the business units as well as the business model. It is also important to establish credibility of the brand concept in view of long-term success.

5. There always has been a lot of discussion about the market segmentation, before creating a restaurant concept. What are the key elements to ensure the product matches the market segment?

    Answer:

    Understanding the guests' expectations and preferences of that market segment and creating F&B products that match the target audience instead of producing what the owner or chef likes. Constantly obtain feedback from guests, review products with an open mind of making changes for improvement.

6. What are the some recommendations you can make to the Marketing and Communications team with regards to Food & Beverage within a hotel?

Answer:

It varies by nation. Using social media in today's businesses as a vehicle for advertisement has great potential and many establishments are turning to social media as a vehicle to create product and image awareness, support, educate and market to guests and potential guests. However, the challenge is the marketing effectiveness as compared to traditional media which the latter is deemed more effective. Notwithstanding to this, the advance in social media technology has also heavily impacted traditional media. Advertisement through traditional media is becoming more expensive unless the establishment has the cash flow capability. Hence, it impacts on the positioning of the F&B establishment and business. Both modes of advertisement are equally important and determining the right mode of advertisement for the different purposes will definitely contribute to cost effectiveness and effective marketing of the F&B Products, for example, with the objective of increasing sale, the traditional media appears to work better while social media marketing may work best for creating brand awareness.

7. How do you think technology will impact your area of responsibility most in the future?

Answer:

Although technology plays an important role and certainly impacts today processes, making everything more seamless, convenient and efficient, machines can only perform limited set of functions and are incapable of human interaction. Therefore, it can never replace the people in the industry where the human touch and the engagement amongst people is most necessary.

8. What other industries do you feel the Food & Beverage industry can learn from and why?

Answer:

Education industry – The food & beverage industry encourages employees to constantly acquire new skills and knowledge to upgrade themselves in the highly competitive environment, encourages creativity and innovation and promotes lifelong learning. Therefore, seniors/mentors in the food & beverage industry play an important role in the grooming of new talents and their role is similar to that of the educators in the education industry where they pass down knowledge and skills to their students, constantly motivate them to do better. In the same way that the F&B leaders can groom new talents to ensure the survivability of the F&B industry.

9. What can independent or small Hotel companies do to make an impact on the local market through Food & Beverage?

Answer:

Since independent or small or hotel companies are not restricted by too many guidelines, they have more flexibility and choices in exploring creativity and innovation in developing F&B Menus. As long as it is something that can differentiate them from the rest of their competitors, consumers are naturally drawn.

10. Your skill is a very particular one, and requires much experience. Apart from that what are the skills needed for a team like yours?

Answer:

A "can-do" and positive attitude, the ability o multi-task, must have the initiative - being proactive rather than reactive, keen to learn and always strive for improvement.

Creating the Menu

The key to success of a menu is, you guessed it, to sell with a solid margin. Rather than describing the best way to build or create a menu, I'd rather go into some ideas that will allow you to help guests choose something that is beneficial for the hotel from a cost/revenue/value perspective. Remembering that the quality of food should never be in question and standards should never be compromised, creativity and culture is something that people buy generally.

When I was studying law, yes law, I was taught many ways on how to best use psychology to address legal issues. I have learned a lot from that and I know many are applying psychological techniques in their industries, even in hospitality. Have you ever noticed that when you step into an elevator, and you press the 9th floor but tonto reach your room 931, that that the buttons start with 6th floor? Suddenly you feel you have been downgraded and and are left looking at your fellow passengers proudly pressing the high floor buttons. Of course there is always that one guy who presses the 15th floor button, sigh. That is psychology; the hotel wants you to believe you are on the high floor. That is also the case with the menu. It even has a name; it's called menu engineering. Very smart. So with German precision, a cost calculation is made on each dish, leaving no space for serving three tomatoes instead of the two contemplated and calculated, or for serve 350 grams of beef, where guidelines state 300 grams per serving. Based on that menu engineering the pricing is estimated, which is then followed by the setting, atmosphere, type of service, etc. The wine list is another one of those things that often has to follow corporate standards, or rather limitations, with purchases that can only be made from preferred suppliers, or even worse, a selection of five wines that every branded hotel has to have on its menu.

I strongly believe that we need to let the guest decide. Guests want to taste value and wine that supports the amazing efforts of a chef. A wine deserves the best dish and vice versa. It is costly but the overall experience counts and will be openly discussed online and offline. Again here are specialists who create wine lists and menus and they tend to be well worth hiring. And once menus and wine lists are in place, guests still like to be guided.

It is hard for people to make a choice. The trick is to make guests believe they have been given a choice, by proposing a favorite cocktail or dish, or emphasizing a daily favorite. You can even see the simplification of choice in tapas style menus; the taster of what's available eases the mind without having to choose.

Of course there is also much psychology in the design of the menu. Some of the menus that you come across are so lengthy that the guest has absolutely no idea of where to start or end. At my first job, we offered only a 3-course menu, each with four dishes. With the main course, a choice of three side dishes was served. It was easy, straightforward, and sexy enough that guests loved it. Apart from the drama of trying to fit it all on the tiny dining tables, it was an experience and a choice was given. When a menu is presented to the guest, he or she automatically scans the menu in a reading the Internet-like fashion, the well known Z-shape. The task for the menu designer is to try to find ways that are not too disruptive, yet clear, to direct the guest to a certain dish. A simple of way of doing that is to create a small box, for example, or print it in bold as the favorite. Personally, I like browsing the menu, and I take my time to do so. I like to be inspired. You can learn a lot from a menu and it will lend a professional to quickly surmise the extent of knowledge of the operations team. Is the overall design is attractive? Is it very personal? Even though menus aim to please, it is almost impossible to cater to everybody. Stay in line with the overall theme of the restaurant or bar, and name it accordingly. It should foster an attractive, cultural, and inviting dialogue between the server and guest.

One thing I have to mention: do stay away from the old newspaper style, oversized menus. They beat every aspect of convenience, and after use by one guest they tend to be covered in sauce or other leftovers.

The kids Menu, Are You Serious?
Innovation and creativity are words often used in the hospitality industry, even key words I would say. There is definitely plenty of space for opportunity in every department of our beloved industry. I work with two amazing guys: a Dutchman, Koen Crommentuijn, and a Brit, Carl Mills, both based in Holland. They are geniuses in their understanding

of the needs of children of all ages. Their original idea for their company Stoerr, was to create toys that are attractive, fun, and promote exercise and pedagogy. They create toys that leave the way to use them to the imagination of the kids. Since we met, we have created Kids' Clubs in all over the world. These are not the usual kids' clubs with a few plastic toys, some crayons, a retired playstation and a little splashing area. This is the real stuff that motivates children to stay, to play, to learn, to exercise, and even to understand food & beverage. I have learned a great deal about kids' behavior as well as parents' behaviors.

The typical kid's menu is... well... do I even have to describe it? Is it the parent who chooses from the menu or is it the child? I wonder if it is the parent who chooses the easy way out, not questioning the intensely boring offerings, or if it is the child who does not know any better than the standard. What the guys in Holland have taught me is that children are creative, open, and eager to try and learn no matter what the circumstance or environment.

So why offer kids macaroni and cheese, a hamburger and fries, spaghetti bolognese, or a pizza slice? I have always thought it was wrong, but now I am convinced than ever. Surely parents want to get the kids involved at a table setting and want them to experience and learn about flavors, meals, and cultures. Of course it depends on the restaurant. And of course every parent needs some adult time during dinner and we welcome the IPad in its full glory. But let's get kids involved when we can.

Times are changing, opportunities have been created, and yet we leave the kid's menu exactly where it has been since I was born. Sure, you can guess my answer to the question of 'what do you want to eat' when I was seven years old. But as a adult now, if I'm asked do you want a Volvo or a BMW, I wonder what happened to all the other brands? Perhaps I have other needs or wishes, but the choice is not given to me, let alone the education about the other brands. The Volvo, well, that would be the hamburger and fries, and the BMW, the spaghetti. Eventually kids will ask, 'Dad. What's on your plate'? Why not start the process earlier? Get them involved and let them be a part of the atmosphere. Challenge them and let the server explain a few dishes. Tell them where and who caught the fish that morning or invite them to the kitchen to show them where the food is prepared. The kids' clubs that the Dutch team are developing don't just offer lunch to the kids, they invite them to cook, in a real kitchen. The cooking is simplified but they learn where the produce comes from and they will eat whatever they create. They made it themselves and they are proud, and can boast to Mom and Dad about what they did. Kids get excited to have cooked in a real restaurant kitchen with people in weird white clothes.

I have not even touched upon the healthiness of food and the need to deliver vitamins and minerals needed for the physical health and cognitive abilities for a child. I won't need to write in detail about this need as you can read about that every day in every newspaper.

Personally I even apply my new rules for kids' menus at home by creating a menu three weeks in advance, together with the kids. We choose a country of origin, and google dishes that match that theme. We then create a list of ingredients and when the kids want they are involved in the actual cooking. Trust me, they love it. After all, they created the menu themselves! We even rate the dishes at the end of the seven days and we pick a holiday or weekend to recreate their favorites. This week chowder was the winner, believe it or not!

Back to the restaurant menu... Have you ever tried a small tapas style course for kids, in line with your restaurant philosophy and theme? No doubt a chef would be immensely proud person to create something exciting for those who form our future. A starter, a main, and a dessert will keep them entertained longer, educate them, and will create a pedagogical feeling, pleasurable for both parent and child. And yes, after giving them that experience, feel free to take out the IPad.

Defining good service
Service is pretty much what defines loyalty or lack thereof. Most of the feedback given online is clearly directed at service that a guest has received. Food comes in second place. With loyalty here, I refer to more than just

the guests who are willing to return, but also to those who talk about their experience spread the word by sharing online and offline. People are more effusive these days as writing online is much easier than speaking out in public. That also means online media can spread a bad word at a never-seen-before pace. Comments on restaurant or bar reviews are incredibly important for continued success. This can also be dangerous and even unfair as the public does not understand that not all needs cannot be met, as every person stepping through the door is different, very different. This is true even though all guests come to a restaurant for the same purpose; to have a great experience.

From a restaurant team point of view, the heart of the operation starts in the kitchen. They might not have the direct contact with the guests, but if the kitchen does not operate well, the restaurant is doomed before the guests have even arrived. The kitchen operation is complicated, bearing many responsibilities like planning, purchasing and staffing. The latter is by far the most difficult, as kitchen staff tends to have a large turnover and high training costs, mainly due to the irregular working hours and difficult working conditions. Kitchens are also finding ways to manage these responsibilities by introducing more catering, or home deliveries, and pick up solutions, creating increased volumes and efficiency, leading to manageable and flexible payroll, and improved purchasing costs. The food is at the core of the smile in the restaurant: the innovation, the style, the flavors that communicate pleasure. The perfect plate leads to a serious effort by a server who communicates this excitement forward to the guest. The energy in the kitchen is such an incredibly important factor, the rest of the operation runs on that. Note that famous restaurants are known for their chef, who offers all of the above. In the past, chefs have been under serious scrutiny as many of them are not particularly a pleasure to work for. In my internships and actual jobs I have had in restaurants, it was certainly without exception in that it took me a while to connect with the head chef, even more so in the middle of the peak hours. And for some reason, as I learned the hard way, you can seriously upset a chef by whistling in his or her direct surroundings, but fact remains, they make your product and concept. Without the food, there is no service.

What is service actually? How can it be defined? Service is the delivery of a meaningful value that leads directly to customer loyalty. There are millions of explanations and descriptions, but the core of service is the means of delivery of the expected and unexpected to the guest, coupled with the customer delivery. I like to differentiate those two types of service for a very important reason. This first is proactive while customer service is reactive.

Proactive service is a delivery that follows a standard that is created to suit a certain market segment or a certain style of guest. This means that a cycle needs to be followed to be very successful.

1. Research

Research is needed not only to find your unique selling point for the concept, but more so to define your buyer persona. The person who will pay for your service, whether it is in the hotel, spa, restaurant or bar. The buyer persona has expectations of your promised service. These expectations are mostly measured in qualitative ways which can be met by the hotel, restaurant or bar. They consist of opinions or statements that become the core of the standards that are presented to employees to be followed. Expectations of customers consist of basic or essential expectations, anticipated expectations, and additional or optional expectations. Essential ones are those that form the product delivery that needs to be met to keep a business going. Differentiation of the service starts with the anticipated expectations, those that will make a guest book you and not your competitor. Finally, the additional expectations are those that exceed the others, they deliver more, and therefore exceed the customer's needs.

Research naturally requires much more than just defining expectations. It also requires a good inside marketer and company strategist. We often get requests from clients who have mentally decided what level of service they would like to offer after they defined their concept. It's much harder but more efficient to do this the other way around. Understand what service is expected and then create the concept directly related to the buyer persona. Remember that developing a concept is only a success when you have the customer for it!

2. Definition of guest expectations

You define operational definitions of guest expectations based on the research. These are specific and clear enough for anybody understand. They will also put you in a market classification which should be followed by all the marketing needed to support that classification and definition.

3. Creation of service standards

Once the guest expectations are outlined well, the creation of the service standards starts. They are the standards that should be recognized by the guest, on the first as well as subsequent visits. Remember that if expectations are exceeded once, the expectations are higher for the second visit, and service levels should be amended accordingly to keep the guest loyal and ensure the best marketing, word of mouth.

4. Education

Education of the service and core standards and the company values are the platform of the success. The reality is that consistency is a very difficult goal and can only be reached with solid education and training. In this case, one size should fit all employees. Education is a fast growing source of value or ROI in the hospitality industry. It is no longer a marketing tool; it is a standard. I have seen many presentations by hotels where they explain that they have the best service on the block. In reality and as mentioned, that leaves much space for interpretation. The best service might mean something totally different for one guest than it does for another, and in the end, we have to please and exceed expectations for all.

5. Guest experience

The guest experience is the result of the previous steps and includes the actual delivery. It is rather difficult to define when service starts and ends. My view is that it starts when you first connect with a potential guest. These days that connection tends to be online. The website is a significant factor and should have images that reflect the buyer persona and expectations. The way the site can be navigated, the flow of reservations, the offers, the text, and everything else are the start of a guest's service and expectation journey. As far as I am concerned, the guest experience actually never ends as people will continue to share, online and offline, for many years to come. Read your news. Engaging the guest throughout is much more than an opportunity, it's a must to be successful.

6. Customer service (loyalty and definition of service gaps) - the reactive service

Lastly, and falling into the category reactive service, service that is given to the guest after the stay, through newsletters, surveys and such are also a part of service. React to complaints, reviews, and online feedback. This shows that you care about the guest's opinion. You want to use their valuable information to improve your service and to adjust to levels that make sure you exceed expectations over and over again. Mostly, hotel, restaurant and bar owners use this as a means to keep communication going, but I would like to draw specific attention to actually creating change. You cannot follow every recommendation, but you can often see a trend, where a need becomes even clearer, or where a service standard requires adjusting to meet the needs of guests. You can clearly define the service gap and make sure that gap does not widen or even worse, start to affect loyalty. A service gap does not always have to have a negative effect. It can clearly also be used to start adding or adjusting services to meet existing and new potential guests.

Guest service is a complicated element for hotel operations, and easy to judge or score externally. Don't be mistaken: your staff is the only way to make things happen, so treating, rewarding and incentivizing them is vital.

Interview
Juan Picornell – Owner and CEO GrupoCappuccino

GrupoCappuccino is a high performance chain of exclusive cafés and restaurants, based in Mallorca, Spain.

Quote on hospitality operations

1. Please tell us about the company strategies and objectives of your company GrupoCappuccino, the chain of Restaurants and Cafés?

   Answer: Cappuccino's objective is to create the best possible experience for its customers, through searching out the most successful hospitality prototypes from around the globe, and bringing them to Cappuccino where they can be developed to fit with the Cappuccino brand, tried and tested. We move forwards on the basis of what works, and what our customers love. In terms of strategy, our objective now is to continue growing in the right measure, but only when the site is the very best in the location concerned, and where our Cappuccinos are not spread out too far.

2. Your brand Cappuccino is recognized all over Spain. What elements in Management are vital to deliver such a consistent brand?

   Answer: We look for managers who are brilliant, sensible, daring and who are always looking to push boundaries and make our service and our concept better. We are constantly questioning everything we do and striving to improve and develop. Our management is imbued with the pride and integrity which we are lucky to have identified in all our staff, and it is through their inherent pride at being part of the Cappuccino family that our managers share my same determination to spread a consistently excellent brand across each of our Cappuccinos.

3. What are the principles of creating a company where service levels are so high, and how is that passed on to the employees?

   Answer: Cappuccino is guided primarily by what the customer wants. A customer is always looking for the very best experience, whether it be for a quick coffee on a sunny morning, or a lengthy meal with family and friends. Cappuccino therefore developed its high service levels out of a desire to constantly meet the expectations of our customers, by finding a prototype that, when tested, was loved by the customers, and by building on that prototype as a key ingredient for future success. Our principles are passed on to our employees through the pride they feel at being part of Cappuccino, and their desire to play their own important part in making our business work.

4. You take an active part in the Marketing efforts through a Blog, a Magazine and you even have your own Music selection. How is the marketing integrated into your organization to make it this successful?

Answer: Cappuccino is very much the product of our passion and inspirations – what it is that makes life beautiful and translating that into a café experience that will be loved and remembered by our customers. It is through our blog, magazine and music that we are able to communicate that inspiration to those who benefit most from it; to give them a more complete and rounded experience which they can then take home with them, continuing their Cappuccino journey as they do so. It is for that reason that we have our Cappuccino radio app, so our customers can recreate something of our magic when they are not in one of our cafés.

Cappuccino's success is built on a matrix of important factors which combine to create what it is that our customers love: it is the atmosphere created by the music, the art and interior design which makes each Cappuccino unique and which welcomes our customers as though to their own home, and our demanding standards which filter their way into creating the very best quality of food and service.

5. You are a frequent traveler yourself, what can Hotels learn from an exclusive chain of Restaurants and Cafés like yours?

Answer: Hotels and restaurants are built on the same core values of service excellence, attention to detail and customer prioritization, and there are consequently many valuable learning experiences which can be traded between hospitality businesses. Much of what other hotels can learn from Cappuccino comes down to good, basic rules of hospitality: Make the customer feel at home; attend to every single tiny detail and keep on going back to revisit whether that detail is still working; constantly change and improve; learn from everything you do; smile.

6. In the many years of consulting we continue to see inconsistency as a defect in the operational process. How do you educate your staff and keep them motivated long term?

   Answer: By always being honest and just. By creating a working atmosphere in which our staff are happy and proud to work, so that they, without instruction, find themselves wanting to better the business and keep service levels high. By ensuring that our staff feel secure, and valued, and by enhancing opportunities for continuous learning.

7. The cost structure within personnel in Food & Beverage remains one of the main factors influencing the success of the company. What other cost factors can make or break your monthly success? And how do they fluctuate with the revenues?

   Answer: Other cost factors of relevance that can affect the success are in first place the food and beverage costs and the control of these consumptions that are essential to the success of any hospitality business. Other costs that can affect the success are the maintenance costs of the outlet (OPEX) and the supplies costs.

8. You have successfully established a Luxury Premium Brand, how will you continue to expand locally in Spain and further into other countries?

   Answer: We are constantly on the look out for the very best sites which will complement the Cappuccino Group and enhance the local environment of the respective locations. Our focus is now on finding two further opportunities in Madrid, one in Barcelona, in London and eventually in New York and Miami.

9. In all your years in Hospitality industry, which are some of the
    main tips, you can give to other entrepreneurs in the industry?

    Answer: Identity and personality are key to forging a successful
    and unique business which stands out from amongst the rest.

10. The Hotel industry is very interesting and lucrative business. You
    are planning to open at least three hotels in the near future. What
    elements from your current operations do you think you will most
    benefit from in the hotel business?

    Answer: The Hotel Cappuccino will be a natural extension of the
    Cappuccino experience, taking all of the key ingredients from
    our cafés (service excellence, beautiful interiors, magical music,
    delicious and high quality food) and translating that into a fully
    immersive experience which the customers will be able to enjoy
    for an extended time. Waking up listening to Chet Baker and
    Paul Desmond on Cappuccino radio, and drinking cocktails to
    the accompaniment of Sade; dining in Cappuccino or our Tahini
    restaurant around which the hotel will be built, or enjoying a
    superb, luxurious service where every detail has been taken care
    of in stunning individually designed surroundings: this will be the
    core of the Hotel Cappuccino experience.

Design decisions

There is a lot to be said for the design of a restaurant or bar. Can you could
do it yourself? Actually, look around a bookstore and you'll notice that
you can buy anything from inspirational magazines to and do it yourself
books that inspire design. Design, or rather interior design, is intriguing.
We all pretend we know a little about it, if not more than just a little. The
New York School of Interior Design has the best description of interior
designers: 'The best interior designers make it look easy, crafting spaces that
anticipate our needs and appeal to our emotions, but in reality a broad set
of skills and technical knowledge is required'. There you have it; interior
design takes a skill and should match the atmosphere, the concept, and
primarily the customer. I believe one lesson often taught is that much of

the design should reflect a home away from home. I totally disagree with that. People do not visit restaurants and bars to experience and pay for something that they can have at home. From a design point of view, guests are looking for the wow effect.

The relationship between the interior designer and the architect is not always the best. The main reason for the friction is that the architect takes on the role of fitting in as many seats as possible to ensure maximum profitability for the facility while the interior designer is focused on aesthetics. Other reasons include that one is hired later and approaches the project after the other has made his or her mark, or that that their visions for the property are totally different. Sometimes the roles of architect and interior designer are also combined and may require another's objective view. Ideally you should always to try to 'sit' in every position or area of the restaurant or bar. Often there are pillars, views of a carpark, or seats next to an air conditioning unit that can ruin an experience. Other elements to consider that can inhibit an experience are the main entrance or exit and other public areas, like rest rooms. These factors can change the opinion of a guest completely, both positively and negatively. I remember a recent experience in Dubai where I enjoyed a lovely fine dining restaurant and then trekked to that bathroom facilities by way of the hotel lobby and into a typical and non-inviting area. There was also a place in London where you meandered through a buzzing cool bar to reach an empty restaurant.

Choosing chairs, crockery, and cutlery is also an additional responsibility. There is nothing worse than a chair in a warm climate with fake upholstery where you literally find yourself sliding off the chair, or those wooden stiff chairs that make your back hurt after 30 minutes. There chairs might look good but are a practical disaster. And finally, the ultimate error is the stackable conference chair, which does not match any design or concept nor does it meet any guest expectation.

The choice of art on the walls is also very relevant. It has been a recent trend to change the art on the walls on a regular basis. That, of course, is a brilliant idea, and in terms of implementation requires a good curator who fully understands the market segment of the facility. Art is an excellent way to keep things fresh and 'change' décor for regular guests. It intrigues people and invites curiosity. Music is another element that contributes heavily to the atmosphere and can influence a positive or negative experience, though the category is often forgotten. Built in sound systems, bulky speakers, and all kinds of electronic solutions can serve as a disturbing factor both in design and to the guest experience. The sound should be optimal and be able to be controlled locally; the choice of music also needs to match the concept. Streaming is by far the best option; make sure you don't ever leave selection of music to employees as they will typically choose their own favorites which don't necessarily enhance or support the concept and atmosphere. Leave the choice of music to experts in the field, there is a significant cost for their services but there is a true return on investment.

Design also can take you right into the kitchen area. An expensive and much discussed cost that requires experience and expertise in planning and negotiating, commercial kitchen operations, and knowledge of hygiene and safety. I will not write extensively about kitchen design, as apart from the planning or an open kitchen layout, the design does not have direct visual impact on the guest. That said, I have seen many totally inefficient spaces and appliances, logistical nightmares, and potential health hazards in the fanciest of places.

The use of materials, the fire escape, the physical placement of the dishwasher and other appliances, should all to be taken in consideration in the overall design. The architect and interior designer also have serious and important responsibilities for safety, security, infrastructure efficiencies, and sustainability. The choice of architect and interior designer is much more than selecting the delivery of creativity, these are jobs that need skill, expertise, and experience.

Choosing the Brand Name
Whether you are creating a bakery, a restaurant, club or lounge bar, a brand should not only match the guests you want to fill the place, but also reflect the concept. You are looking for guests from outside as well as within the hotel, this already puts you in a challenging position, as they might not

reflect the same market segment. An example is a lunch restaurant, that needs the local corporate lunches, but at the same time needs to be the restaurant that hotel guests choose for dinner. Let alone the fact that often hotel guests also will have breakfast there. It is a challenging task, but can be solved by understanding the concept development that I described earlier.

Some ideas that could help the naming process:

1. Consider the local area
   Naming the restaurant or club can often be linked to the area where it is situated. A great example is the Harbour club in Amsterdam, at the harbour. It is an attractive name as it associates with freedom, relaxation, sound and feeling of water and the boat life. The menu reflects the name as the the name reflects the local area. The perfect fit for success. Another successful and fabulous process in naming is to highlight often a forgotten area, take the old harbour of Sydney or the meatpacking district in NYC, now the trendiest areas for hotels, restaurants, bars and clubs. The branding has been particularly strong in these areas and have resulted in fast growing development and extremely popular venues.

2. Live history
   Investors have since particularly 2008, with the financial crash impacting many companies resulting in endless job cuts, that investments in office buildings are no longer delivering what they ever did before. Office hotels are popular, with large turnover, but a solid cash flow comes from hotels, with the restaurant and bar facilities. This has resulted in investors looking for new opportunity, particularly in conversion of historic buildings. Typical examples are old fire stations, storage places, or prisons that are no longer in use. Naming them by what they used to serve adds to the excitement of the guest.

3. Reflect your concept theme

Following the concept development closely the naming will often follow by reflecting the theme. An example is the Chinese wall, if you have a Chinese themes restaurant, original it might not be, but recognizable it will be. Another great example is the Birch Coffee in New York city, they have kept the design, you guessed it in a rustic style, using birch wood as main theme. It certainly stands out from the crowd.

4. Deliver personality

Naming also gives opportunity of a local who laid the first stone, a known poet, or artist, or even the head chef, known for a certain known dish. You can find places like the Oscar Wilde Bar in the Café Royal Hotel in London. Another example is Elliott's Oyster house, originally known as the Elliott Bay fish and Oyster Company in Seattle, USA on Pier 56.

5. Make it memorable

One last element to the success related to naming is simplicity and making it memorable. Now that booking and checking out the facility online has become a natural first step in our lives, visibility, loyalty and word of mouth has become more important than ever. So naming your place 'The restaurant on the corner' or 'The living room' is perhaps not a good idea from a search point of view, and 'Canavacciuolo' for an Italian restaurant might be rather difficult to remember.

Don't follow trends

Lastly in this chapter, I would like to lift our industry by learning from other industries, but also recommend to leave the comfort zone. Our industry is not known to be the most creative and yet we work in so many countries, with so many cultures and meet new people every day. Sure you cannot please everybody, but we are talking to much about trends.

The surf and turf is back, the burger is becoming a trend, so let's create. Creation is not complicated when you have live examples, in fact copying is easy, however setting a trend, looking for something that will develop in the future potentially has a lot more success than following some successes found in other parts of the world. Take fashion, there are basic needs, like T-shirts, hoodies, jeans, but those who set trends, create something new and unique will get the attention they deserve, that will eventually not only sell what they have created but also the basic needs. Trends can be described as a direction in which something is developing. This means that understanding the market, the movements and potential future of the business is vital to adjust accordingly to be the first. I would like to highlight a number of elements that I find are most relevant within hospitality, and invite to not follow trends:

• Individuality

The first time I went to a fashion show in London, I was amazed with how ridiculous and unwearable some of the items were, and yet this repeats itself fashion show after fashion show. But looking back there clearly is a point to this, namely to show individuality. Same as a car show, where the future of the automobile industry is displayed with new slick designs that are not even close to be put on the market. Hospitality can learn a lot from the retail industry. When you look at overall sales of one clothing brand for example. It is not the items that were most likely turning heads on the catwalk, it is the 'normal' standard items, like t-shirts, blouses and pants, that create cash flow for the company. Same goes for the hotel, restaurant or bar, the also need to create that individuality that is needed to draw attention to the entire concept, that will still make a lot of money of starters, deserts and drinks.

• Different

Looking for something that is the future, something that is currently not available, is a task that is not as straightforward as it seems. With design, the menu or the type of concept you can challenge competition. Even something as simple as pricing can create a difference. Even though we should stay away from creating pricing wars, like we often see in the struggle for sales of hotel rooms or spa treatments in the city, there is a lot you can do with making a place more accessible by adjusting pricing and presenting a more affordable or pricier menu. Daring to be different, is a strong component of setting a trend.

- Dictated

Dictated is an element of trends that is driven by marketing. It is a question of supply and demand. When you are at the supermarket for example, you are extremely tempted to buy the 'special offer' luring at you at the cashier. Even though you had no intention to buy that product, the supermarket created demand. A typical example when asking a room service supervisor, what is the best sold item on the menu? You will get the answer; the burger. The burger is a must on the room service menu. It is dictated by not only the number of items sold (demand) but also by the head office of the hotel company (Supply). What would happen if that burger would not be on the menu. I believe some have tried, and replace it with a local dish for example, or a healthy option, but the trend is a dictated one. Every where in the world the burger is a trusted, familiar dish, that is in general consistent as well.

- Identity

Identity is a part of the trend, that can make a significant impact on your business. At early stage, already when you are creating the concept for your restaurant, you will create an identity. The identity gives a solid chance of standing out from other concepts, only if the core values and mission are fully followed and implemented. The identity is also extremely important in the branding of the place, as through logo and font type you set a standard for the communication internally and externally. Recently I have noticed the need for old posters, old commercials a la Mad man style. That is a very cool trend that will not last, unless you are in an old marketing building, however creates an identity which sets one aside.

- Memorable

Setting trends is not an easy task, but when you succeed you create a memorable experience for many. Roof top bars, are totally cool right now beginning of 2016. The 20 best rooftop bars in the world, I just received in a newsletter. The views, not the bars are often what makes these successes. So look around, what is attractive, what will people remember, and even more so, is there something others have not thought about, that you can own as the first.

- Functionality

Unlike that very odd item on the runway I mentioned earlier, a trend is something that has value of functionality. There needs to be purpose, or creation of a feeling that the guest feels comfortable with, or even more so needs. Trying to set a trend that does not carry a value for the guest, is a total waste of time.

- Monotony

A monotonic trend is perhaps more of statistical use than anything else. But by measuring certain data, you can see an automatic reaction of the guest, which could very well lead to setting or creating a new trend. A simple example of monotony is trying to get people to start queuing at a buffet from the left instead of the right, total confusion follows. The latest trend however is to create portion or tapas style items on the buffet, to improve a better flow of the buffet, rather than the large queue we all know. But in this case there is cost of labor and tools involved. By measuring actions from inside and outside the industry we can learn a great deal that can be applied to drive loyalty to a business.

- Trending cycles

If you are an eager investor in company shares you will know there is a cycle that is being used by share analysist. Every so many years a drop in shares appears, as well as a rise. It is not set in stone, but there certainly is a trending cycle. This most suddenly is the same for our trends. Take the industrial look that became so popular in 2105. Will that disappear? Yes, absolutely, will it come back? For sure! Understanding these cycles will or can put you aside from the competition.

In this chapter I have focused on delivering a fresh look on our Food & Beverage department, by mainly looking at our business with an objective pair of glasses. The question remains, how would this business be run as a stand-alone, what efforts or functionalities, what recruits are needed to make it a success. In the chapter following I will speak more about leadership, which can make or break a business. It has to be understood, get away from the ordinary, try and break the standard approach to running a F&B outlet within a hotel operation. The world has moved on, and will continue to do so and the online impact of your business has already taken a huge role in deciding whether you are a success or not. Are you prepared?

Chapter 4

Lead it
A stakeholder's analysis

In this chapter, I will focus on leadership and management within the hospitality industry. Having worked in the industry and also outside the industry, I have come across numerous management and leadership styles. I find them hard to define, after having studied and read potentially over 100 books about leadership and management. Within the corporate hotel industry, there surely are guidelines for personality, skill and education but whether those are reality, I doubt very much. Nothing wrong with that, as one personality suits a hotel in a particular location, with a different working culture better than the other. The typical career path to become general manager of a hotel suddenly has changed and will continue to do so, like a lifecycle.

When I started working in the industry, GM's came from the accounts department. They had good knowledge of numbers and could apply that to all areas within the organization and look fabulously intelligent when presenting the yearly budget to leadership at the annual corporate feast.

A few years later the trend changed, after all what does all those accountants know about room operations? Running a hotel 24/7 was not for everybody, always on call, always on the move, managing people from all levels within the organization. Help with check in, try and get rooms ready in time, assisting with finding last minute extra personnel, and ordering last minute linen for the bathroom. Understanding and speaking with guests, communicating all the good and the bad to employees, with the eternal smile. Yes, the track to become general manager had changed, the rooms division professionally pulled the longest straw. But not for long, all these people in the organization had not seen anything yet. The real stress and guest contact was in Food & Beverage, this was hard core, they knew their stuff, were trained as waiters from age 15, well experienced in the most stressful situations and kept their appearance stylish and professional. They worked crazy hours, had great knowledge of people and knew their numbers too. They created a new path to the gym, plus they delivered a great party at the annual budget presentation too.

Not for long, all these operations, all the success and great effort needs to be sold. The sales and marketing teams that always takes the blame for slow business and always celebrating in their nice suits, enjoying dinners and trips seemed of value. They are the ones who drive the business, write contracts with the large organizations to secure room nights and filled seats in the bars and restaurants. They were knowledgeable, always motivated, positive and were the new generation General manager. With the backup of the operation and finance team, they were great presenters and certainly not afraid to change a few things within the operation.

Now in 2016, it's a pretty good mix and the cycle has gone around a few times, however, a new generation has appeared recently; the millennial generation. I just read an article about the importance of a mentor, how millennial should use a mentor when they have recently come out of some sort of leadership internship. Smart, hungry people for little cash. Inexperienced for sure, but with the help of a mentor and clear guidelines they are fast tracking the GM roles. Not sure if the annual parties are that exciting any more, but the hotels P&L will make up for that.

A good boss
I was told once by a very smart successful and British lady (now Branding for one of the best hotel luxury companies) that, if you stop learning from your boss and you think you know more or are better than your boss, you

need to look for another job. She is also the one who told me you should never choose a job for a boss. She meant that a boss can or will always move on, so better choose the job that gives you most pleasure. I fully agree with her first statement and have found it hard to follow her second advice.

I am one of those who has learned most things from my direct reports and peers for that matter. The experience of working closely on a project and daily operations while creating new opportunity with a group of people is extremely motivating and educational. Naturally, it requires a lot from you, as you need to drive not only yourself but also others. I strongly believe as well that one needs to differentiate the task clearly, for example, running the daily operation is a separate ballgame from doing a revenue generating project. Sure, they are reflecting each other, however, work strategies are significantly different. So, rather than describing directly what a good boss is, I challenge you to start with yourself. You might not have the ambition at all to be a boss, but you have to be successful on your own.

Start to understand who you are, your strength, capabilities as well as your weaknesses and challenges. It's a great means of defining what kind of boss you can be, also the type of boss you wish to work for or you think you can learn most things from. Still, what defines a good boss? What differentiates one from the other in the hospitality industry? Rather than defining a good boss from text book phrases and jargon, I would like to highlight some of the elements that the team and I have come across in the hospitality that can make a serious impact on the employees and the overall business.

Visionary
Spelling out the vision of the leader is extremely important. The description has to be totally clear, and hold all elements that can make working towards this vision easy to understand and straight forward to implement. A boss with a vision, often repeats and highlights these elements, to create a working atmosphere that leads to a solid work stream by all team members.

Motivation and motivator
Motivation starts with the person him/herself. Someone who has to motivate others needs to firstly, be self-motivated. A motivated boss will

easily reflect the passion at work place, as well as the vision of the company. Motivating others is only then a natural communication process.

Goal oriented

One element that is still lacking in many meetings or simply unclear or too difficult to reach. I can't tell you how many meetings I have joined where the goal of the actual meeting was not even stated, an agenda was missing or lacking a timeline, just to name a few. There is absolutely no point holding a meeting without a serious goal. In our industry and in many others, we insist in having a morning meeting every day. These meetings differ tremendously from GM to GM. Some are short and useful, most are tedious and incredibly useless, lacking focus and action, leading to repetitive endless information without a cause. Don't get me wrong, there is a point to the meeting, but only if objectives are set at the end resulting to change or an action needed to correct or improve a service. This leads me to the next point, all too often there is a lot of firefighting going on, rather than finding the root cause and looking for a solution that is permanent.

Leading change

Change is hard and can only be successful with full drive of the boss. Change starts with the employees, stating why there is a need for change, gaining buy in as they will be the ones who will implement change. Again, goals set need to be clear and fully understood. It helps to get the employees involved in the decision making, but the right information and communication is already a fabulous start of the process. I will come back to leading change later as it is so incredibly important for the success of an operation as well.

Timely

There is simply nothing more demotivating than having a great vision, setting goals, action planning and nothing happens. Ideas can be found anywhere within and outside the operation but if they lead to goals or actions that are not implemented in a timely manner, then motivation is totally lost.

Rewarding

Will a simple thank you do? Yes! In many ways a "thank you" is a sign of recognition of success. It's so easy but too often forgotten, in the hectic life of a boss. Within Hospitality, we are so used to the employee of the month or the year. It's beautiful to show that the boss cares, that attention is shown to those who perform according to the company's vision or have reached a goal or delivered incredible customer service. Of course, financial or non-financial incentives are solid ways of rewarding, they also help build that self-esteem which is much needed for success.

Honest

A word that sounds so straightforward but is sometimes a challenge to apply. A boss has daily interactions with stakeholders that influences the business from many angles. Personally, I have had directions from an owner which is very different from the corporate organization I was employed in. Still you have to implement it, find a middle way that works for both, and eventually implement it. Communicate it to the colleagues. Honesty naturally is the best and only way, and the communication is eventually more based on trust and a solid relationship.

Respectful

Walk the talk, a phrase that probably has become Hospitality jargon. I feel it goes beyond just that. Respect is a way to show that you care as a boss, about each person. It's time consuming but extremely rewarding. It strengthens a relationship within the team, gives space to discuss, share opinions and views on business. Respect is something that needs to be earned, you don't just get it.

Listener

A good boss listens, hears positive and negative feedback and uses it to make a change where needed or simply create an open and fair relationship between the employee and the company.

Implementer

Idea generation based on experience is readily available within the organization. These ideas can come from one on one reviews, customer interviews or surveys, employee satisfaction indexes and many more. A good leader listens, analyzes and forms a team where needed. Unfinished projects and ideas that are not being understood or actions that do not serve the purpose are a total waste of time and reflect badly on a boss.

Fun

Excitement and passion at the work place are keys to success. Even though tough, every working process, meeting or plan should be fun. After all, the workplace is somewhere where we spend at least 5 days a week. Imagine going to work without experiencing fun.

Team player and stake holder

A team player is someone who involves others to form and implement goals and processes. Someone who understands that giving and taking energy is normal in reaching happiness at work has the pillars of team play right. Every employee is a stake holder, somehow they influence the success of a process. Stakeholders vary in culture, personality, personal goals and have to be understood to enable them be part of the team effort. A boss can and will have to lead the way.

Leadership rules

Now that I have characterized some traits of a leader within hospitality, I would like to go deeper into what a leader stands for, the role of a leader and what the future holds for a leader.

Ken Blanchard, a successful American businessman states 'In the past a leader was a boss. Today's leaders must be partners with their people; they no longer can lead solely based on positional power.'

Leaders cannot do without management, the difference according to the Guardian is that "Management is a set of processes that keep an organization functioning. They make it work today – they make it hit this quarter's numbers. The processes are about planning, budgeting, staffing, clarifying jobs, measuring performance and problem-solving when results did not go as plan."

Leadership is very different. "It is about aligning people to the vision, which means buy-in and communication, motivation and inspiration." The leader has the role of motivating and inspiring people to reach a vision created for the company. Leaders are always under great pressure to perform, as there are numerous measures that can put their position into question.

Leaders have some controversial characteristics, in some cases they need to lead, in some cases they need to be a politician. Depending on the hierarchy or whether the company is a public one, the behavior can be seen in many different ways. I am not convinced there is a perfect leader, as all stakeholders including personnel or management have different expectations of that behavior in various circumstances. That does not mean that we need a Dr Jekyl & Hyde scenario, but for example a presentation about the financial situation to management might have a different voice than those to shareholders.

Politicians
Series like Homeland or House of Cards, highlight in particular American Politics. In these series you can identify that a politician spends a lot of effort on defending a specific case and thus, his or her position. A leader is more focused on the result, requiring quicker decisions and less politics. In the hospitality, leaders are mostly great politicians, they develop relationships with their management as well as the the hotel owner or management company. I respect the leadership for defending their teams to drive the hotel to one vision that in most cases, is to be followed and not set by themselves. They are the great combination of a leader and politician.

Working with people
Probably the most important trait of a good leader is to recognize and act upon the value of people. With people, I mean those externally like guest or press, as well as internally. Clear and apparent communication skills are needed to drive people to the best results and to exceed expectations. Internally the leader needs to build trust and appear honest and straightforward, while respecting personal and corporate values. People are a large asset, as well as a large cost. Ineffective leadership leads to frustration and even boredom. Regular updates or useful meetings are

therefore, keys to the success. This is a very time consuming exercise for a leader, but should by no means be underestimated.

Diplomats
This skill is required to be able to represent the vision, customers, guests, press and naturally personnel. The leader needs to be sensitive, honest, trustworthy and communicate tactfully.

Technology
Change is continuous and technology takes us places we have never seen or understood before. A leader needs to understand the potential of technology and all the tools within, that can drive a business and even more so, stand out from the crowd. Trying to understand the technology and the value thereof is not enough. A leader will help to invent, support and implement technology in and outside the industry. Technology drives efficiency and will influence decision making for the business. This can be anything from choosing a hotel booking system for a hotel, to a CRM system that drives the digital marketing. The IT manager in a hotel is still often seen as a cost and sits muffled away between the fans of the server, or hidden behind the accounts receivable clerk. Statistics pave the way to success and personnel does no longer have to sit with a black pen highlighting potential corporate clients. Within our industry, we are far to reacting and tend to focus on making sure the printer works, rather than creating the bills they are needed for. Within our industry, the IT manager is also a role that includes tasks that are not relevant to the growth of the business, but rather to purchase enough licenses, make sure the systems work together.

Technology is about innovation, meeting and exceeding guest's expectations. Many years ago, I was totally impressed with the system at a luxury hotel in Los Angeles, offering buttons to one call solutions, and open curtains automatically. They certainly were the first hotel that I came across that had that solution, however, private homes already had that way before as well as the car industry with their remote key system. Standing out with technology is not easy, and it is very expensive, however, the return of investment might exactly be what the hotel needs. Learning from other industries and looking at what the future guest might need is what is key to success. Some large corporate hotel chains are now hiring trend analyst, either to support the digital marketer or to deliver technology driven ideas. The leader will need to learn and adapt to make this happen and potentially fix his own printer when the paper gets stuck.

Setting priorities

The job of a leader never finishes. When they come home, have a meal and check their emails, there, mailbox will be flushed with new corporate standards, questions from owners, an issue with a guest, resignations and anything else that needs decisions or immediate feedback. Important for a leader is not only to manage the schedule, but to categorize issues and opportunities in importance. Having owners, they often get the priority, however they will understand most delays. Setting priorities by a leader is also a form or communication. Management or owners for example will understand what is important to reach the goals, and stick to a vision based on the priorities of their leader. Of course this only works if this is communicated well and effectively. Remember the GM who could not be reached for days or weeks in the budget period, or the one who potentially spent 80% of the time communicating up rather than down the chain? Would you choose to work for a GM like that? In the first example, it could mean a lack of organizational skills, lack of people skills, a highly politically influenced person or someone who has not kept up with technical developments within budgeting or yielding, just give a few examples. Setting priorities is much more than allocating task by importance and time, it is a means of communication.

Mediators

Perhaps, more the role of the managers, but certainly a trait that is a need to work in a team towards common goals. There are many disputes within an organization that can hurt the motivation of not only the people involved but also those surrounding them. The mediation skill of the leader is therefore, one of the key behaviors that will impact the organization.

Observer

In our vibrant industry, dealing with guests every day, we need to observe, listen and understand the feedback we get offline and online all the time. Observing gives opportunity to discover and address a potential change in a process. All too often, ideas, complaints are listened to or solved on the spot. This can have a very positive result to guest loyalty, but the root cause of the issue remains. Ideas are heard, now they need implementing. The leader has incredible opportunity to observe every day, requiring an operational skill that means going out on the floor meeting employees and guests, asking questions. Once ideas and issues have been explored, they need to be part of the innovation, or process improvement methods that should be in place in any hotel. Preferably those who have an idea implemented should be rewarded to promote this type of communication.

Decisions, based on finance and data

The financial acumen of the leader can seriously impact decisions. In my role as a consultant, before I even got to visit a potential client, we read and received data, any type of data that has the potential to show variation in the business, preferably by department. The data is an incredible source in the hotel industry, which is underused. There are benchmarks in the industry, like food cost, personnel turnover, profit margins and such, however, looking deep into internal and external data, like city reports or TripAdvisor gives a good inside information on volumes or guest feedback. It is the task of the leader to implement and decide fast and ensure they are sensible and communicated well.

The leader has a role to engage in innovation. As you could read before, hotel *Innovation* are taking this serious now. Since exceeding expectations of guests has become more and more difficult over the years, a hotel can differentiate to innovation. In this book, I will dedicate a chapter to innovation, but a leader has to manage the innovation process and is fully responsible for implementation.

Long term

Leaders come and go, particularly if you look within the hospitality industry. Therefor the General Manager tends to take decisions that have a short term impact on the bottom line for example. That makes our industry vulnerable, as plans and implementations are not registered and even more so, not shared. I have worked for a large corporate organization, with many 4 and 5 star brands. They create success by sharing best practices and making sure that anything from root cause to controlling can easily be copied to other hotels. A very efficient way of forwarding success. I found it one of the most useful tools, when visiting hotels all over the globe. Unfortunately, not every hotel has a leader who thinks long term, when pressure is on short term performance and decisions that quickly affects the hotel's overall performance. Apart from measuring success financially, there are many more tools currently used, like guest satisfaction, or employee satisfaction and the famous secret guest concept. Key for a good leader is to not only make long term decisions, but document them, so it can be followed through by the person following.

Interview

Stuart Birkwood

General Manager – LeMeridien Abu Dhabi

Your quote on the future of Hospitality:
Back to basics; it's a simple business…by people for people. No need to overcomplicate it.

1. You have many years of experience in Management and Leadership. What are the core 3 elements for a successful Leader to pass on to management and how can they ensure that their objectives are met?

    Answer: Listen to your guests, listen to your associates and listen to your instincts!

2. What are the principles of creating a company that leads the market place, through changing and yet deliver consistency to customers?

    Answer: Don't say 'if only'.

Over Communicate, be open to criticism, build trust, get the business out of the comfort zone, admit to learn from mistakes, work as a team.

3. What type of Hotels do you feel are setting the standard for guest experience and how will that change in the future?

    Answer: The B&B market is showing how very small, individual, family owned establishments can deliver exceptional guest care & Experiences through personalization, attention to detail and individual service.

4. You are a frequent traveler, what kind of benefits or elements are you looking for when you book a Hotel and what do you bring back to your organization?

    Answer: Fast Wi-Fi (does not have to be free), Personalization, Recognition, an uncomplicated stay

    On time, first time

5. In the many years of data collection, measuring and analyzing, where do you see the largest opportunities in the future for Hotel Management?

    Answer: Attracting better, greater, more skilled & devoted talent. How can we enhance hospitality as an aspirational career for the best academic talent, who can by themselves, rethink the business.

6. Differentiation is a key term for any product or service. There are numerous new brands being created to attract new generations. What does that mean for the Luxury Hotel segment and the property owners?

    Answer: Competition drives business forward in new ways of getting ahead and this can only benefit the customer in the long run. Luxury is not only physical, it's also about experience, something unique to do, see and feel.

7. You have been successful in both small companies and large corporate organizations. What are the biggest differences and how can they learn from each other?

   Answer: Communication! Alignment of Strategy! Not to grow too big or too fast, keep a small feel in a big company e.g. care for your people and don't miss the details.

8. In all your years in Hotel industry, where do you feel the most financial opportunity is missed and what should the industry do to change that?

   Answer: Staff training & retention; Customer loyalty & retention. Invest and see the rewards going forward.

9. The Hotel industry is a very interesting and vibrant industry, what are the elements that Senior Management should address to ensure this remains the case in the future?

   Answer: Seek inspiration from external sources and other industries and concentrate on the core hospitality of the people we serve, manage and lead.

The positive attitude

It is interesting to read that French fine cuisine still ranks top 100 with the Michelin guide and yet a French restaurant has not ranked number 1 or 2 in the world's best 50 restaurants which is an international concept that launched 15 years ago. What kind of conclusions can you draw from that? It might mean that this well-established cuisine is starting to get outdated or that chefs are not necessarily the best leaders. A leader has to be very diverse. Two years ago I saw the cartoon Ratatouille, a movie that is based on the fact that no one can cook, not just anybody can create and that a restaurant might appeal to one but not to the other. With the variety and great interest in kitchens these days, the numerous cook books, the

Television shows, even at home, we have the opportunity of increasing our knowledge and skill. The creativity in the kitchen is limitless and clearly there is an appetite for unknown foods or ways of preparation that was not there before.

Recently, I was at a new hotel in Amsterdam, with a highly skilled chef for dinner. Without exaggerating, it was by far the worst experience. I don't know if the restaurant was outsourced, or run by the rather new hotel company itself. Many seats were taken and the design of the restaurant was cozy, stylish and rustic just like the millennial would like it. The service, the quality of the food, the menu and even the drink service was far below standard that I would never consider going back there. I actually wrote a very critical note to the hotel and never got a response. Later, I checked online for the ratings the restaurant was getting from others. We were not alone, the ratings and comments are by far the worst I have seen in many years. If there are so many matters completely dysfunctional, you can wonder who the leader behind this operation is, the restaurant manager, as well as the General Manager of the hotel. The staff was uninterested, unskilled and the quality of the food was a disaster. I would say that this leader is most likely failing on most of the behavioral aspects that I described earlier in this chapter.

This bad experience, believe it or not, could have been turned around, in my case anyway. If I would have received a note back, explaining the actions that they are undertaking, the appreciation for my feedback and perhaps even an opportunity to try them again and give them a second chance, I would have given it. But they simply do not care, the average checks probably covered the ignorance of this leadership.

It brings me to a trait of the leader who deserves a dedicated area within this chapter that even though there are internal and external factors affecting the business, can still move a business forward. Do you remember your first boss that told you only the problems, or only the negative things? The one who never celebrated success or passed on recognition, the one who never greeted in the morning or the one you never even saw.

A positive leader communicates on a regular basis with their employees and guests or clients. Showing dedication to reach a vision and making sure there is buy in from the colleagues throughout the organization. Trust me if guests in a restaurant for example gives negative feedback that trickles down incredible speed to all staff in the entire hotel, that is damage and very difficult to control. Once the vision is set, a clear path on how to get there needs to be laid out. This means that, everyone needs to be involved and no matter what, they need to be allocated task as part of the team, to be able to achieve the goals. The positive attitude of a leader towards the team is therefore an essential part in the organization. Even negative criticism can be uplifting by a leader who is positive to make and create that change. Setting goals for teams also means a timeline needs to be allocated and measured. So that success can also be celebrated, a change in the process can be noted where needed and also rewarded where possible. A smile can do wonders and people need it. They need guidelines and timelines to enable them perform.

The leader needs to be that motivator, standing on the side or being actively involved to support the team. There is a reason why personal trainers have become so extremely popular. Going to the gym is a pain in the ass, it takes a lot of time and motivating yourself is not always so easy. A personal trainer, motivates, smiles, gives clear goals and the results follow and even though you might hate them after 50 pushups, afterwards, they are your best friend. You feel good, your body shape improves, you feel fit and you even want to go back and get some more. The score card is your measurement, but the way you have been lead through the process really makes the difference.

The leader of the future is kind, straightforward, can communicate well, adapts to internal and external factors easily involving the team; yet, be decisive and strong. The team clearly has a responsibility in gaining respect too, but the work place is so much better with a positive leader.

The objective consultant
So far in this chapter, I have focused on all the traits, characteristics and habits of a leader. Having been in the industry for a long time, I can easily

confirm that most General Managers we work with welcomes change when it's clear there is a financial result that follows. It is widely understood that the industry is rather old fashioned in many ways and that the need for understanding the core of the business is greater than ever, to keep the guests loyal. But there is much more to it.

In 1993, I wrote my first book, where I described my life as a student in Holland. I wrote the book with grandfather's type-writing machine. Fighting for grades and making sure I passed the modules in the allocated 4 years. I lived in the most bizarre house with 3 others and the living circumstances were let's just say, not doing the mind a lot of good. Performing in these circumstances will suddenly prepare you for real life situations as a leader. The book was most likely never published because it would affect parents dramatically. A big part of the education was work experience and an internship. I did my placement in a very fine boutique hotel, The hunting tower Hotel in Perth, Scotland.

A part of the book was also about the thesis I had to write for the hotel. I had to do a marketing plan for the expansion with small cottages. Matching potential guests with the cottages was certainly not an easy task, in the middle of the early 90's recession. The client base was vast and loyal, but low seasons seriously damaged the hotel. With the cottages in mind, the hotel was aiming for the English with as serious interest in fishing and hunting. I want to share a page out of the book that is until today extremely relevant. In fact, I started the book with showing this image on what factors influenced or would influence this hotel.

I identified Economic, technical, public policies, competition and cultural circumstances as some of the main areas. Remember this is written over 20 years ago.

The economy impacts every hotel, describing this environment would help us identify our existing and also new market segments by understanding spending behavior, also, identifying and recognizing the economic cycle. The economic cycle is important for hotels to understand. They are described with words like depression, upswing, recovery and peaks. The economic cycle is a reaction on all the internal and external factors within a market. It is hard to predict, but there is a clear trend. As a leader, the reaction and proactive actions are vital.

Additionally, I analyzed and tried to predict the technical behavior that was extremely rapid already and I remembered at the university, one of the classes was learning how to type, two hours a week on a typewriter and that was electronic, believe it or not. Working there operationally also taught me so much about technology and the opportunity of businesses that would unveil if there would be a dramatic change in system, bookings and internal communication. Handing over the hand written orders from the restaurant with my handwriting, caused a few headaches in the kitchen. 20 Years later, technology has become a part of our life, in many cases, a company's vision and has taken the road that I predicted back then but in much faster pace, forms and shapes I could not even imagine back then. As I am writing this, I am listening and steering a tune on a Bluetooth system focused on my reader, researching online and offline. That looked very different many years ago and will look totally different in the future. Technology, hiring skilled staff and allocating financial resources are part of a leadership decision that are critical.

The public policy was in this case particularly important and relevant because of the expansion of building into the forest and also, to ensure that the hotel or guests have the right documentation to hold guns for hunting, or fishing for example. Keeping an eye out for legal aspects in an expansion or new build can lead to serious hold ups.

The competition teaches us a lot and with current technology, there is an incredible source of information available on the internet. We can start understanding why the competition is offering a certain weekend package, why they have so many suites, why the restaurants are always full or why they take so many wedding bookings. Competitors do the same with you, so be first, be different, remember your vision and your unique selling points. Learn from other industries, how they communicate and connect with guests. How they differentiate themselves from the others in the market. It will be the source, the key of how your marketer can address your market. And whatever you sell, don't sell service, it's a lame misunderstood way to compete as you are not the judge of that, your guests are. It's only the way you exceed great service that counts. I literally need a paper bag, when I hear a General Manager say we have the best service in town and statistics totally point in the other direction when its stated as a unique selling point.

Competition can and will help you make decisions, but don't underestimate the speed it can change and if you have identified a new concept or idea, how quickly it can be copied.

Lastly from the graph is culture. Already then, the culture was a main value and now even more so. People want to experience locality, understand a culture rather than just getting a taste. Leaders use culture as a source of marketing and sales or even design and experience. There is pride in cultural differences that is much more obvious nowadays more than ever. I recently passed a place that was probably one of the first American café's in Amsterdam. The sign outside said, Doughnut since 1939. It certainly made me believe they had been there a long time and they are proud they are still there. It is a great way of establishing and recognizing a culture and consumption will follow.

The part of the old non published book of 1993 paved way for observation and techniques I have acquired since. Later, this was sharpened by the Six Sigma education that was much about objective processing too. As a consultant, the conversation with a potential customer is much easier when this is understood clearly. Since this book is all about making hospitality sexy, I want to share a few more details that affect the business significantly and also examples of where opportunity is much closer than expected.

4 Ways hospitality leaders can impact bottom line effectively

As a leader there is direct access to an incredible source of information, namely management, staff and guests as well as statistics. By listening, interviewing and understanding statistics, many ideas can turn into solutions creating good news for the bottom line. A General Manager, can see opportunities by just looking at the Profit & Loss Statement objectively.

I have been asked on many occasions before the first face to face meeting, do you see any opportunity in our profit & loss statement? So far I have not once answered negative and also because other industries for example retail, have less resources to play with. After all, most retail offer one or a few core products. Hotels offer rooms, service, design, location, loyalty programs and so forth. Some retail companies are very smart; there find an opportunity and play into demand that is already out there. Many clothing brands sell attributes like socks. An example of a company that has turned that around is the concept called Happy Socks, established in 2008, a playful company that plays with colors for socks and now starts selling an entire range of products. They found a niche in the market, based on a very loyal customer base; we all need socks, well, at least for now.

Below you can find 4 ways of addressing the hotel in an effective way.

1. Yielding/Pricing

If you are a picky shopper you will notice that one packet of eco butter will have a price different from one supermarket to the next. There is a reason for that. Of course it could have to do with the fact that, the supermarket has different owners under a franchise label supermarket chain, which gives them the right to price as they wish. But it has more likely got something to do with supply and demand. I know the bottle of mineral water in the minibar is a crucial point of discussion, should a hotel give it away instead or put the price up even more, since the product sells like hotcakes? And back to the butter, the supermarket in question might be geographically located in an area that has a serious interest in ecological products and are willing to pay extra for it and additionally, would not notice the extra Dollar the supermarket has put it up with.

Pricing is a sensitive issue, you might risk a loyal customer or guest if you suddenly put the prices up. Hotels are doing the right thing by hiring a yield or revenue manager, but for smaller hotels there might not be a need. In fact, for some hotels a simple excel sheet that everybody understands will do the trick. The excel sheet should tell you about expected occupancy (demand) in a certain time period, so that prices can be adjusted accordingly. Another very important part of pricing is the price allocation of rooms. Hotels have different room types and guests are willing to pay for a better room. A room with a view over the car park is worth less than a room overlooking the ocean, just like a room with a separate working for example. This gives opportunity for not only different pricing, but also upselling, at time of reservation or check in.

2. Sales

Sales is an extremely important element to revenues. The sales team or management should do anything to get contracts with local companies to ensure a continuous stream of sales that covers the monthly basic costs. And it can be that simple to join local network event to make new contacts that contribute to the hotel's innovation or client base. Its not complicated, but often forgotten.

3. USP Value creation

I launched a restaurant re-opening with my colleagues once in the middle of Wimbledon and rather than focusing on press or local advertising, all the marketing funds went to a fashion show with a tennis theme. It was a great way of innovating and getting attention to an otherwise rather boring hotel restaurant opening, straight after the sales guys got out to get lunch contracts with local companies of whom many were invited to the party as well.

There are many concepts or ideas a hotel can implement based on innovation, ideas from guests and staff. The leader needs to be willing and needs to be part of the implementation.

4. Outsourcing

For many a painful word, as it will include tough decisions and allocation of resources, it might not affect immediate cost savings or increased revenues. So what about thinking smart, looking at other industries, where a company actively starts taking in new clients in the accounts or housekeeping department. Rather than just focusing on the hotel, there might be a local company who needs laundering services or want to outsource their finance solution. Naturally there are also the common outsourcing ways, like cleaning. There are now hotels that more or less outsource everything like reception services, restaurants and run the hotel with a small management team. Price reflects value, so in some cases this might be a great way to address cash flow issues.

5. Cost reduction

Some guests or corporate clients are simply not worth it. They either do not keep to their volume promises or only give your business at low rates when you are fully anyway. Time to thank the business and say goodbye.

Cost reduction takes serious focus from a leader, as the temptation to look at personnel costs is high. Cutting staff might not always be the right decision, keeping in mind sickness levels, the already high stress levels within the industry and the service promise that a hotel has to guests. Employee savings should be followed by a process focused analysis. Who is needed, where and in which area? Does a certain position create added value to the service delivered? Or can it replace by technology.

Another big job but certainly worth it is, the review of all the contracts. I experienced firstly that contracts can be way too lengthy. Recently, I came across a 35-year contract with a laundry service. Make sure those contracts are done, finished immediately and renegotiated. Other contracts like, PR or IT also needs to be revised. They often come with a monthly fee that is not properly used. Remember, outsourcing requires supervision from someone within the company. Other contracts also have small costs that keeps returning, but are not noticed. Examples are, license fees for software's that are often per computer. Has there recently been a count of computers? A stewarding company had contracted taxi fares for staff leaving after 11pm. Guess what most of the evening staff were doing close to that time? Contracts are serious opportunity to save costs, without damaging your guest service.

Leaders taking the business offline again

We are living in a very exciting world, where everything changes quicker than one could ever think only 30 years ago. There is a wealth of information available at our finger tips. There are new ways of communications available that are only just being understood. So what happened to all the leadership theories, all the methodologies that have been presented to us by the many writers all over the world? I for one get excited by new reading material that is about the psychology of intelligence. Not on how you make a decision, but more about the process that gets you to make that decision. That is a learning, a learning of people and how they make their life interesting. That's what it's all about, happiness and behavior. In the tube in London in the old days, people cramped into one cabin, leaning against each other, reading the daily newspapers, were somehow still communicating, smiling, looking at each other and getting to know each other. Opinions were truly communicated in a kind and honest way. Is that something that is disappearing? Are we afraid to speak? To communicate freely? Are we losing the emotional attachment? Like everything else, I am sure it is a cycle. Surely, our emotions will steal people away from short messaging services, where opinions count but are spread without thinking twice, leading to potential damage. Emotional intelligence is about understanding own and other people's feelings and applying it to thinking and behavior.

Naturally, emotional intelligence can also be used to regulate own or others emotions, to cheer them up or calm them down. The book by Daniel Goleman, with the same title is a must to read and in fact was crowned by The Harvard Business review as one of the most influential business of the decade. Daniel has opened up for leaders and managers to learn a skillset that is so extremely important for any industry and in particular our industry as we are dealing with people around the clock. Leaders who are ready for the future are also prepared to learn from others and apply it first themselves and then educate others. Leaders build leaders, that's the only way forward and it's the only way for a leader to be successful him or herself.

Now, what is occupying a leader more, to keep updated on emails, to read the news, to sit in meetings or be in front of the guest? To be honest,

I think it is one of the most sensitive and hardest things to judge. All I know is that it's extremely easy to get lost in this continuous stream of information, let alone all the Social media that comes with it! When walking down the street now, browsing the net, you miss out on the beauty surrounding you, you forget to ask questions, you forget to listen or to be part of the atmosphere. Recently, I was in a fine dining restaurant, with 4 guys as we had promised each other to leave technology in our pockets, many other tables had the shining tools on the table. Even a couple that looked to be there for romantic purposes were more interested in what was going on in the world than looking at each other. Is that the behavior we have to accept? Or is it the behavior we have to simply adjust to in small efforts. I wonder how much time is spent on social media by employees on a working day, but I also wonder how much time is saved by using these tools. I wonder if it's a tool or if it's a fashion item. I don't have the answers, but everybody else seems to have. I remember walking around with one of the first blackberry's, one with this little wheel on the side, very practical keyboard and a light that started flashing red when you received a mail. It was pretty cool and fast in the beginning, later I understood that you were online all the time, always reachable. Now that is routine, a part of life and many get frustrated when they don't get an answer the same day. The days of phone calls are over and the need for silent coupés on trains are disappearing. My mum calls me once in a while just to see if all is ok and to make sure I received her sms. But I miss them, these calls, they mean communication. Even though you don't see the person, you hear and feel emotion, a reaction that is needed to respond in a sensible way.

Leaders have the opportunity to transform this online world, use it to the best, but never lose touch with the guest or the employee outside the virtual world, as they are the ones building the business.

Planning to lead and leading to plan
The last part of this chapter is dedicated to the calmness of the leader, to cope with all the factors that influence the working day. When I was in a sales role, I wondered what a General Manager's role would look like. So I took a few days out of my working life, left the private life out and tried to understand how that day would look if I had 350 employees, 7 direct

reports, owning a company and a corporate head office on my back. And in the meantime, I would have to develop and educate others. What does a schedule of a General Manager look like, is it even possible to have a schedule?

1. There are numerous of planning tools and apps available for your phone that are indeed very useful. After reading many books about how to work efficiently, I still have a simple rule that works extremely well. Plan the night before, make sure your calendar has no surprises and leave space for last minute urgent matters. Planning is not hard if no external disturbances would occur, but they do so, for it is essential.

2. Plan right- Don't leave the nasty stuff for the last, that really is not a very motivating and inspiring end of the day. Try and do the ugly stuff in the morning.

3. Use the people with the right skills. Sure, there is need for control, but there also needs to be trust. A leader has an opportunity to surround him or herself with amazing people, who have great qualities in solving issues or are ready to take on new challenging tasks.

4. Always take time to develop yourself- Learn from others, use the many sources of information that are readily available, but also continue to find and explore in many other ways. An example is, an IT event I was at, recently. A room full of programmers talking a lot of jargon, people looking for investors, people with ideas, people with large companies looking to invest. I was quite surprised when the organizer said he was going to pick 30 people to stand up and tell the others why they are there. Naturally, I was picked after 10 people had done a 2-minute speech on back end programming and some other stuff that was totally uninteresting. For some reason, whatever I said must have been so interesting that lots of people came by to talk about their ideas and asking advice on how to work their dreams. I followed up with two meetings and one of them got a successful investment. And I learned a lot that evening, I learned how programmers think, what their thoughts on success are and what drives them. I can apply that in my working career and plan for it.

5. Always take time to develop others- Life as a leader can be very lonely, so there is no better way to ensure that your team is and stays close. Involving others in your decision makes your team proud and feel respected. Plus, this is fabulous to create other leaders around you. Making sure they are part of the plan is a great opportunity for growth, personal as well as the companies.

6. Build new relationships- Leaders are pressed for time, but joining a sales call gets the leader to understand the market place, joining a call with a supplier gets a leader to understand market pressure. Local networking events are available almost every week. Leaders learn from others by communicating and can share thoughts, ideas and get inspired.

7. Leaders need to recognize success and understand limitations. Knowing and understanding the pressure that can be delegated to others often comes from understanding and respecting his own limitations. The role of leading to plan is associated to passing on the right tasks, within the right timeframes and rewarding accordingly. Its only when a leader is able to manage their own planning, that he/she is able to manage others too.

Leadership in hospitality is a task full of joy, compassion and requires enormous dedication. The way a leader in our industry has opportunity to be close to people every day and also be the stakeholder in demand for many other parties, you can say it is a challenging role, but most certainly one most satisfying I have come across.

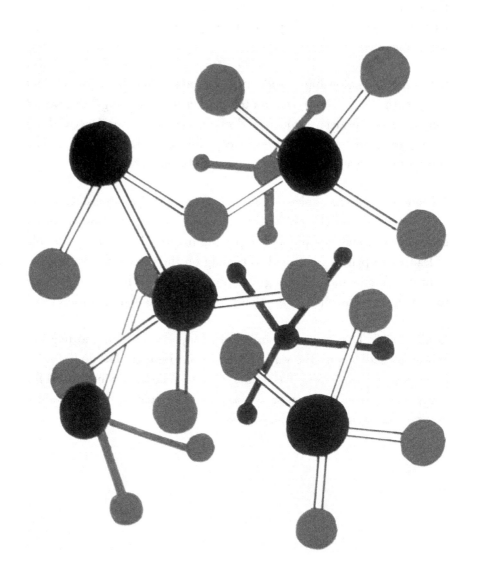

Chapter 5

Innovation wonders
More than just a thought

One of the main reasons for my blog www.jeroengulickx.com is to make the reader feel a part of an industry that is not only sexy, intriguing, but also a very innovative industry. And I would like to inspire and educate simultaneously to maintain the strength and attractiveness of this business that takes time and a lot of text.

In my many years of consulting, I have come across many ideas and inspiration. Every day I meet people within the hospitality industry or students who want to be a part of it. They are mostly vibrant, energetic, want to travel, experience culture, learn and be operational and active. Yes, it requires a certain person to work in this industry. A common way to share inspiration is through images, for example Pinterest or Instagram and blogs. Popular bloggers, no matter what their main subject is, even though mostly fashion, almost always mention travel as their hobby or include it in their occupation. Why, I am not sure, but showing that you are a global personality must be of importance. Showing a pair of legs with an umbrella drink becomes a highly like or loved fashion item. Personally, I love following bloggers who go through locations as most people are flicking through pages in a book. I also get inspired by travel images of new design hotels, or places and cultures I am not yet familiar with. I share them with my team or clients.

Innovation is described as turning an idea or invention into a service or product that can be sold or that will lead to sales. Innovation can be expensive, and outsourcing is often a great plan, as objectiveness is key to success. Idea generation however, is readily available, with the hotel teams being an incredible source for potential innovation. Your hotel team, your operational team, often has ideas through listening to guests, issues that keep arising or opportunities that they also find from external resources or simply experience. When interviewing, we very often come across amazing ones, for innovation or simply to solve issues or deal with challenges. My company Mocinno International, is all about driving change, creating niche, developing marginal excellence and with it the solution can often be found right within the team.

In this chapter, I will be talking about Six Sigma, Lean and blue Ocean strategies as well as give some examples of innovation that are based on interviews with hotel employees, results of feedback of customer reviews and most certainly other industries. Before I start with going further into Six Sigma, I would like to share a personal experience that has an innovative approach to deliver to the local community, a feel good social responsible approach to running a hotel.

Article
The good experience and the good hotel, taking education to the next level
Jeroen Gulickx www.jeroengulickx.com

Working within the luxury hotel segment always gives a certain value and excitement for every project. It makes consulting harder, as much, more attention to detail is needed. You need to keep understanding and deliver maximum value for the consumer who is willing to pay that premium. I have traveled the world and still do the selection of most projects myself that suit the team best. I am fortunate to work within hospitality, working with so many people of so many cultures. Flying to places where I have created friendships, and experience new things every time I visit.

The trips besides great amounts of joy and feelings, also mean traveling to countries that are in social or economic difficulties, or worse. They bring emotions of controversy, inequality and certain opportunities.

This reveals much space for people's care, as people need or are looking for education, development, career building, social affairs, or even more basic elements like self-esteem, food & drink.

This time, my travelling took me to Holland, where I was born, where I grew up between many cultures and controversies that makes this one of the countries that everyone must visit. The way it treats the tourist or business traveler is far beyond many expectations. A total different feeling, architecture, infrastructure, sites and history are reflected into the day-to-day lives of the Dutch and their visitors. I am proud that acceptance of this all is such a great asset for my fellow countrymen.

Choosing the place to stay

When I have a choice of hotels, meaning the client does not decide for me, it depends often on the mood I am in or the reason for the trip. I like the strong service hotel chains, when I need the comfort, the guarantee that everything will be smooth, from check in to check out. More so I, now choose more of a local experience, a smaller brand, a brand with a vision that reflects me, not just the reason for the visit. Though I do require certain minimum standards to be able to be comfortable with the stay.

All that Amsterdam

Amsterdam offers a wealth of experiences, most known to many, which have very little to do with business or hotels altogether. The small streets, the canals, the architecture, the numerous activities one can do every day, like a boat tour, the most amazing museum visits, climbing walls, diamond factories, Heineken experience and naturally, shops make the city extremely attractive for short as well as long stays. Every time I visit, I am amazed with all the new cafes, restaurants and hotels that have popped up since my last visit. The reason for visiting is often to see my family but recently, because I opened an office in Holland April 2015, Holland offers an amazing platform for business. The cultures and great variety of nationalities deliver skill, knowledge and willingness to change, adapt and learn. I can't explain exactly why, but the freedom that the Dutch have in their approach is what creates the warm hospitality everywhere you go.

The Good Hotel

In all the years of consulting within hospitality since 2001, I have been dependent on people, employees and all stakeholders involved in the operation. On the data that they deliver, on their skill and knowledge, within service, technology, design, architecture, legal and the so many other factors that keep a hotel or hospital running. One element that keeps returning is education. With education I mean, everything that needs to be trained, refreshed or developed, as the industry advanced fast and expectation from guests or patients are becoming higher and more developed, which makes it hard to exceed. Service is something that has changed dramatically, even in the last 10 years. Cost cuts resulted into short work process, fast deliveries, with fewer colleagues, yet keeping standards according to the brand and company's vision in line with the low retention in the industry, making it even harder to deliver to the promise that you made or want to make to the guest. Education is key to make sure that everything communicated is understood well, and implemented. That is not an easy task, since not every person receiving that, has the same way or speed of learning.

So I want tell you about my recent experience. I stayed at a hotel in an area that I am not at all familiar with, just a few minutes from the Central Station. When I arrived, I realized the hotel has amazing views over the water, in fact it is a floating hotel, around 150 rooms. The rooms are small, are warmly decorated and have all the businesses or leisure travelers require. They are cute, yet practical. The lobby and public areas are large yet cozy; communicate your need to be there, work there, eat and drink there and socialize. When I checked in, the staff was pleasant, warm and efficient. I went to my room to quickly freshen up for a meeting in the lounge. Again the service was friendly, helpful and efficient. I experienced this throughout my stay and was always greeted, smiled at. One thing I noticed most besides me feeling extremely comfortable, there was trust and honesty which was incredibly refreshing. The service is real, from the heart. Only the day before I checked out, I read the welcome note from the CEO and understood the vision of the company supporting education for those who can't afford it or where it is unavailable in different parts of the world. With the city of Amsterdam, they have selected, trained and educated people in need of work from Amsterdam, who are now working at the Good Hotel in Amsterdam. Clearly, this explains the warmth and trust that you now receive as a guest. Knowing that your support to this and many other initiatives from the Good Hospitality Group makes the next hotel booking for your trip just so much easier.

http://www.goodhotelamsterdam.com/

Six sigma and the hospitality industry

In the example of my recent experience, we can define Innovation as turning an idea or opportunity into reality. That is what innovation is all about, whether that is successfully deployed is another matter, but opportunity does not always need to translate into an economic success.

Six Sigma is a process improvement methodology using all kinds of tools and techniques. The goal of implementing Six Sigma is to improve the final service or product delivery by seeking to minimize or make redundant steps that do not add value or cause defects in business processes. It is a method that was developed already in 1986, for Motorola and fully implemented later in General Electric by the role model of Six Sigma, Jack Welch. As you will understand from this, the initial Six Sigma model was developed for the delivery of a product and not so much for the service industry.

The tools and methods are very identical and the implementation of Six Sigma has the following objectives:

1. Emphasizes the need to recognize opportunities and eliminate defects by customers
2. Recognizes that variation hinders our ability to reliably deliver high quality services

3. Requires data driven decisions and incorporates a comprehensive set of quality tools under a powerful frame for effective problem solving
4. Provides a highly prescriptive cultural infrastructure, effective in obtaining sustainable results

In short, Six Sigma consist of tools and methods that can be applied to any industry with great financial success and delivery of improved satisfaction to the guest. I have applied tools and methods since 2001 and used it with my colleagues in the company as well as educate the clients to use some of it and apply the thought process. Six Sigma is extremely valuable for start-up hotels as well as existing standalone hotels or hotel chains. One of the biggest successes within Six Sigma lies within the use of Best practices. A successful project can easily be copied to sister hotels and the detailed processes can be changed when needed, as internal and external circumstances change continuously. Six Sigma sends an alert fast when something in the process breaks, as long as the tracking is done properly.

Six Sigma opens the door for data, use of data and collection needs of new data. A simple example is a client that we assisted with their bathroom amenities into the Hotel Industry. In the initial meeting, we were projected a very successful company ready for international growth, a solid line of products and great sales. A rather new company, so marginally not yet a success. Using some of the Six Sigma tools, we found quickly that there were 3 peak sales times in the year to only one supplier resulting in dramatic stock levels, bad cash flow and no effort in marketing or sales was implemented since the sales was 'good'. Another example is a hotel client in Rome Italy with a great Food & Beverage financial picture. Note that, normally with Hotel consulting, we look at financial situation and other hotel data before the visit, like segmentation and margins. When looking into the numbers and splitting revenues into breakfast, lunch and dinner, the revenues came out of breakfast for almost 76%. Lunch and dinner were a large cost and very little next to no interest from guests outside the hotel. An example of non-value added step in a process is something we probably almost every day come across. When you eat organic apples, have you noticed a sticker on every apple? The apple is still the same and yes, it is a confirmation of the apple being organic, but what is the value to the consumer? Picking that up from the crate where you found it and it says organic apples, is that not enough? Instead there is waste, for the environment as well as a cost. It's simply annoying to try and peal the sticker off, if I have not eaten it yet.

By now you might be asking yourself, what does Six Sigma have to do with Innovation? Often and as one would expect they actually conflict, as Six Sigma is all about improving efficiency and productivity. Aiming for operational excellence will decrease the opportunity of taking risk within the hotel, which are needed to be innovative. Doing the right thing is not the same as doing things right. Innovation is all about change and hotel or hotel company who is using Six Sigma will be more focused on innovation that actually brings success, whether that is an additional service, product, branding and so on. Innovation combined with Six Sigma will ensure focus on new market segments, using new techniques, operational procedures or even the entire business strategy.

Six Sigma is a methodology that calls for education. The tools, not all but many are complicated, there are systems like Minitab to be used and it's often only a Green Belt or Black Belt who can only use the tools. However, the methods are not all that complicated and invite for every process will be reviewed, with new processes to be analyzed and tested before they are launched or implemented in full scale.

Six Sigma exists in 5 important phases. I will describe those and use an example of a potential implementation of innovation based on the Six Sigma methodology into the hospitality which has not been tested, but I believe can have huge impact. The 5 phases DMAIC, consist of Define, Measure, Analyze, Improve and Control.

Define
The first phase of the DMAIC process is Define. The only way to start with a Six Sigma is to get to the bottom of a problem or opportunity. I want to be clear that, even though problems are easy to find, this is a great start for any innovative hotel. However, problems are very often turned into

opportunities and innovation. A problem is often based on data and when it is not data, should be collected to confirm the problem. An example of a problem is that, all the rooms ending with 35 (like 235, 335 etc.) are the largest rooms, but we have never sold it at the price allocated to it. Data tells us that this room is sold last or hardly ever sold at all. An immediate reaction from most management would be to drop the price to lower levels and make sure it is occupied. Six Sigma looks at it differently by clearly defining the problem (in the next phase) to this. That can either be done by collecting new data, by asking front office staff or the guest why this room is of no interest. Once an operational definition is made based on the findings, you can take the next step. In this example, it could have been that the room is next to the elevator, has no view, staff does not know how to upsell it or many other reasons. The next step is to understand if this issue is severe enough to tackle and if it will make a serious change to the business. All kinds of innovative ideas also pop up, like what is an extra service that we can offer to make this room more interesting like a play corner for families or a display of art and selling it as the art room. Once the management has agreed that this issue of importance should be handled, resources need to be allocated. Together with the allocated team, a detailed goal statement is created followed by drawing a process map called SIPOC (supplier, Input, process, output, customer) or Deployment map, that describes a high level map. This high level map describes which departments and steps are involved. Finally, we have to describe the customer and their requirements (Voice of the Customer). These requirements will be most beneficial if they are measurable, like numbers or percentages. I will not explain all the tools that are available, but most of this can be done in simple ways by interviewing or collecting data. Note that, gut feeling is not relevant and even dangerous here as this is the base for a project to be successful. Also important in the define phase is that, customers can be both internal and external to the organization. In the simple example later on, you can find some of these details.

Measure
The measure phase is all about quantifying the problem or opportunity. Data collection is continuous and is being refined to prepare well for the next phase. Identifying the root cause here is essential as it will also tell

you the baseline. Establishing the baseline is needed to measure any type of improvement in the future. In the last phase control, I will come back to this. In this phase, the team can start defining the reasons which might cause the problem, and also find new ways to collect existing or new data to confirm these reasons or in Six Sigma called root causes. Note that, specialists will use tools to ensure that the data collected is reliable and not based on assumptions or opinions. With regards to the room 35, data that can be collected from the front office technology. Things like when was it booked, and by whom or how? Was it a family? Was it booked through reservations and can we interview them to ask reasons for booking, or denying the room type? What is the sales process? Is the room too close to an elevator? How many people typically occupy this room, is it only sold when occupancy of the hotel is over 90%? Are there any complaints from previous guests about this room? And so forth.

Analyze

Analyzing the data collected in previous stages is the start of a potential change as you can identify opportunity. This is an opening for innovation. This phase is all about happiness, as this is where you start recognizing how your hotel can increase revenues or decrease costs and also deliver improved guest satisfaction resulting in loyalty. This is also when the selection of the team in the first phase becomes critical, as they are all potential stakeholders that will influence decision being made in this phase and the next one. The data is being inspected here and with the team, a brainstorm is initialized to narrow down the vital opportunities or problems. In the room example, the team could have come with a number of causes, like the room is not bookable online, there are only families staying in these rooms and willing to pay the premium; yet the room is not made for families because there is only one sink or no space for an extra bed. The project now takes a solid turn, turning data into opportunity. The team recognizes steps that needs to be taken to fill this room year round, leading to higher occupancy at the rate established. The Cause & Effect diagram is a great tool to classify the results of the data into what is most impactful for the hotel and the guest. The typical hotel organization will start here, leaving out great opportunity by missing and not quantifying data.

Improve

The brainstorm or use of other tools in the analyze phase will result in potential solutions, innovation or new project ideas. This phase is about the implementation and verification of the solution. Even though in the previous stage potential solutions have already appeared, in the Improve phase you have to move from quantity to quality. The improvement plan should be detailed but also gives opportunity to be creative and find solutions that are not the most likely ones. It can occur that potential solutions actually conflict as well, in which they need to be weighed up against each other or even tested. What follows is a clear new process map that has to involve all the team members as well as everybody who is involved in implementing the process. Internal communication is of extreme importance to make implementation successful and get the entire hotel on board with the change. A change that needs to be tested and piloted to ensure success. The baseline established in the earlier phase, is used to see and understand the shift that is needed to deliver the optimal guest service and improved process. A possible pilot as for the room 35 type could be to actively start selling the room as family room, packaging it with a kid's experience, online as well as off line, or making adjustments at small cost to the room to make it an art room and adjusting the pricing accordingly.

Control

Potentially the most beautiful part of the process is to track and measure how successful the project is. This is a phase that in most implementations is ignored. The Control phase is a process that over time, typically 12 or 18 months, gives indication of steps in the implemented process that work or don't work. When it works, it should become a part of the best practice documentation and when it does not work, there should be a change made directly, to avoid this happening again in the future. This management or monitoring is often done by the team member accountable for the project, often together with the financial director. Creating a best practice will help similar process in other departments or in sister hotels. In the case of room 35, tracking is simply done by measuring type of guest, occupancy and average rate as outcomes and for example, how many bookings come through the newly created web offering.

114

Besides Six Sigma, more and more companies are implementing Lean. There is a clear relationship between Lean and Six Sigma. Simply said, Lean is a method that is applied to create more value for guests or customers with fewer resources. These methods are mainly used in production processes, eliminating waste or unneeded steps in a process. The ultimate goal is deliver perfection and value to the guest or customer. The key elements of Lean are as follows.

1. Focuses on maximizing process velocity
2. Provides tools for analyzing process flow and delay times at each activity in a process
3. Centers on the separation of 'value-added' from 'non-value added' work with tools to eliminate the root causes of non-value added activities and their cost
4. Provides a means for qualifying and eliminating the cost of complexity

In other words, Lean is very useful within innovation. It teaches how to start, implement and steer a project and make it accelerates the best and fastest possible way. These days, Lean is and can often be combined with Six Sigma, particularly within Innovations as it takes away uncertainty and uses tools to work smarter, rather than harder. Within Six Sigma, after each phase, there is a checklist of minimum requirements that are needed to be able to get to the next phase. This checklist is called tollgates and will leave no space for essential parts that have been forgotten.

Healthy innovation within a hotel, using Six Sigma.
In all the years within hotels, all the research that has been carried out with regards to hotel gyms is endless. For many years, a hotel gym has been a must have service. According to London Hotel Insight, in London, 75% of the guests even when there is a request for the gym, do not actually use it. I will give you an example of Innovations that my company has put together, but not yet implemented in any hotel. I am 100% convinced however, that it will be once I take you through a number of the Six Sigma phases of this particular turning complaints and data into innovation.

Defining, measuring, analyzing, improving and innovating.

A number of issues both from a guest point of view and a hotel point of view are very evident with regards to the hotel gym. For a hotel operator, the hotel gym is cost only as it is very hard to deliver a return of investment. It is a service that hotels feel they have to offer the guest, as the demand and certainly the expectation exists. Personally, I also want the hotel to have a gym or pool, even though I try and make it a habit to explore the city by running through it too. The gym takes space, which could otherwise be sold as a room for example. A gym has to be maintained, water and towels have to be supplied. That is a cost to the hotel, which they cannot pass on to the guest. From a guest point of view, the state or size of the gym is in the top 10 of the overall complaints within hotels, based on one large research project I was part of, with a large hotel chain. Further data collection told us that over 90% of female guests do not use the hotel gym. Reason given is because, they do not feel safe; the gym is smelly or dirty or too small, in that particular order of relevance. Men do want to use it mostly and 52% actually select the hotel only if it has fitness facilities. Out of the guests that are using the gym or fitness room, over 40% were unhappy with the facilities or that the machines they wanted to use were not available as typical gym hours are between 6.30-9am and 5-7pm.

Enough data to conclude there was an opportunity both for the hotel as well as the guest. The hotel gym is clearly not delivering what it should. So we put a few people around the table, someone with a gym/exercise background, a yield manager, a hotel general manager and myself. And we came up with 'The 1Sq Meter Gym'. Rather than offering a gym that does not at all deliver to standards even when it is available, we came with an in room gym that would exercise all part of the body. We selected a partner 'Casall' a Swedish design company developing training equipment and clothing. They developed a designer ladder, available in several colors, allocated a number of equipment that you can attach to the ladder, a mat and exercise ball. They even offer an app that you can use to train preferred time periods and intervals. Recently, we launched this concept as 'The smallest hotel gym in the world and your guests will love it'.

Advantages:

1. Guests do not have to bring gym clothes/shoes
2. Exercise is available at all times
3. No need to visit a separate gym
4. Cleanliness aspect
5. Feel safe in own room
6. Ability to charge a premium for an exercise room
7. Access to an app as personal trainer
8. Low installation cost
9. Sales of equipment (third party revenues)
10. Great marketing opportunity, taking the health avenue
11. No separate gym room needed, even though still recommended
12. Reduction of complaints, leading to improved guest satisfaction
13. Partnership with a well-known reliable brand

The 1Square meter gym is yet to be piloted into hotels, but clearly in this case, complaints and low scores in guest satisfaction, collection of relevant date have resulted into what can be great innovation once tested and tracked.

Innovation as the engine of the hotel

In 2004, I was part of one of the largest innovation projects at Starwood Hotels & Resorts. A team of 10 people had about 3 days to interview over 300 people in countries all over Europe. The goal was to collect as much data as possible to create a minimum of 3 innovation projects for the company. The experience was incredible. The impact of meeting all these employees from all levels within the organization was immense. The reaction from the employees was extremely positive as they felt listened to and their opinion counts more than they ever felt. They were kept updated on the entire process and the ideas that came out eventually were implemented by 3 different teams with great success. The success was based on real life ideas and experiences, the communication process throughout and the final implementation were proof that ideas can easily be found within the company as well as from external resources.

With the help of one of my dear friend Juliana Cavalcanti De Andrea, I interviewed one of the frontiers in innovation, Pedro Do Carmo Costa.

Interview
Pedro Do Carmo Costa
Director and Co-founder Exago
Interviewed by colleague Juliana Cavalcanti De Andrea – Clothing and Uniform designer

You quote on the future of Hotel Innovation
'Someone, somewhere is inventing the idea to dramatically disrupt the hotel industry. So before that someone does it, think about how YOU can change the rules of the game. It's your game after all.'

1.   Please tell us about the objectives of your company, Exago?
Answer: At Exago, we believe that organizations have significant untapped potential within themselves – in their people. Working with companies across sectors and continents, we've learned that the answers to most strategic or common day-to-day business challenges already exist somewhere in your organization. Leadership only has to create the environment in which these answers can surface and be implemented.

Exago helps companies embed this innovation culture and capability. We develop solutions based on software and services that allow large companies to engage their collective intelligence in solving critical business and strategic challenges.

2.   You have had a number of clients within the Service and Hospitality industry. What were the biggest surprise and moments in your view?
Answer: This is an industry rich in orthodoxies. Looking at the highest-level business model and comparing it with other industries, nothing seems to have changed substantially in the hospitality industry over the last hundred years. Due to the sector's conservative and capital-intensive nature, most modifications have been incremental and mainly adoptions of the inevitable. The pace of change in the hospitality industry is much slower and less dramatic than the world or consumers' pace.

I am also surprised by the fact that, some of the biggest changes in the industry have been led by people from outside this sector, particularly in more recent years. These includes, social networks allowing for genuine hotel-guest interactions and online booking engines and travel intermediaries that pressure hotels to develop more aggressive discount pricing. Other key transformations are couch surfing, peer-to-peer on Airbnb and new accommodation options that have forced the creation of innovative services to conquer an increasingly demanding clientele.

3. What type of innovation is available for Hotels, and what are the basic needs to collect data?

Answer: Several types of innovation exist for which we can construct various definitions, for example, technology innovation and process, product and service improvement. I would rather use a simpler framework, one that defines two types: incremental and disruptive innovation.

Incremental innovation is about the everyday changes that we explore and implement. It's about becoming 1% better every month, every year. It's not only about the top line but also efficiency. Hotels are good at this, improving facilities, making processes more efficient, adopting new technologies and systems. This is pretty much a rat race in the sense that, we can't stop doing it. Stopping is downgrading. And those who cumulatively deliver a higher hit rate for incremental change can actually differentiate themselves from the rest and grow faster in margins and revenue.

Disruptive innovation is about reinventing our business model. It's fundamentally changing one or more of our business model's dimensions: whom we serve, what benefits we provide, how we deliver those benefits and how we sustain that differentiation. Great examples of disruptive innovation are everywhere – Amazon, EasyJet and Apple. Or take Uber's fresh, an example of the ridesharing service now operating in over 200 cities worldwide, which has been lowering taxi fares, creating turmoil in that once stagnant business and generating the need for taxi companies to reform and quickly explore new paths and services.

4.   From capturing ideas to actual implementation, lots of steps need to be taken. Where can you see the biggest opportunities within hospitality? Answer: Most innovation processes follow some or all of the following steps: discovery – where you identify challenges or explore new insights that can unlock innovations; ideation – when you generate ideas around these insights or challenges; elaboration – where you put some meat on the bone (i.e. you iteratively turn ideas into proposals and ventures); experimentation – when you test the assumptions behind ventures to de-risk them and finally, scale – where you launch the new concepts to the market after adjusting them. I think hospitality can outrun other industries in two of these steps: discovery and experimentation.

Discovery is about anticipation, unlocking insights about markets, customers and technologies – which lead you to great ideas and opportunity spaces. The insights around under-leveraged assets are what led to Uber's opportunity space. Hospitality is a face-to-face business in which customer's proximity is the ideal way to observe your audience and extract signals from them. Being so close to customers and being consumers ourselves (experiencing good and bad things), you should be able to extract insights faster than anyone else.

Experimentation is about de-risking. When we strongly believe in a venture or business opportunity, we need to ask what the key assumptions behind this opportunity is. What are the things that might cause this to fail? They typically relate to the benefits we deliver, our ability to deliver them and lastly, the ways we can capture value (i.e. make money). Once identified, we have to test these assumptions before committing significant resources, through simple experiments that rapidly and cheaply confirm or deny the assumptions, assessing if the risk is manageable. Because of the nature of hotels as networks of connected physical assets, running experiments in stand-alone units is easier. Then, if tests show a venture will succeed, take it to the next phase. Not many industries have a configuration that allows this.

5.   Clearly we can learn a lot from other industries. Which industries are facing similar challenges for innovation and what are these challenges?

Answer: Several industries are facing similar challenges, including guest profiling, cost reduction imperatives, price model rethinking, evolving customer needs and expectations (with more sophistication), increasing competition and the need to reinvent experiences.

Some of these industries are not necessarily the usual suspects:

- The airline industry: As a whole, it has faced low costs competition and diminishing margins, learning to segment itself into low-cost, regular, Net Jets and luxury options – to create different value options for different targets. More directly related to the hospitality industry, the exclusive Four Seasons private jet experience takes travelers around the globe, with personalized itineraries, which is a bold example of what can be done to reinvent experiences.

- The real estate industry: Red Fin turned this highly inefficient sector upside down by creating 'customer advocates', making the entire process faster, easier and worry-free, with lower commissions and technology leverage. The company placed consumers' needs at the centre of its business. In this way, Red Fin managed not only to change the real estate customers' experience but also, to produce a cultural shift in the relationship between companies and customers.

- The music industry: Streaming platform Spotify sent strong shock waves and provoked intellectual property discussions throughout the music industry – at the same time, democratizing the market and leveraging many thousands of artists. But, the firm's also notable for its flexible pricing and subscription model, offering different levels of services to customers.

All this proves that, the shift to digital network creation and to targeted and more personalized consumption models seems inevitable. Consumers now can voice their likes and dislikes. So the hospitality industry has to find channels to grow and consolidate this new relationship and create services that enable customizable guest experiences.

6.   How can Senior Management adapt to change, within and outside the Hospitality industry?
Answer: To stay ahead of the innovation game, senior management needs to provide direction, incentives and processes.

Direction is about sending a clear message to everyone that innovation is not just a fad (and acting accordingly). This is actually your organization's differentiation engine.

Incentives moves people and help align everyone to the innovation credo. Getting to work every day, your employees need to think, 'How am I going to be measured today, this week, this quarter?' If clear incentives for innovation and a long-term perspective don't exist, you're wasting everyone's time.

Finally, you need processes. You can't expect serendipitous innovation. You need structured processes to go from insights through to ideas, opportunities, experiments, ventures and finally, value.

Senior management can also:
-    Bring external input: you can create an innovation board and invite externals to your industry to participate. You'll get quite unorthodox perspectives and some very interesting insights. You can use this board to evaluate ideas, insights and ventures.
-    Build your capability and process: leadership, process and incentives are mentioned above. You have a budgeting or booking process that wasn't built in a day.
-    Get started quickly and build on your successes.

7.   Your company is all about engaging employees, how will employee engagement change in the future and how can Hotels adjust to this?
Answer: We believe employee engagement that attracts, retains and leverages employees' knowledge is a key driver for any company's future. The more engaged your workforce, the higher the volume of contributions (of ideas, insights and collaborations) and the higher the chances of hitting a home run. As a result, you capture higher value.

This sounds like a pretty simple game, yet some tricky questions are left. How can you boost engagement levels? How can you streamline the idea evaluation process?

On the one hand, everyone's attention is being solicited by his or her business, social networks, and personal interests and so on. Making your innovation process appealing is as important as it is hard. To attract and keep your people engaged in common challenges over time, you have to develop good communication plans, adopt clever incentives and a gamified idea management platform, recognizing valuable contributions with leaderboards and digital currency rewards (which participants can exchange for material prizes).

On the other hand, we've learned that grinding out hundreds of ideas kills innovation. Idea management platforms using predictive markets mechanics have proven to be a highly efficient way to collect and assess high volumes of ideas. They allow you to engage your people in shared challenges, collect all their ideas and activate your company's collective intelligence for a collaborate selection of the best ideas. This also makes sure you don't get swallowed up by bureaucratic monsters – having to analyze all the input received.

With Generation Y (people born during the 1980s or 90s) and Generation Z (those born at the end of the 1990s and into the beginning of the new millennium) hitting the market and overcoming various orthodoxies and employee engagement will become more and more paramount for any industry's future.

8.   The Hotel industry is one that circles much around cost and ROI, how does this affect Innovation, and implementation thereof?
Answer: Cost and return on investment (ROI) are great business metrics, and they've led our businesses to what they are today. However, you have to figure out how to balance these metrics with others that allow you to explore some out-of-the box opportunities. Most innovations especially disruptive ones are difficult to evaluate using traditional metrics. Think of some of the big innovations we've mentioned, like Amazon, Easy jet and

Apple. Applying the 'ruling' metrics of the day would have killed these opportunities, yet they succeeded and changed their industries, sometimes dramatically.

Most innovations are today driven by customers' pains, unattended needs, potential trends and unleveraged technologies. Make sure you use these to establish new metrics and balance them with cost and ROI.

9.   You yourself are a frequent traveler, what are your biggest obstacles when booking or staying at a Hotel and what could be learned from innovation?

Answer: As a very frequent traveler, I've realized that I adopt different personas all the time. I can be a quite functional traveler who needs a simple place to bunk before a meeting, an experience seeker who looks for a boutique hotel or, increasingly, a great apartment via Airbnb (often more expensive than a five-star hotel) or a luxury traveler who aspires for good room service sensu lato (e.g. exceptional food and beverage, spa and location). Depending on my persona, I use distinct gateways. I think consumers have acquired more power than ever. Choice is at the tip of their fingers.

As a consumer myself, I see good changes, but mostly incremental ones. I always experience a thrill when I pop the card to open the door. That first impression can still cause shock or disappointment. Consumers have gained more power – hotels less.

On the negative side, especially in the US, the penny and dime charges are an insult. I still feel like the prey, with the hotel trapping me in all possible ways.

10.   Will the Hospitality industry remain a sexy industry in the future to work for, and what needs to happen to ensure that?

Answer: Absolutely. In the future, wine will come in tetra-pack packages, some with plastic caps and others with real corks and consumers are happy with all of them: unique offerings for different targets, different wines and uncommon packaging for every taste and persona. Personally, I believe that finding the right balance is the key and each hotel needs to understand where it wants to position itself. Wine will always be sexy and so will the hospitality industry.

As you can understand from the interview with Pedro, there is no more excuse into delaying any innovation effort within the hotel industry. The best time to start is today. The management has limitless access to data and information that can be used now, to create serious disruption in the hospitality industry.

Blue Ocean

Competing within the hotel industry is fun, there are so many ways in which a hotel can differentiate themselves. Compare it to a product like a t-shirt, colors, round neck, long sleeves and perhaps not so much one can change to compete. I have learned most of Sales & Marketing in my years in London. London has on almost every block in the center at least 10 hotels within the same category, looking for the same market segment, stealing business from each other. When in sales, out looking for contracts, it was evident that negotiation skills were one of the most important elements in getting the contracts. Nothing much to compete with, service, room types and other offerings were certainly not any different than the others, let alone disrupting any traditional offerings.

The Blue Ocean strategy is a systematic approach to making competition irrelevant. The brilliant book 'Blue Ocean Strategy' by Kim and Mauborgne, is in many ways one of the best books when you are in a situation as described above, but also when you are creating or launching a new product or service. In this book I will not get deep into Blue Ocean, but rather want to explain why and how using the blue ocean can get innovation within the industry going.

Blue Ocean strategy splits up into two areas, the red ocean and the blue ocean. The red ocean signifies competing in an existing market space and the blue ocean signifies creating an uncontested market space. So rather than taking the hotel or department into an existing market, with a blue ocean strategy you actually define an entire new market space where there is no competition yet.

The red ocean:
Competes in existing market space
Beats the competition
Exploits existing demand
Makes the value-cost trade-off
Aligns the whole system of a firm's activities with its strategic choice of differentiation or low cost

The blue ocean:
Creates uncontested market space
Makes the competition irrelevant
Creates and capture new demand
Breaks the value-cost trade-off
Aligns the whole system of a firm's activities in pursuit of differentiation and low cost

Within our industry, there are numerous examples of Blue Ocean companies. Starbucks, a coffee culture that was created many years ago, catering for people who want a consistent good cup of coffee in a relaxed, homely atmosphere. Starbucks was founded in 1971 and now in 2016 has over 23,450 stores, worldwide and about 13,000 of those are in the USA. They created a new market space, demand through opening a number of places in the same location, and in 2016 they will even open their first store in Italy, Milan, a country which has always had their own coffee culture and was most sceptic about implementation. The pricing of the coffee is high and so is guest satisfaction. Their coffee making is Lean, a different person takes the order, passes it onto the cashier and finally a trained coffee maker, barista will make the coffee in exactly the same way every store does. They make it interesting to return by offering new beans or seasonal coffees (and they got the best granola bar ever) and of course the loyalty card. Sure now other chains have entered the market space that Starbucks have created. But with the rigid cost structure, ultimate guest delivery, they will continue to be hard to beat.

Kids Nanny Service. A few years ago I was introduced to a Dutch company run by Rachel Pietersma, that seemed simple; a nanny service offering nannies to hotels. Turned out this extremely successful company had a lot more to offer. Apart from ensuring that all the nannies have all the qualifications needed to handle children of all ages, the CEO herself carries out all the interviews personally. Her expectations and demands are very high and have much to do with pedagogy, education and attitude. The company started in 2010, as a kid's party service and since then has expanded all over Holland with 90 nannies who serve hotels, corporate clients as well as private families. Hotels don't just get a nanny who comes with a suitcase full of activities for the kids. They actually propose an entire outdoor activity plan, like a visit to a museum, or zoo, ensuring that the children get a feeling for city and country they are visiting. Additionally, the company offers a variety of languages like Chinese, Russian, Spanish and English.

They have expansion plans with regards to technology and in 2016 they will start recommending family friendly hotels, to further tighten the relationships they already have with the hotels.

Le Pain Quotidien, started in Brussels in 1990. Founded by a chef, who was dissatisfied with the quality of the bread that was available. By purchasing furniture of a local market and implementing a large long table in the middle of the store, he is also the originator of the Communal table. Le Pain Quotidien, marks itself as well as a breakfast restaurant, creating a culture that is mostly only found in hotels worldwide. Now they serve salads, pastries and have an entire range of retail products like chocolate spread. Their head office moved to the USA and they strive through an excellent Franchise set up. The concept will continue to grow and has great potential to be integrated into hotels as well.

AirBnB, an effort that started in 2008. They do not project themselves as Hotel Company, but as a website. A website that connect people who are looking to rent space or have space to rent out. Sure, the original thought was most likely to compete in the vacation stay market, but has grown quickly into a global site where people can put up their place for rent and now available in over 190 countries. A smart alternative, to the hotel industry and again with an extremely small cost margin. Most of the funds go to marketing efforts with much success. They project a safe and verified channel, making sure that the apartments or residences are let out by trusted individuals. An entire new Blue Ocean approach to stay with limited but satisfying selection levels, like does the apartment have Airco, a pool etc. Also a very transparent way of pricing and booking.

Happy socks also established in 2008, in Sweden came with the idea to satisfy the need for so many. Socks that create happiness and launch that into a market space that was not existing yet. Sure, there are many brands that carry socks as part of their portfolio, but they are either not specialists or they are simply boring blue and black socks. And you have to admit, you smile when you see people wear those. The dots, the colors and stripes invite for a happy reaction. They challenged the existing buyer, created something that is eye-catching and does most of the marketing itself. A brilliant example of Blue Ocean is thinking and implementation.

There are many such examples, so I want to finish giving an example of a hotel concept that is Blue Ocean. Ace hotels is a company that was established in 1999, in the USA. It is a chain of hotels that currently has 9 hotels in the portfolio. They created a new market space by ensuring that each hotels has the style and design that reflects the location, in line with my previous description in the chapter eat me. The Ace hotel in Seattle is in a former Salvation Army halfway house, another is hotel in London's art district on the site of the original Shore ditch Empire Music Hall, the latest opening was in the YMCA building in Pittsburgh. Ace hotels market themselves in a very clever way, staying in touch with the guest through event calendars, keeping the hotels fresh, energized and human as they state in their vision. The website is fun and inspiring and invites for a revisit. Ace Hotels is creating a special relationship as well through creating a tight link with retail. They recommend products that carry their own name, which are very cool and also link to audio, travel related items and art.

Best practices
Innovation is not only about creating something new, it's about identifying existing and new opportunity and making sure that it can be repeated.

That requires structure and discipline from top management, as well as all the stakeholders. What's working in one hotel might not always work in others, only data will tell if a project with success can be copied and implemented in another place. A best practice is a method or process that shows consistent results of improvement and contains steps, tools and data that can be used again and again to improve the way organizations work and develop.

In retail, it could be the way each store is opened, the purchasing process, the pre marketing, the communication, the hiring process etc. Naturally, starting with the process that is impacting the industry most financially or from a guest point of view will have to be tackled first. A current and very typical development we can see is the environmental industry. How water can be reused, or how governments can deal with water pollution and implement clean air programs that work across the border.

Within hotels, working with so many different skills spread out over all the departments, there is a lot to be learned from each other and there is a great opportunity to register and document success. Even though many hotels have corporate standard with regards to for example, purchasing processes or branding, there is a lot of decision making left to each individual hotel. Also every culture, department might have different history and of course different service requirements. Also, inconsistency and turnover of staffing and management makes it hard to keep the consistency. Typically, a general manager get replaced every 5 years in the hotel industry. This means new views on the business, which can and will affect the service to the guest, as well as internal and external process.

I would like to share with you some of the best practices that have implemented into hotels since 2001, which have affected the bottom line and service greatly. They are either based on an opportunity or have risen because of operational issues.

Group booking process
Issue: Slow response time

Solution: By improving the booking process, following a lean approach, the response time to bookers can be decreased significantly.

Results: Looking into the booking process has created opportunity within allocation of groups, displacement of groups, denials of groups, improved forecasting, improved pricing methods and improved internal and external communication.

Yielding
Opportunity: optimal pricing and occupancy
Solution: By improving the way the room are priced, according to seasonality, city trends, historical data, future trend analysis, use of systematic tools, third party websites, upselling techniques and training, the average rate and occupancy have great potential to increase
Result: Yielding creates flexibility in pricing, last minute as well as in advance creating the best possible pricing and occupancy levels.

Sales & Marketing
Opportunity: Optimal planning and communication
Solution: By creating and implementing a long term marketing plan, taking into consideration all departments, there is continuous flow of information that can be communicated internally and externally.
Result: In more loyal guests, improved operational knowledge, improved pricing, improved staff planning, good view on budget allocations

Procurement
Issue: significant annual increases in costs
Solution: By streamlining the procurement process and purchasing process, the hotel has opportunity to decrease short term costs, revise contracts, understand outsourcing opportunities, licenses, improve communication, improve re-use and accounting procedures.
Result: Significant financial savings are made by streamlining processes, getting by from department head, renegotiating contracts and choosing alternatives.

Human Resources
Issue: High staffing costs

Solution: Engaging all department heads in scheduling, understanding results in low occupancy periods, data analysis, use of scheduling tools, training in tools, systems and tracking, the staffing can be streamlined and show only marginal movement in line with revenues.
Result: Improved staffing levels resulting in improved communication, lower costs, improved employee satisfaction and better use of systems

Food & Beverage
Issue: Complaint on pricing
Solution: Value for money creation through optimizing menus, amending the restaurant concept, outsourcing of the cleaning and stewarding.
Result: reduction of menu size, improved purchasing costs, decreased cleaning costs, improved concept through simple changes, more attractive promotions internally and adjustments in the pricing levels.

There are many more examples of best practices, the above mentioned resulted in great direct results as well as numerous side effects. Guest satisfaction is always number one, and through streamlining and listening to guests, there are many ways to react and be proactive.

In this chapter, which you will understand is very close to my heart and should be really close to every employee in the hospitality business's heart, I have described how innovation is much more than popular word. It can result in many changes that are both needed for your business to survive but more importantly, get your hotel or department to stand out and disrupt the industry. Data and people are the best resources to start a change that is needed. Changes are continuous, so I suggest to lead the change. Using the numerous tools described in the chapter will create control and energy around change.

In the next chapter with the title 'Delivering the dream', I will focus on guest satisfaction and customer service, what it means and the value of it.

Chapter 6

Delivering the dream
Leading guest satisfaction

The hospitality industry is by far one of the most controversial and exciting industries when it comes to guest satisfaction. Before I thought about my reader and the purpose of this book, I created a map or work flow to facilitate the reading. The order of the chapters and subjects were an important factor in the process. I actually contemplated even writing about guest satisfaction, mainly because the entire book really has a purpose of educating the reader and everything about delivery to the guest; whether that is design, services or simply sleep and food. I decided to write anyway; while traveling and speaking with not only regular travelers and naturally hotels management, there is quite a lot that has been misunderstood, as well as opportunity being missed because data is unclear or our minds and gut feelings are telling us one thing and the truth is significantly different.

An example is a large project I once worked on. The project was about analyzing data that was collected from travelers after they had stayed at a hotel. Many hotels want a solid indication of guest satisfaction per hotel and be able to benchmark against others in the group, but clearly also recognizing and highlighting strong and weak elements within the hotel. I remember before this project that I too, just like many General Managers, took this guest satisfaction index very seriously. And so we should, but there are many sides to this data that are not satisfying enough for an analysts who is looking for correlation, standard deviation or sample sizing to name a few. Then there are also outside factors that can play a significant role in how guests rate the hotel. Think about the weather, a rainy New York for a business trip is no fun; even more so travel related matters. For example one might book an exclusive resort, for an extended holiday, but the entire island, the flight and local experience might be everything but luxurious. That creates conflicting expectations leading to confusing ratings. Recently, I have started looking into what tourism or destination agencies are communicating towards the international public. Pretty pictures and videos of the most magnificent area of a country or destination are often not what it's really like. Some might only have one sandy beach which is so crowded, even a German would not find space for his towel at 7am in the morning. The tourist office has an incredibly important role in identifying and marketing a segment that matches the service levels of the destination.

Going back to the data analysis, the group working on the project were looking for correlation between answers of the data. There was none, or surprisingly few, we tried to look for every angle possible. Some very surprising results for example were that, value money is not correlated to satisfaction. Yes, you read that right, there was no sign that if the score for guest satisfaction is high, the value for money would also be high. Another interesting example is that, cleanliness of the room was not influencing the quality of the room or the other way around.

In fact how can we actually measure guest satisfaction, if every guest is different, if every service given is given by different people? There are ways and of course we can learn from all the surveys as you see and understand trends. Rather than going into much detail of data collection or the definition of Guest Satisfaction, I'd rather share ideas, concepts and knowledge of what really is of value for the potential guest. How to read your guest, how to share information and how to communicate internally as well as externally to ensure your guest will be a loyal one.

'In order to succeed, we must first believe we can' Nikos Kazantzakis

The product

The only way to understand the guest is to start identifying one that suits your product. Leadership needs to fully admit the qualities of the product. Whether that is the hotel, the building, the spa, the bar or the location, there need to be a match with the customer and the product. In recent years, the Spa has become more of an amenity or must have than anything else. So are we wrong with building a spa in every hotel? Yes, absolutely we are, as it is not an expectation for every traveler, so is it a service? Yes, it is a bit, if your market segment is not asking for it, then you will run it with a loss and start cutting costs, creating a low value experience for your guests, who do wants to use it. There is a reason why so many spas are losing money, it is not part of the core business and promoting a receptionist from the hotel to be a spa manager is seriously a bad idea, without any relative education or experience. A bit further in the book, I will focus more on the spa element, for now it has to be understood, originally the spa is meant to be a retreat for people who needed rehabilitation. It still is, a good spa only has one focus and that is to heal people. So if your identified market segment is looking for a spa, you will have success and in fact, if you do it right, it will be the marketing tool to attract people to the other facilities the hotel has to offer.

Another element is of course the location, or age of the hotel, a non-renovated hotel in an unpopular area of a city cannot pretend to be anything else. Even though in recent years, you can see for example with the W hotels, that they are opening in unexpected daring areas, with great success and creating a buzz to old and underdeveloped areas.

Take also the concept boutique hotel. When I started working in the industry, the boutique hotel concepts was not such a big thing as it is now. The corporate names were setting the standards for the hotel industry. That is changing and will continue to change significantly. People are looking for a local experience, easy to find, easy to book and yet giving the loyalty points that they are looking for. Some companies are striving to represent these boutique hotels, like Small luxury hotel & resorts or Design hotels (in lesser format). They are offering hotels with a certain niche and charge to be part of their portfolio. The hotels have to meet certain standards set by the company to ensure a certain physical equality.

Article
Published by 4Hoteliers.com
Jeroen Gulickx

Have boutique hotels broken the code?

The trip
The trip by car on the windy road in the Cotswalds was amazing and of extreme comfort. We were driving a Rolls Royce silver shadow, from London to a little town in the South of the area. I remember the car as if it was yesterday, it was a green shiny color and the petrol was more expensive than the dinner that evening. When we got to a small village we parked the car in front of a little post office where I asked a few people passing whether it was ok to park there, to which they responded, "The parking attendant only works when he feels like it, so we have not seen him in years". Moments later, we arrived at the most picturesque place. The town close by, Crudwell had a small lovely hotel in it, the first time I came across a boutique experience.

So what is boutique and why is it so popular?
Size is clearly of importance, and of elite standard.
Boutique is a French word and means shop. Historically, the French are known for their delightful small and exclusive shopping solutions. That's why we love Paris and the small streets, with the great variety of shops it has to offer. A hotel could be the same, a small place with something specific and exclusive to offer. Condé Nast Travel gives Paris as the ultimate location for boutique hotels: 'Paris not only has more hotels than any other city in the world, it also has some of the most beautiful and most celebrated. But its famed palaces don't have a monopoly on looking fabulous. Thanks to a vanguard of boutique pioneers, you can stay in a room created by Philippe Starck, Christian Lacroix, India Mahdavi, Marc Newson, Pierre Le-Tan or Sophie Calle for a fraction of the cost of a night at one of the grander big-hitters. And while these new and revamped hotels aren't always

conventionally swish, they offer a quirky take on this most visited cities. Rooms in Paris, especially those in historic buildings, tend to be small. Lifts too, can be cramped and soundproofing is often an issue. But if you're counting your pennies and are prepared to carry your own bags, these super-value finds all under £200 a night - from a fashion favorite in the 1st arrondissement to a minimalist masterpiece in the 20th - are worth every step.

Looking beyond size and standard, the reason for boutique's existence could very well have much to do with the creation of a hotel concept that offers recognition or the feeling of being somewhere different, something that others have not tried or experienced. The trend in marketing agencies is similar, moving from a large corporate agency to the smaller niche agencies calling themselves boutique. Sure, it has something to do with knowing and wanting to understand more about the locality, the area, and knowing exactly where the experience comes from. But perhaps that also comes back to recognition. We feel we get more, if others know what we are looking for or if we know the product we buy, eat or experience is a local one of good quality. We also have the need to be looked after and not become one in the queue, again like some companies feel when they become a "small" client of a large marketing agency. Or for example, when a guest is only recognized upon check in or out.

The Value of the boutique hotel

How we select the elements that decide for us to choose a boutique hotel can and will vary. Recognition is one factor that plays a role and the level will of course be different from stay to stay, but it is potentially one to differentiate a boutique hotel from another hotel.

An element reviewed often is Value, its big word related to brand, cost, experience, balance, philosophy and ultimately experience. In all my years within the travel industry, people become harder to categorize, resulting in values that are hard for hotels to understand and to adjust or offer their services accordingly. However, developing hotel concepts becomes a cleaner cut and perhaps fun, just because market segmentation is widely spread and opinion is readily available from the end users, through online reviews, booking engines and corporate companies moving to online travel services. With the creation of boutique hotels, value is the core business model, playing into those wishes or thoughts of the guest.

Eventually, that is what it is all about apart from loyalty programs or location. Boutique hotels have an opportunity to deliver and exceed guest expectations, just because they are small and can add this incredible value, which is exactly what the small boutiques in Paris's little streets have done for so many years.

The product is perhaps not as static as I described earlier as there are also lots of amendments that can be made, but they mostly require investments or even outsourcing. So the duties go beyond that of the hotel, since location and destination are not always reaching the optimal levels of tourism.

The destination
Selecting a destination for a trip has become a totally different experience. Over 90% of people look at the internet and look for more information on the hotel or the city it's in. This could be anything from how to get around in the city, the safety of the destination or what to enjoy locally. These factors can make a traveler decide whether to book, if of course they have a choice and it's not a work related trip. Travelers need to feel an association with the destination and that is often not something that the hotel can directly influence. Of course, some destinations have a better reputation because of their history and historic buildings, like Cape Town or Rome. You can read more on technology, apps and online booking in the chapter about technology. For now, I want to focus on how hotels can help or push the destination management companies, tourist agencies and governmental institutions. Particularly the governmental institutions sit on incredible data they receive, for example from airports. They are doing all this data collection to be able to steer projects that drive tourism and business to their country. It is difficult to judge whether they are successful in the actual implementation. What I can confirm is that, I personally do not think that every effort is made in attracting the right customer. I keep

coming back to know what you can offer and to whom; Just have a look at some destinations who are seriously well represented like Florida. They are visible at tourism fairs, have contracts with Public relations agencies worldwide, have a great welcoming and informative website and all because they are upgrading their image to attract a younger crowd, with good incomes. They are successful, hotels are being built in Miami, prices are rising and global airlines have started flying directly to one of their bigger airports. Same with Mallorca, the Spanish island that was for years in decline has polished up their image, improved infrastructure, identified a customer who wants to spend and enjoy the beauty of the island. In the last 5 years, Mallorca is blooming, real estate prices are climbing, beautiful hotels are being built and others renovated and rebranded. The destination needs to create one or preferably a number of unique selling points that is attractive for the consumer.

Also, more and more you see that typical points of recognition are disappearing, like the phone boxes of London or the buses of Malta. They are not unique selling points, but simply great tools to market. All too often, you now see images that really do not reflect the destination or websites, that is to say the least unattractive, unclear and not informational. I asked Doug Lansky, a key note speaker who travels worldwide how he feels destinations can make a real difference to the hospitality industry.

Interview	
Doug Lansky	
Travel writer, Author, Key note speaker	

1. Please tell us about your objectives in changing the way we travel?

Answer:

I want it to be a good experience for travelers for years to come and for that to happen, some organization needs to step forward and provide some quality control. Outside of Disney, this role doesn't currently exist. Hotels look after their guest and so does good restaurants and airlines… but there are a lot of bits that make up the traveler's journey in that destination that can affect their overall experience. What we have are a lot of marketers making campaigns and asking for more visitors on social media, but we need to take care of the end-to-end experience of the visitor and provide some new brand-aligned "products" to attract new visitors.

2. You have been part of many events as a speaker and participant. What is the biggest eye opener for many who attends your presentations?

Answer:

That the best marketing is a great product and that they have a vested interest in helping to improve that. If you don't have a big draw, all the web design and Tweets in the world won't be of much help.

3. How do you believe hotels can influence the selection process of travelers?

Answer: You can have a top end hotel, but if the destination is aiming at low-end visitors, that can limit your success. One of the big roles of the DMO (Destination Marketing Organization) is to define the brand of the destination. If you want to have a say in the brand direction, it makes sense to either get involved with the DMO's decision making process or work within the brand that they've selected.

Of course, you can also reach out to your target market by finding some key local partners. For example, if there's an art collector's conference every year and you have a top end hotel, reach out to the organizer and offer a package.

4. Hotels continue to focus on customer retention. How will the digital revolution continue to change customer's behavior within Hospitality?

Answer:

Here's one thing that hotels can do tomorrow and it won't cost them a thing; use the internet to connect their guests with like-minded locals. So let's say a guest checks in and the person at the front desk ask if they have any hobbies/passions and let's say the guest says "fencing." The front desk can say: "I see we have 5 fencing clubs in town... if our concierge could make arrangements for you to join one of our local clubs for a practice and provide you with some equipment to borrow; all without any cost, would you be interested?"

If you can help a guest have a unique, authentic experience and do something they are passionate about and make some new local friends, that's an incredible service that may win their loyalty.

5. There always has been a lot of discussion about marketing for a destination. What are the key elements that creates success for a destination?

   Answer:

   1. An amazing and unique experience (or site)
   2. No overcrowding
   3. Good service and infrastructure

   There are really nice hotels and restaurants everywhere; that's not what typically gets people to book a trip. When their friends ask "How was Barcelona/Tokyo/Rome?" They're not typically asking about the hotel. So, it's vital to all stakeholders that the core of the destination offer amazing things that don't let them down (due to overcrowding or bad service).

6. What are some recommendations you can make to hotels with regards to connecting with Destination Management companies?

On one hand, you can't wait around for them to help you, they are working with various initiatives and campaigns. On the other hand, it makes sense to get involved and see if they're looking for partners for any special projects or have some great offers for co-op advertising opportunities.

7. What other industries do you feel the Hospitality industry can learn from and why?

Answer:

Disney may make a large percentage of their money in their hotels, but they know that people are coming because of the theme parks and rides and they add new rides every year. Their hotels offer great convenience and perks for those who want to experience Disney's attractions (special hours for entry and other accessibility features like direct stops on the monorail). And Disney keeps an eye on carrying capacity and even closes their gates a few times a year when it gets too crowded.

Imagine how that would look in a city, you push (read, support) the destination to create great experiences with great service, position the hotels so that staying in one enhances the actual attraction experience and makes payment easy (or "magical" as Disney would say). In other words, hotels could make deals with top attractions for early or late extra opening hours (maybe just 20 min before or after main entry) and then, let them charge drinks/ snacks to their hotel room (or something as easy).

You don't want the destination to feel like Disney (with no locals and no authentic culture and no soul), but you want it to work as well as Disney.

8. Destination management, tourism offices and similar often government funded organizations are dealing with traditional marketing and strategic methods, what is your recommendation for urgent change?

Answer:

The landscape has shifted. The things they are working on now are not in my opinion, the best use of resources. Less than 7% of visitors, for example, ever use the DMO's website and nearly all of them check 20-40 other information websites. Every destination has between a dozen and 100 good information websites (Lonely Planet, Rough Guides, Time Out and loads of others, plus blogs and apps). If a DMO shut down their website, I don't believe they'd lose a single visitor. Same with Tourist Offices. Now visitors have smart phones and Wi-Fi – they have as much information in their pockets as the tourist offices have. And when visitors goes into a tourist office, they're not spending money any more. The visitors are already there in the destination spending money. Give visitors Wi-Fi and let them check their phone in a café while they have a coffee. If they really want to ask some local question, they can ask at their hotel or even ask someone on the street.

Better for the DMO to help work with private partners to create new brand-aligned experiences. As Apple will tell you, the best marketing is a great product. Hotels know this as well. But destinations haven't figured it out yet. Destination needs to think of themselves as a hotel on trip advisor and try to improve every aspect of the visitor's experience.

It is clear from Doug's answers that there is much opportunity for improvement and that there are many ways that Hotels, museums and all other attractions can do their bit to change the way to attract and deliver what the travelers are really looking for.

Customer service

The industry is continuously changing, not only ours, bit also other industries. Customer service nowadays is widely misunderstood. Just browse some retail sites, some hotel sites and click on Customer service. In that category, you can find information on booking, shipping terms, how to get in touch when you have a complaint, when the expected service did not match the actual delivery. The interaction with our guests is extremely important and we have lost a lot of the contact we used to have since technology and online booking took over from particularly, the initial interaction with the guest, namely the phone call. I would like to differentiate the customer service in pre, during and post service.

The pre service experience is changing rapidly and will continue to do so. The way we are now communicate with our guest before the stay, is or rather can be much more efficient. Since many companies are now processing much more information about the travel habits of the guest, there are better ways to connect with them, through newsletters, direct mail, sms notification or social media. Also with the loyalty programs available, a booking can be made much quicker than ever before. There is so much written about the customer experience, particularly after the stay and yes great customer service after a stay will get you good word of mouth and can be the last experience with the hotel.

The pre customer experience is all about creating an impression to the potential guest or guest who has already confirmed. Many say that, the personal contact is so important even before the stay. The booking trends are saying otherwise, as many direct bookings to hotels are coming through third party websites still, like booking.com or hotels.com; mainly to get a quick overview of pricing, location and star rating of the hotels. There clearly is not a lot left of the pre arrival experience, or is there? Travel agents worldwide are losing leisure as well as corporate clients. Within leisure, there is a clear trend for a need for tailor-made trips, both for the all-inclusive and luxury market segments.

The direct contact before the stay has become more important than ever. Over 90% of people traveling, check out the website before they travel. On the site they are looking for a story, for an advice that can make them excited. Even through email, coming from third party booking sites, there is a lot that can be done to meet the needs for the travel, to guarantee the best possible experience for the actual arrival. Even more so, through social media and content marketing, the communication with the traveler has limitless opportunity. You can learn more about this in the chapter on marketing.

Customer service during the stay is clear and probably does not need a lot of description. Once again, the importance here is not just the actual service that is expected, but more so, to exceed the expectation of the guest by asking, listening, leading to potential interest to join the loyalty program or sign up on social media tools. Staff should be much aware and trained well to deal with guests and get them committed and loyal to future visits or pure marketing.

Post stay customer service is what is mostly understood with customer service; it's when an issue has risen and needs to be turned into an opportunity. By solving an issue fast and efficient, guests often can be turned from being annoyed to being more committed than before. The large opportunity in post service also lies in the continuation of the relationship between the hotel and the guest. The freedom to speak can be found all over the internet and on every mobile device. How often do we see people complaining on Facebook about lost luggage or a full length review on the internet about a stay? It takes a dedicated and smart person to answer or react to those comments and leadership to acknowledge opportunity. Not everybody should be dealing with guests without the proper education or skill. Mistakes are easily made, communication is not hard and problems are often not identified clearly.

The selection of the person in charge of taking care of customers should be selected carefully. I have listed a number of minimum qualifications of this particular staff members.

1. **Clarity**
   Acknowledging and clarifying the opportunity or issue leads to the ability to resolve or create change. Someone with this skill is an expert in communicating and identifying the root cause of whatever the guest is telling us. Only when you find the root cause, repeat it, clarify it and send feedback to the guest that you will create a connection. Once the root cause of the issue

or opportunity has been noted, this needs to be communicated internally as well. The customer service agent or staff member is the greatest link to making changes either to prevent errors from happening again and/or to create a change that can impact the service that the hotel is offering in the future. The support and understanding of management is the key in this process.

2. **Friendly and positive**

Kindness is something that is not always an easy trait, particularly when an angry guest needs to be calmed down or listened to. Important in this is the listening skill, but also the smile and the positive attitude. Making notes always helps when you are in front of a guest, just like making eye contact. Friendliness is a natural habit of most of the employees in the hospitality industry and a requirement in this role.

3. **Knowledge of the service**

As a frequent traveler, we have all come across the most potentially annoying experience of asking employees about a direction to the restaurant, opening hours of the gym and the answer was incorrect or unhelpful. As an employee, there is a need to know more about other departments, details about the hotel and all the service elements that comes with it. To deliver customer service, the education and core values are most important. Training is required for all staff naturally and here even more so.

4. **Ability to read people**

In hospitality, psychology is an important factor. Reading people is one element of psychology that creates trust and openness. Trust is required to get the best out of a guest who is either upset or has a story to tell. Reading people means verbal and nonverbal communication, both off line and online. It takes a professional to read people

5. **Focused**

Another skill is focus, taking time and making time. Focus is to give time to a guest or specific subject. This means putting a timeline in place that is realistic and useful for guests and also for internal follow up purposes.

6. **Goal oriented**

    Customer service is about setting goals, striving for results. Once feedback from a guest has been received, a goal needs to be set. The goals need to be clear and followed through.

7. **Confident**

    Internally and externally, the employee is required to show confidence with offering solutions, which requires knowledge of the hotel and service delivered.

8. **Persuasive**

    In order to communicate well with the guest, Including getting positive as well as negative feedback, there is a need for persuasion. To get down to the core of the issue or opportunity, the guest needs to open up. That is a challenge mainly when the guest is upset, but also when information is hard to find.

9. **Improve**

    This quality is required to ensure that, need for change and improvement is recognized and communicated.

The future of communicating with our guests

Now that I have written about delivering the dream, I would like to highlight more on actual and potential deliveries that can be considered by hotels. Firstly, I would like to write the ultimate delivery, sleep followed by the recent and definitely future trend of hotels selecting organic amenities for their guests and finally, why hotels are offering bicycles as an alternative to taxis.

Sleep as the main driver for more than just guest satisfaction

Many years of searching for the best possible sleep, hoteliers keep awake at night.

Teams have applied a process driven method, based on data and data collection, called Six Sigma to many hotels and organizations. The teams were, and are still attempting to understand the correlation between making a choice of a hotel and actually booking the hotel.

What are the reasons and as an hotelier, how can we influence others that, understanding the process of getting to the decision is more interesting perhaps, than the actual booking. Why? Well, because those are the guest that will return, they made a conscious decision about the hotel. So with regards to sleep, which really should be the main driver for a stay at a hotel; what does this entail, and why is it needed so much?

What Keeps the Average Guest Awake?

About a third of a person's life is spent in bed. On average, that is about 8 hours a day. Good rest and recharging is needed to lead the hectic and complicated lives that humans choose to live these days. Whether you are an executive traveler or one on a leisurely trip, sleep is key.

Analyzing sleep is not such a great mystery and also quite easily done with many scientific methods. The polysomnogram and the multiple sleep latency test are just a few examples. They are carried out in a closed environment by Doctors and specialists with help of sensors, wires and monitors, to collects data like blood oxygen levels and breathing events. The results are not far from what you would expect, events before sleep, like food & beverage and also, closely related noise, surroundings and the actual bed we sleep in. So what is the hotel's solution for offering a better sleep?

There is no point discussing noise, as every hotel room has its own noises – flushing toilets, squeaky doors and floors. And what about the other guests with the mobile wake up clock next door, the high heels on the wooden floor up stairs, and the neighbor singing 'Simply the best' from Tina Turner in the shower and finally, your partner in the same bed. Anything over 40 decibels keeps us awake, or disrupts our sleep.

The surroundings can be slightly more controlled by the hotel, those being related to light, temperature and increasingly, focus on space and design, intended to make the guest feel comfortable. Light and design, sure, but in my years of collecting data, temperature was in the top 10 of the guest complaint list. Even though specialists recommend a cool room (under 19 degrees Celsius), temperature is still a very personal choice. The reason temperature was so high is because, we are all extremely different and very often the room is too warm. A too warm room results in irregular and reduced sleep, mainly because at night our body temperature also sinks to the lowest.

Scientific testing of sleep in a hotel room is therefore probably not so often tested; there are simply too many external factors. Still, we learn from our data that deep sleep is needed and we try and learn more about how we can deliver-on sleep to the hotel guest.

Market research, by J.D. Power in 2012 about overall hotel industry ratings and the survey shows that hotels need to start paying more attention to the complaints as overall scores are dropping year on year. This was revealed in Forbes magazine and on top of the above findings, prevention of the problem is one of the things that increases the overall guest satisfaction and ensuring that in room equipment, furniture is clean and everything is working.

Following the research from Six Sigma, doctors and hospitals and J.D. Power' market survey, we can find out that, it is time for hotels to take sleep to the next level and assist in a person's health and offer and influence one of the solutions that really deliver guest satisfaction; a bed that works. As guest, you spent most time in there, it needs to be comfortable, deliver and exceed the guest expectation!

The relationship between the guest and the bed is a personal matter and while hotels are looking for the best solutions, here are some facts and thoughts:

- The body weight changes annually about 0.3 kg, pregnancy changes shape of the body almost daily.
- A normal bed changes its shape as it gets older and used.
- The hardness of a bed varies on the sleeper's degree of muscular tension, and which also impacts the flexibility of ligaments and joints
- To have a customized bed can prevent back problems
- A good bed prevents pressure/bed sores (decubitusprofylax)

- The results of good sleep are numerous, with brain power to be the main driver needed for success, efficiency and memory.
- Beds should offer optimal pressure relief
- Optimum hardness of the bed or mattress is key to sleep
- The bed or mattress should be made of materials that breathes and removes moisture from the body.

More facts really are not required; hotels can take learning in all this and start influencing the decision process and eventually the booking. No more data is needed, guests don't care; they just want sleep; that's what they pay for.

There is an opportunity here to perform in a direct way and impact the delivery to the guest without back doors or great marketing tools, but by simply giving them a promise.....a great sleep in a great bed.

Will Hotels offer guests organic bathroom amenities? Should they?
Finally, the word is out, bathroom amenities face a new challenge; guests with an opinion and increased knowledge about skincare.

Recently, I was discussing food with a number of people in the organic skincare industry and one example struck me, a normal apple bought from the supermarket in 1930 had more than 80% less toxics in there as the regular apple you buy today and had double the nutritional value. The reason the discussion came up was because, we wanted to understand the bigger picture of the health and wellness of our body. So what can hotels contribute directly to our skin?

What is skin?

Skin exists of three layers and is considered the biggest organ of the body, which is about 15% of the total body weight. With regards to the composition, the skin exists of 70% water, 25% protein and 2% lipids. Each one of the layers consist of different types of cells, the outer layer called the epidermis renews itself every 3-5 weeks. We can help the renewal with scrubs, soaps and popular mild peels done by professionals in the Spa or Treatment industry.

To keep the skin looking young and fresh is determined by the type of product that we apply. The objective is to keep away toxics. The second layer of skin called the dermis, plays a key role in that too. The dermis is important for the body to be able to breathe and nourish the skin. Only products that actually remain there and are natural enough to penetrate the first layer can improve this layer of skin. The third layer called subcutaneous tissue is the main protector of our body and serves as an absorber and heat insulator.

The bathroom amenity a benefit or decision?

In research by MSNBC, the question was asked to guests, whether they would choose a hotel by the type of amenity. Many of the comments and answers were related to the brand of the product and own label products. The brand impresses and leaves memory, the own labeled brand does not leave a mark. Beside the brand, the smell gets very high marks. The choice of hotel reflects the wish for attention detail and really exceptional toiletries. So a luxury 5 star hotel should be carrying a product that impresses. But is it a decision maker? Do we change choice of hotel because one has a product that suits better? The answer remains to be seen and is not clear so far, because it is very individual and depends on expectations that come with the hotel brand and size (small luxury or boutique for example). One element came out very clearly, which is that for frequent travelers, the toiletries can sway the decision on where to stay.

Organic right up there amongst the requirements like smell and brand?

Organic products are finding their way into the society and becoming a significant alternative to what we see around us. Probably, we are becoming more aware via media of the implications to our body of normal products.

The reasons for choosing real organic products for which every ingredient has been checked are many. The ingredients in many amenities to avoid are:

- Sodium Lauryl Sulfates
- Ammonium Lauryl Sulfate

- Myreth Sulfate
- Siloxanes
- Derivatives of Lauryl Alcohol
- Propylene Glycol (*Antifreeze*)
- Olefin Sulfonate (*Deodorized Kerosene*)

Finally, some more facts from an article in Body stream that points towards the use of organic products:

33% of personal care products have been linked to cancer

48% are reported to be potentially harmful to the reproductive systems

60% of ingredients that can act like estrogens or disrupt hormones

Most chemicals have not undergone any safety testing

The skin absorbs things easily and in general is exposed to over 168 hazardous chemicals each day.

Hotel guests do not choose the products, hoteliers do, unless the demand changes instantly. Luckily, they are taking sustainability and waste like bottles very serious. It's costly using certified and clean organic products, but surely in 5 years, the guest does not want anything else. A product a hotel or spa is proud of, is the only way forward. And even though not in top ten reasons for choosing a hotel, I believe the guest….has already chosen.

Emotion in Motion – Taxi Please
Traveling is a true pleasure and our bodies are getting used to the change of eating habits, sitting in confined airline seats for over 8 hours and the time difference is not an issue. Let's look into some basic advice and elaborate on the most fun part – the exercise.

The facts

The center of Disease control and prevention advices on how to prepare for a trip, what to expect, eat and drink and suggests to bring anything that can protect you like sun block, repellent, limited alcohol use, and respecting the host countries rules and regulations.

Besides the prevention here is some detailed advice on staying healthy during the trip, from the International association for medical assistance (IAMAT)

The dos

- Drink boiled or bottled water, or use water purifiers / tablets.
- Wash your hands regularly and thoroughly with water and soap or use an alcohol based hand sanitizer, especially before handling food.
- Eat thick skinned fruit that you can peel yourself, such as oranges and bananas.
- Eat well cooked food while it's hot.
- Use anti-mosquito measures, including sprays or lotions containing DEET.
- Wear seat belts in vehicles and a helmet when riding a bicycle, moped, or motorcycle.
- Stay fit and be well rested.

Avoid

- Ice cubes in drinks.
- Unpasteurized milk and dairy products.
- Shellfish and large fish.
- Food from street vendors.
- Excessive sun exposure.
- Contact with animals and insect bites.
- Swimming in fresh water.
- Unprotected sexual contact.

Staying alert after the trip is also highly recommended, as you will be able to notice when something is affecting the body as a result of a happening during the trip.

Bike your way through the stay

So let's pick up on how to make exercise and the overall stay fun and see how we can stay fit and stay fit in style. Hotels are converting rooms to gyms and clearly taking the offering extremely serious. Yet it is up to the individual to look and understand all the alternatives.

On an average business trip, exercise tends to be forgotten, taxi's are right outside the door and meetings rule the days! The best way to see the city is by foot or by bike. You can see the signs, bicycles all over the city provided by hotels and hotel maps with walking routes. Bugaboo the baby stroller brand, even provides stroller friendly routes.

Walking is of course great even though it is a low impact form of exercise, and is in that sense also closely related to bicycle motion. Impact is the amount of stress the activity puts on your body. The bicycle gets you faster from A to B and has the significantly better health effect when cycling on unleveled roads. Both forms of exercise come with good burning of calories, riding the bike burns 140 calories in 20 minutes, compared with 110 calories during a steady walk.

Style and exercise

But let's be honest, traveling in style comes with a bicycle and walking is rather uncool. The bicycle dates from 1817 when Baron von Drais invented a 'walking' machine that helped him get quickly around the royal gardens. In 1865, pedals were applied directly to the front wheel and the velocipede was reality. Much later the pneumatic tire was invented by Dunlop, and made biking finally a comfortable experience too.

So now the selection is huge, with the sincerest apologies for the taxi companies. Hotels can offer anything from a vintage, a stuffy but charming city bicycle, to a mountain bike. With the selection of the bicycle, hotels awaken to an entirely new opportunity to reflect their brand in the city and reflect the guests, needs and demands.

Leading guest satisfaction

In this chapter, I have focused on elements that can and will influence your guest's decision to return to the hotel. The one element I have not written is the service element of people. The reason for not including it is that, it should be the first thing anybody should think about to create guest satisfaction. We are in the service industry and without good people we wouldn't even be in this industry.

The internal customer of personnel is where it all starts. If they are not following a vision and delivering the core values that have been developed by the management, there is no point even getting into this business.

Much of what you read before goes straight into the delivery to the guest. In short, I would like to mention a number of elements that will predict a positive internal guest satisfaction or employee satisfaction.

1. The vision needs to be clear and understood, as it sets the path to consistent core values. With consistent, I mean, employees can handle situations and conflicts as well as receive and deal with positive feedback, in good and bad times of economy.
2. Motivation is led by management, through continuous communication with the employees. They need to feel involved, aware of a potential change in the economy, a planned renovation or anything that influence their daily work. I remember, well with the introduction of yielding which was pushed down the chain and many people in reservations, sales and front office seriously struggling with how to handle this internally, let alone how to communicate different pricing levels to the guest. The communication of something this big has been poor in many hotels or hotel groups that I have worked with, even though it impacts the revenue stream dramatically. It is a positive change giving both guests and employees opportunity.

3. Think and act long term creates great value to employees. They want to understand, they have chosen the job because they want to be involved in the company and make it a success together. Short term results are naturally also of great importance for employees, as they need to be celebrated, but long term strategy creates a tight team.

4. Interaction within the teams from different departments, leads to, mutual understanding of departmental goals as well as individual challenges. Promoting this interaction through workshops or educational efforts, will strengthen each employee as well as the effort to get to the same objectives that have been set by the management.

5. Education within Hospitality and perhaps also with other industries is potentially one of the most vital elements of motivating the internal customer. By having regular updates on how the business is going and educating personnel on trends, skills and knowledge, you will not only create a team that will be able to deliver service, but that touches on all the elements mentioned before, working as a team towards common goals.

6. Finally, people need individual growth, recognition through incentives and the ability to see what the future holds. A career path for each individual is therefore, a way to acknowledge these needs. They should be recognized already in the recruitment process, not only to attract the right candidates but also, to confirm the commitment to each.

Good scores within employee satisfaction are directly influencing the results of the guest satisfaction, there is no doubt about that. Even though when I was involved in a large project within Six Sigma, there was no statistical relationship that was evident. Main reason for that is that, guest satisfaction surveys are not all about the service and as stated before, service is such an unclear operational definition. Service means something different from one person compared to another as well as all unrelated subjects, like quality of the bed or cleanliness that cause scores that are hard to measure.

The reason for measuring guest's satisfaction has much more meaning than just finding opportunity or addressing issues that occur before, during or after a stay. One great reason for measuring guest satisfaction is, to ensure that guests come back as finding new ones is much harder and much more expensive than retaining guests. Tools for retaining guests is and will become much more so driven by technology. Digital marketing driven by CRM gives endless opportunity to communicate with guests in an efficient and effective manner, through social media, blogs, newsletters and content marketing. The ones that stand out are those who focus their digital marketing and personalize it as much as possible. A good example I recently experienced, was a downgrade from Gold status, since I had not reached the number of flight I need to maintain this status. All I received after having being a very loyal customer for over 10 years, was a new credit card sent to my home address and how to activate this card. The airline has lost an incredible opportunity to do anything they can to keep me loyal, with last minute efforts to get me on board or extending the gold status for another few months. Even a nice letter or questionnaire could have made me excited to choose this airline again. Instead, I feel dumped, not needed as a loyal passenger and for sure, it will not be priority to fly this airline again in the future. Now they need to find at high cost, a passenger to replace my loyalty. This was a great opportunity also to get my feedback, to find out more about my travel habits and to adjust the future offering accordingly.

Another reason for measuring guest satisfaction and dealing with it in a professional and efficient manner as described earlier, is to ensure positive word of mouth, one of the strongest marketing tools. McKinsey's research showed that, unhappy customers tell their story to 9-15 people. The internet and freedom to express has become incredibly hard to manage for hotels, with the social media that is used by so many, that it requires resources that are often not available. Efficiency and direct response is therefore of essence.

Measuring guest satisfaction is extremely important and only effective when dealt with directly and taken seriously by management and resources are allocated. A second chance is hard to get, with the tremendous competition and ever growing choice available to guests.

Chapter 7

Housekeeping sleepers
A clean cut approach to clean tiles

The internal or external inspection, one of those stumble blocks in the final review after a surprise or secret inspector had stayed at the hotel. Yes, they still exist and whether it is an inspection for Guide Michelin or local rating board, they will always trip over the Housekeeping efforts.

I remember having a boss who was so surprised that the inspector had not found any hairs in the bathroom, that he went to check himself. He was very happy to say he had found a few and that the inspector had missed them. In fact, he found some more stuff in the room that was missed, like a layer of dust on the back of the TV (no, they were not flat in those days) and in the bathroom was missing a small wash towel.

My nearest friend pointed out to me what a beautiful word Housekeeping is and how meaningful.

The employee
Housekeeping is the department with the highest percentage of sick leave, in my years as a consultant I even registered an average of over 40 working days a year, at a number of large properties. With a standard of between 14-16 rooms to clean per employee, the physical and mental demands are big. Expectations are high, irregular working hours, on your feet all day,

carrying, lifting and awkward working positions are some of the challenges that come with the job. Mentally there is inventory, planning, standards and the complexity of self-motivation as well as working as a team and naturally working under high pressure, with lots of simultaneous guest check ins and outs.

Working in the Housekeeping requires a lot of training, like how to handle chemicals, efficient working, guest communication, brand standards just to name a few.

Often, the role is seen rather prejudiced as a dirty job. Fact is that, I have worked with many highly educated and skilled people, lawyers, doctors who are not able to find a position at home and move away in the hope for work and better conditions, often sending a large portion of the wage to support the family. Luckily those are often the colleagues who bring true pleasure to the workplace, with serious dedication, motivation and happiness and they have a lot to teach the westernized cultures. However, it can be a dirty job, cleaning up after people is never a joyful experience, certainly because when people in general are away from home, the sofa becomes much more than a comfortable place to sit in. In a hotel, a sofa is attacked with chewing gum, spills of red wine, becomes a playground for children and armrest become bar stools, basically all the stuff that would not or hardly happen at home. Reason for bringing this up is that, there is opportunity in strategizing this department, by revising the department, structure, changing roles as well as responsibilities and challenges the ancient old traditions faced, not only here and there, but literally everywhere in the world. No matter what brand, what size, what location, what type of guest, the age of the hotel, the department's rules and regulations are set in stone and copied again and again.

The outsourcing solution
Starting with the hot potato in the industry. The housekeeping department is a cost, that's the traditional way of looking at it, that's how it is presented to the owner or companies and the more a hotel has saved compared to previous years, the better. Sure cleanliness is a measure, guest happiness and employee satisfaction are measures. But the winner above and beyond

remains the financial performer. Like many other industries, goal setting is an element that is a minimum requirement for employees to be understood to perform. So what are goals for a housekeeping department? Where do they come from and how can they be measured for success? I mentioned the most important one; financial performance.

Who sets that particular objective? The General Manager does, with help of the Financial Controller. Fabulous one would think, but where does that come from, is that based on history, size of hotel, type of property? Indeed those are factors to determine the budget. And you guessed it, is that enough? A question not asked enough as most of the calculations are standardized, based on years and years of tradition, practices that are not questioned enough. And above all, my team has hardly ever seen those objectives being communicated to the Housekeeping employees and trust me; that is not the only line staff who hasn't ever heard the management objectives. You may think, sure but surely, experience is a serious factor in that too? Now don't get upset, tradition and best practices play a large role, but objectively a best practice is only good enough when its results are continuously questioned and measured.

Setting the financial goals are a basis for developing a department that in fact can be a standalone as well as part of an entire picture. Should we even call it housekeeping? It really is an integrated part of an overall service or final delivery for guests and colleagues. What better way to look at it objectively, than to have the department be evaluated and measured by a potential external partner, who can come with a cost calculation and structure that has the forecasted results with regards to financial performance. A review from an external source is a very healthy process for any hotel, small opportunities or low hanging fruit can be spotted quite quickly through rigid methods and use of tools.

What happens is the following, the potential outsourcee presents themselves as an amazing company and has all the questions ready; how many people are working here, what areas do they take care of; like kitchen public areas, rooms, meeting space, how many people work at night, what are the current issues? and so forth and so on. Mostly the outsourcee has already established a team of employees and clients. This offers great flexibility and mobility within a city, ensuring time efficiency and optimal use of skills. Results are obvious for any hotel, cost savings, improved flexibility, decreased maintenance of relationship, decreased planning effort. And by far the most complex and difficult part, the scheduling, interviewing, training, rewarding, and implementations of all the laws and regulations. In particular, Southern Europe and the Middle East has rules and regulations that can be extremely difficult for companies to manage.

So what's keeping any hotel of outsourcing? Outsourcing is complex, much more so in the hospitality industry, main reason being the service element and just as important, the variation in occupancy and business levels. The service element, which I have explained in more detail in the human resources department is extremely complicated. Everyone is different, every person has a different expectation and definition of service, guests and employees. It's incredibly difficult and much effort has to be made to create a team, train a team, not just within the housekeeping department, but as part of the entire hotel team. Training is not enough, sure the brand knowledge, complaint handling etc. are a vital part of the skill set, but there is also motivation, product knowledge and communication, which are often an issue when outsourcing. However beautiful, it seems to move responsibility to another player and safe costs, these are factors that play a large role in the final delivery of the service.

Accountability cannot be outsourced

That says it all, however wonderful it sounds from a cost and efficiency perspective, truth is, control is lost, accountability is becoming a vague definition, or grey area. Even when responsibilities are clear, the actual delivery to guest is becoming nothing more than a promise. I can't tell you in how many meetings with outsourcees I have been, where I got the yes and Amen on deliveries, which simply never came true. I understand, don't get me wrong, because when all the previously mentioned elements have to be understood, implemented, trained and documented, there is a cost involved. A cost that has not been taken into consideration in the initial calculations. It's not all black and white, there are outsourcees with great success, who have control over motivation, education of the brand and communication. They stand out and win accounts.

Besides housekeeping, there are many other parts of the business that can successfully be outsourced, like valet parking, concierge services, security, stewarding and finance. My advice is to keep control over the service, when outsourcing is on the table. Make sure you make not only the right calculations, but also set the correct expectations. This means that you cannot lose control over the process, it means that accountability lies with you and the management team and should at all times remain there. Outsourcing 100% is a total mistake, keep control over 20% of the business as a guideline. Make sure you review working schedules, to make sure efficiency remains and preferably the same team returns to the hotel as much as possible to create a team within the entire hotel, not just the department.

Another important thing is to keep aligning responsibilities, review results on a monthly basis. Adjust goals and objectives where needed, in line with the business levels in the hotel, changing markets, or management instructions. Measure success and reward accordingly, like reduction in use of chemicals, increased guest satisfaction, improved cleanliness or guest feedback about a certain employee.

The housekeeping solution

I can't speak about this enough, and you will notice throughout the book, that I strongly recommend to start looking at each department or outlet as a potential revenue generating source. Whether that is a direct or indirect source, a product or service. The management needs to decide how to define this best. It is a struggle many companies have already, an excellent example is Public Relations. Ever since ROI is an abbreviation of the now, PR has been challenged with how to present a client brief that has a financial value against it. I am a strong believer in PR, but have serious doubts with the monthly retainer concept that is driven by the company or persons that has no relation to the hotel or hotel goals, in fact a bit like the outsourcing solution I wrote about before. Make sure you keep control of about 20% of the process, regular reviews are a part of that.

There is not just one solution, there are numerous, but start moving away from seeing the housekeeping department as a cost centre simply because it already sounds horrible and gives a nasty taste in the mouth, as cost is something we want to decrease and get rid of. News for you, it's there to stay and the more you cut in it, the nastier it gets, unhappy employees, bad tools or useless materials, unsustainable chemicals that ruin the environment and your furniture and eventually decreased guest satisfaction. Yes, you might reach that striking goal of decreasing the costs compared to the year before but on the long term, you lose, big time. That's something you have to explain to your boss, tough. So start implementing a change, make it a department that is fun, invest in it, create objectives that can be measured, start to innovate. I will give you some examples that are much more than fun, they are ways to improve guest satisfaction, create an additional revenue stream and reward teams and individuals who create success for you. Lead them, manage the processes as you should.

Love to share some examples

1. We are all individuals

Define goals, collect data, measure, innovate, implement and reward the hell out of it.

Like I wrote before you work with people, everyone is a genius in their own way. Every person wants to learn, to be motivated. That means individual goals are extremely important like your sales team or middle management. There is a lack of individual goal setting, not just within the housekeeping department but throughout the hotel. This has much to do with the standardization and repetitiveness of the job itself which I will explain later. This leads to the ability of management to schedule any person within the department into a specific role. Scheduling is therefore a much easier task, particularly in a busy hotel with many room types and long hallways. Naturally this has a positive result to the cost, if applied properly. But it has a negative result on the motivation of people and staff.

The number game

There are a number of ways to change goal setting, firstly it is important to build in fun, a goal of cleaning 16 rooms (note I still do not know where that industry standard of 16 has come from) is not fun. However changing the goal to cleaning 14 rooms and receiving an incentive after that, for every additional room will change perspective. The goal remains, but the delivery is much more motivating.

Room types

Divide the rooms into categories and use scorecards. Almost every hotel has room categories, divide the goals for that specific day up, into floors, room types. It creates variance, which is needed, different rooms have different cleaning procedures, different types of guests, different atmospheres and room designs. The score card system will score room types. A standard room could be 1 point, up to a suite at 4 points for example. This creates different goals for every day, making the day a lot less repetitive. A total of 16 should be reached for example and again incentives helps. The management can also do competitions with the score cards, like who cleaned most suites in a month for example.

Beyond the individual

You guessed it, team goals have extreme impact on an individual and it accelerates efficiency and effectiveness. Competition is great, and more fun when done in a group, so rather than sticking to that number, create a team target.

Besides the daily goals, there is much more to individual goal setting. Within the annual performance reviews, friendliness, happiness, personal growth, are reviewed. Many of those are difficult to measure which makes them less interesting for the management, but by no means less important for the individual. For example, a career plan is a necessity in personal growth, and when followed through by the company, a wonderful means for personal motivation.

Goals need to be clear, the individual needs to understand why 16 rooms need to be cleaned, what impact she or he can have on the operation of the hotel, how happiness reflects on the guest, what cleanliness means to the management and guest, how the use of chemicals can affect the environment. People are intelligent, they need change, their mind needs stimulation, above are just a few examples of what can be reached. Recognizing skills, individual skills are extremely important, it might lead to promotions or cross departmental moves. You will be amazed how individuals in the department never get the questions; what is your background, or what is your ambition?

2. Cross education or work

Housekeeping is fun, it's our job to make it fun. Understanding the housekeeping culture is not easy. I learned so much theory within the department from big fat books, like sanitation management or pages full of how to schedule standards within cleaning per star rating, but I learned most from practice. Living the department is much more than an experience. You can feel the international spheres in the rooms, communicate with colleagues and guests from all over the world, whilst applying the tools that are available. I also noticed that when I was working in the department, other department were frowning upon the department.

That is something which is not unexpected, however, it's one of the elements that can be phased away, by introducing cross work opportunities. That is an implementation that carries a cost, but will motivate and increase understanding of what others do in other departments. It creates respect and improves personal relationships outside the daily environment. Cross education or work creates change, a company culture that also helps individuals create their personal path. An opportunity so easily created, that will have numerous potential positive results to the entire hotel team. In some cases, these implementations result in job changes and a better personal fit for individuals, decreased recruitment costs, better skilled personnel and improved overall performance, impacting guest and overall employee satisfaction.

3. Rock the boat

Pride. Housekeeping is cool, so make sure you reflect that. Get rid of those lame, black and white uniforms that hang on your knees, reflect boredom, and are anything but stylish. Jeans is perhaps extreme, but we all have pride and walking around in baggy pants, mostly shared with other colleagues is anything but cool. As long as the guest recognizes staff, and it's part of the brand standard, that really understands the guest, make it something that you would want to wear.

4. Show personality

When I walk through a corporate landscape office complex, I almost start shivering. A while back, I was invited to assist with branding for the second largest construction company in Scandinavia, to make their real estate division sexy. When I interviewed in the head office, with a number of key members of the team, I realized that this company needs much more than a new brand that attracts private people to purchase homes from them. I explained that to start creating a personal warm inviting brand that people will buy from and later call their home, it needs to start right there in that office. Sure you can see a few personal touches, picture of the family, a calendar of dogs, and a separation wall covered in colorful post it notes. To put it diplomatically, the totally wrong environment to start from and when I presented that as a starting point for this large organization, I never heard from them again.

It's not difficult to understand, I write best with music on, or read best in comfortable chair, or shop when I feel I can't concentrate anyway and need to get stuff out of the way. I dress for the occasion, to feel important, confident, relaxed or calm. So create these opportunities for your housekeepers.

Flexible dress code

Dressing well motivates, keeping certain standards and yet giving some freedom, or giving the option to select from a pre-negotiated item list gives a housekeeper the feeling that she or he is meaningful and important and that the organization cares. It should be a comfortable clothing and the more personal, the better! It will create confidence, pride and reflect on the daily work and eventually the guest.

Music motivates. Recently, I started working with a company that creates music that aligns with a hotel's branding vision. They create amazingly smart solutions, and when you enter a lobby, you immediately feel a part of the hotel, the atmosphere. Music plays a big role in our lives and it sets that tone for a feeling or emotion. I remember talking to someone in operations at the Metro in Brussels. They had incredible amounts of violence in their Metro stations and we started playing classical music through their speaker system. It created a calm and sophisticated atmosphere and decreased aggressive behavior and violence.

In the years of experience, I have seen many housekeepers turn on the TV to get some music going, totally fine. Build on that, give every housekeeper the opportunity to listen to the music by supplying them with an iPod or similar where they can listen to programmed music to both motivate and stimulate work behavior. Better yet as one of my closest friends indicated, get them to create their own playlist, there are tons of ways this can be achieved these days!

5. An individual as part of a team

Within Six Sigma, the process improvement method I was taught in 2001 and applied ever since in many situations and departments within and outside the hospitality industry. Six sigma has taught me many things, like how to collect data and how to validate and apply it. How to base many decisions on facts rather than assumption, as well as leadership and manage net styles. The tools and methods can be applied for all stages and departments within a company, small or large, startups or an established company many years in the market place. The team also applies a lot of the tools to create inspiration or innovation, often learning from other industries.

Chapter 8

Financial crackdown
Tricky business

The finance department, some call it the heart of the hotel, some call it a ghost house, some are afraid of it, some can't spend enough time in there. One thing is for sure, that the department has an opportunity to make a serious difference to the organization.

In this chapter I will reveal some of the assets of this departments and some opportunities that the entire finance team as well as hotel team should consider. I will not write about what they should be doing, as to be honest, that would be both standard and already hundreds of books have been written about it. I would like to challenge the roles, challenge the unit or the department. Steer them away from just routines; find new ways to make the department, a little sexy.

I remember back when I started working in the industry in Sales, things were a little different. There were no mobile phones, there was no email system and even more so many corporate travelers were not allowed to use credit cards for hotels, as their companies had set up credit with hotels. Great for cash flow indeed, and the credit control job paid back very fast for many hotels. Now you can imagine how many times the sales team had to be in the finance office, at that time and still often called the Accounts department, to negotiate credit for clients. There was nothing more frustrating than to have signed a contract with a new client and having to get approval from the credit controller. The credit controller had no great system other than Dun & Bradstreet, or similar. New companies were hardly a part of that system, so sales people ended up in heated discussions with the controller, and often the Director of Sales and Director of Finance had to be a part of it too. Often sales won the discussion, since we all realized that business pays our salaries.

That brings me to the Payroll Clerk. Yes, you have seen those mafia movies where people sit in a little box, with a glass window. The guy wearing a see through white shirt, with shirt armbands and braces would give you a check or hand over cash once you've passed the slip you received for your hard work over to him. That role you don't see so much anymore, even though the payroll role still exist in many hotels, particularly the larger hotels working with lots of extra staff.

So what is changing and why? And how can hotels adjust to the market place to stay ahead and keep the costs to a minimum.

I remember having numerous discussions with multiple brand property owners. They were and are still wondering why some management companies have to have 6 people in accounts whilst others can do with only 3 or even sometimes 2. It is hard to explain to them, even though it is easy to understand. It has much to do of course, with which part of the finance department can be outsourced or centralized (even called insourced). But also, the responsibilities vary from hotel to hotel.

You have just seen a few of the challenges and I am sure you have identified some opportunity already as well. I will focus on setting goals, measurements and ratios. Additionally, I will talk about revenues, pricing, the role of the department in the hotel, the educational task the department has and finally the procurement role, one that has been under discussion for many, many years.

Objectives
Through the many years of travel and consulting as well as being in charge of small and large operations, the most beautiful part of my job has always

been to work with people. People from different background and cultures have taught me more than I would ever be able to from any book. Setting objectives helps with every aspect of the business and also, will steer all personal achievements.

Setting these objectives for most department in the hotel is more like a regular or even a daily occurrence. The finance department seems to however, not be a big part of this. The finance department has goals, like making sure the invoices are sent, everything is registered correctly, that materials are ready for revision and more of this boring stuff. But the goal of how do work better as a team, or anything else that is not directly finance related seems to be lacking. Perhaps, it is hard to be creative as well, or that the image of the finance department is all mistaken. I would like to show you that the finance department can be one of the most fabulous engines that drive the hotel.

The finance department is not just a number crunching department. It needs to be a department full of communicative people, who want to be involved in the many decisions management or department heads need to make. With financial information, the power of being able to influence the business is large. The way business decisions are made are often based on the financial results. The task of communicating that information internally is the main job of the finance department and the people in it. Employees should join departmental meetings, innovation sessions, workshops and branding efforts. The transparency of the numbers and results need to be understood well by others, as they can have immediate effect on how the business is managed. For accounting reasons, most of these people have a certification that is required to do the bookkeeping in a legal and efficient manner. In the goal setting of the finance department, the following objectives should be included in the personal goals as well as the departmental goals.

1. Build in an analytical effort in the data collected: Analytics drive decisions and the department should take on this responsibility of asking for data when it's not available to them from HR or Departmental heads. Analyzing existing data is a logic step

towards change. On almost every visit, the team and I do ask for financial data in advance. It says a great deal about how the hotel or department is run and an opportunity can be identified easily

2. Communicate information and data: Data that is available on Food & Beverage for example could be of great value for other departments too. Sales can use this to create a marketing plan, housekeeping might learn from the scheduling results, or room division can use the same purchasing policies. There is so much information to share and give and as long as finance is part of key decisions, they will be more open and transparent with numbers in the future.

3. A small team form part of a bigger team: Hotels are the worst example of the finance set up, they sit in dark offices at the end of the corridor, or in the basement. They are not involved in the large 'happy' remainder of the teams. That starts internally of course. Every effort should be made to make a department feel comfortable by setting team goals, arrange kick offs, ideas or innovation sharing and celebrating success. Once the confidence and importance of the department is communicated, the team can enter the large operation and be part of departmental meetings, client events and much more; that will motivate the entire hotel team to understand the value of finance.

4. Creating a key account culture: Every person in finance is dealing with crucial contacts like suppliers, bookers, third party engines, purchasing and so on. These relationships can and will result in better pricing, regular offers, improved knowledge, improved processes and much more. Their relationship are a vital element of the overall well-being of the hotel.

With clear objectives, any operation will do better setting objectives, short term as well as long term will result in team work. A small reminder is that objectives needs to be smart, Specific, Measurable, Attainable, Realistic and Timely. There is plenty of reading to do about setting objectives on the internet. The finance department should not only set objectives internally, but clearly be a part of the entire hotel goal setting.

Measurements, standards for the industry, ratios

The hotel industry is probably known for all the numbers, the ratios and standards. Not only from an entirely property level, like liquidity ratios, or financial leverage ratios, but also within the hotel. Like a standard, it would be the 40% food cost, or 80% room's margin. I totally believe in standards, however, they should clearly be revisited as they can vary incredibly; depending to the city that the hotel is in or the country, the social costs and so forth. The classification of the hotels sometimes define that too, like a resort should have different margins than a city hotel.

An important element and exercise based on Six Sigma has always been the analysis part, setting a baseline that actually makes sense. I can't tell you how many times I have been asked, 'Do you think we are doing well' or 'great numbers in our restaurant right'? That's very difficult to answer, always will be. Again, I am not saying there should not be any industry standards, however, they should certainly be challenged. And every department should be successful financially, why operate it otherwise? An unsuccessful hotel restaurant, losing money every month is a waste; both for the guest, as it clearly adds no value, or for the hotel having to manage payroll and stock which is not needed. Instead of putting standards in place, run a project that tracks the pain, the root cause and change it accordingly. Guests don't care about the numbers, they want to eat in a fun, affordable restaurant with a great atmosphere, with lots of other people. Only that will create your numbers and ratios. Luckily, the finance department is willing to share the information needed to base decisions on. Setting the baseline based on data will give the ratios needed and the industry standards can be amended and used as a guideline.

Forecasting, pricing and revenue

There is a very well deserved annual process that involves creating the budget for the year following. It is an intense process that is prepared by many stakeholders. These budgets are set to assist management to make decisions about operations. The goal is to ensure that all team members are aligned with at least one of their departmental financial goals. Typically, the process starts with each department doing their own budget, followed by the largest part of the budget which involves rooms, normally done by the Director of Sales as he or she should have information about the future, what is in the books, events and happenings in town and much more data.

A large part of the process is to set the pricing of the rooms, the menu and all other revenue generating departments like the spa. Once they have been established, the occupancy and sales needs to also be established. Over many years, there has been an automatic increase in budget, also based on guidelines from the corporate offices. The finance department has a clean overview of what is happening based on passed data and will make sure that, the budget gives the best picture to reflect that and will challenge departments that introduce changes to the numbers.

The budget should reflect a realistic picture of the future and should be adjusted at least monthly by adjusting forecasted numbers influenced by occupancies and advanced bookings. This will ensure that management can adjust the cost accordingly, like staffing and stock levels.

In the chapter Innovation I, specifically emphasized the subject Six Sigma. The finance department is heavily involved in process development, which is why I interviewed Frank Braun, in charge of Process Management & Optimization at WMF AG, who is working closely with the finance department.

Interview Frank Braun
Process Management & Optimization WMF AG

Your quote on the future of Hotel Process Improvement

Today's excellence is just a faded memory tomorrow. Exceptional hotel experiences are rooted firmly in constant improvement and constant change; unless you are sold out, you have room for improvement.

1. Please tell us about the objectives of your department at WMF?

     Answer:

The Strategy & Process Management team was created to manage, analyze and develop processes designed to achieve a high performance organization. Its main goal is to identify and deliver growth beyond the current business by using continuous improvement in concepts, tools & infrastructure.

2. You have incredible experience in data collection. How do you compare the value of the data in the hotel industry as with for example, WMF?

Answer:

Data is not just a collection of guest feedback questionnaires and anecdotal references. The Consumer Industry base their decisions on evidence, hard data to guide and grow business. Sales, manufacturing, shipping, and costs are meticulously metered and tracked to provide a hard troth for decisions to be based upon. The Hotel industry or service industry for that matter still has to catch up on the process metering; while output data such as RevPAR and Net-Rooms-Growth allows to monitor change, not enough data is available to change the outcome of anticipating customer requirements.

3. What are the core principles of Six Sigma for the service industry and will they change in the future?

Answer:

Although Six Sigma is rooted in manufacturing, it works just as effectively in the service industry by cost-effectively translating the manufacturing-oriented tools into the service delivery process.

In manufacturing, problems lie mostly within the process and in a service environment, the problem is often the process itself. Service industries are full of waste and redundancies, it is fairly easy to apply relatively simple statistical and lean tools to reduce costs and achieve greater speed with less waste.

The biggest most limited commodity in the service industry is associates and that commodity will become even scarcer in future. Six Sigma will change from process improvement to strategically prioritization, which processes and delivers the best ROI based on the quicker changing demands of the customer.

4. Which one of the 5 Six Sigma phases in Hospitality is ignored mostly and how does that compare with other industries?

Answer:

There is a significant difference in the testing and implementation of solutions in between manufacturing and the service industry, such as hospitality. Improve as a methodology step, depends on smaller scale testing and evaluation, as this can lead to further change or improvement in product or service. Especially in highly complex environments, it is essential to take the learning from the Analysis phase and translate it correctly into the right solution; even modifying it so it fits even better to the problem at hand. Hoteliers are by nature impatient, which I view to be a good thing, since they strive to be better every day. However, with this comes the danger to overrule the facts at hand and implement what they think is right, not what was needed. In Sales, there is a saying: the worm has to look good to the fish, not the fisherman; this is also true in process design.

5. The Hospitality has a very biased and subjective culture, what are the key elements that management needs to adjust to change this?

Answer:

The success of Toyota and Canon can be partly tribute to their understanding that, higher value can be achieved through better cooperation between the functions and associates in a workplace. They are using a very successful form of "knowledge management" asides from trained and learned knowledge in form of figures and instructions; let associates decide based on subjective and intuitive circumstances. They profit from the implicit, common sense knowledge of their associates by valuing the interaction between them. In hospitality, associates need to have a degree of freedom in deciding, thus, offering personal service that guest grave for. Not everything can nor should be regulated from top down.

6. How can Hotels establish a consistent and improved relationship with their customers and what is the most important elements in the organization influencing this?

Answer:

Hotels by definition are a home away from home and exist to provide for essential human needs: shelter, food, security. Getting these basics right is the foundation for all other interactions, regardless of the segment(s) a hotel is aiming for. The majority of the investment in form of money, time and of course associate resources should be tasked to provide a hassle free environment along those pillars both for external and internal customers. Avoiding lengthy complicated processes, lack of transparency and non-availability of guest facing associates will automatically raise the confidence of guests in the hotel and therefore, the likeliness to return. Additionally, with the increasing shortage of associates, hoteliers must decide which offer can be sustained, meaning delivery as promised. Constant analysis of work processes will become more important in the future.

7. Within Hotel strategy, which one of the departments or elements of the business show largest opportunity from a customer and financial point of view?

Answer:

In today's wired world the key to success lies in acquisition and distribution of information. All guest facing departments from Sales over reservation, Front Office, F&B and Housekeeping are not only sellers but also information gatherers. Making intelligent use of your sources, analyzing and distributing the information appropriately lets you decide which opportunities are presenting itself and can be pursued. This ranges from upselling based on check-in interactions, observing guest behavior (or patterns) to influencing key decision makers. Translating information into revenue is more profitable and quicker to achieve than the same EBITDA impact of cost reduction. Information is the currency of success.

8. In tracking business improvements with our clients, we found that 84% of incremental profit came from revenue related projects rather than cost related projects. What is the reason Hotel management keeps their focus on costs mainly?

Answer:

Cost is perceived easier to steer in view of EBITA growth. The largest cost contributor in any hotel is typically labor; in operation, the easiest problem solver is to add labor for improving service quality. Management is trained to operate on a low cost base, which in itself is not a bad thing, however, revenue is franchised largely to Sales by definition of job title. Hoteliers are very conservative; a more entrepreneurial philosophy is yet to be implemented in the daily operation. INSEAD, co-developed a decade ago the Blue Ocean Strategy, simply a method to adjust the value proposition of an offer and look for a business that seemed unlikely to materialize with conventional approaches, looking for the so-called non-customer. First, applications like the Formula One hotel chain focusing on travelers near highways in the lower segments or Citizen M with its clear focus on design and style. Embracing a start-up mentality will work in your favor and as an additional benefit, it's much more exciting than controlling only cost.

9. In project management and process improvement, it is vital to work in teams and a variety of stakeholders with complimentary

knowledge and skills. How is that handled at WMF and what can we learn from that?

Answer:

WMF has a very detailed and rigorous framework of project management guidelines and process tools. Projects are decided on merit and ROI, chartered are assigned with the needed resources. For important projects, this is happening on executive leadership level, along with clear defined responsibilities. The success of this approach shows the importance of business leadership standing behind all project work and process improvement. Delegating the responsibility to a lower function and not being involved will stop all efforts quickly. Involved sponsorship, supported milestone meetings, effective governance of project selection has to be lived on every level of the organization to ensure success.

10. Lastly, in project implementation, what are the skills needed and what is the role of Senior Management in this?

Answer:

Project management, leading to successful implementation of changes or new product or services needs a wider scope of hard and soft skills. Knowledge of Project methods and project organization is important to do the job, it needs to be accompanied by personality and leadership paired with communication and moderation skills. Projects are done by teams, by associates, and they have different needs and reasons to drive and implement projects. Establishing a community of such experts with the needed support will prove more cost effective than just 2 or three sole operators.

With reaching the actual implementation phase followed by a period of process monitoring, the actual work of the project team is done and the new process, service or product becomes business as usual, thus, the responsibility of the department that it is meant for. Senior Management has to recognize and support this handover to cement the new accountability plus its responsibilities. Lastly and most importantly, celebrate your successes, make it public, internally and externally; success breeds success. Allow on the other hand also, room for failure. Nobody wants to fail, but nobody delivers great projects all the time. However, once your company establishes such a culture, your successes are soon the rule.

Procurement

The role of procurement in the hotel operation and often the account team is not an apparent one. Often hidden away in the basement near the loading bay, we find a few employees in charge of what I would call "the engine of the operation". This tiny department is seen as a cost center and often confused with the purchasing role. To clarify the purchasing role which is a part of the larger procurement role, it's defined as the actual handling of a purchase, from taking an order to placing the order with the supplier, finally receiving and storing it and making sure that it gets to the right department.

I will focus on procurement, because it's a process that starts with sourcing suppliers or vendors, establishing contact, evaluating the supplier and finally negotiating the best deal. Since the purchasing role is most often a part of that in hotels that are not part of a large corporation, I will include that in procurement.

Highest quality at the lowest cost is for most management team the credo and main objective for the procurement department. I wonder if that is the right objective, in fact I will show why I believe there is much more to it.

In general the actual position has become dull, suppliers are easily accessible with the internet as search tool, a few mails and you can get the prices down with 30%. In some cases, when one of my team members has been part of the negotiating process, we have gotten a discount or so called kickbacks or marketing fees, before meeting the potential supplier.

The supplier or vendor;
So let's first understand the supplier. The reason for it is that, I want you to form an objective view of what they have to offer before I go back to the actual hotel.

The supplier has a need. That need is for a procurement or purchasing officer to find his or her products.

How would they do that? There are all kinds of events, trade fairs and shows one can attend, in the hope that the guy with the wallet passes by. With many business cards printed and after the trade fair, you receive 90% of emails from suppliers that want to supply to your product. Maybe it was not the right trade fair? Sure, but reality leaves not much space for co-incidence. Hopefully the 10% that is of value pays for the stand and all the business cards that were printed. Sure, I am not saying all trade fairs are like that, but the competition is indeed very tough at the fairs.

There is another option, create outstanding marketing materials. We have learned that content is of essence, offline as well as online. The website is however, carrying a much more important element, which is to have the company site user friendly, simple and SEO sure, meaning valuable content. There is where most suppliers go wrong, the buyer is misunderstood and there is lack of valuable information that leads the hotel to find the supplier. Logical probably, as you want the procurement officer to understand and know about your product.

What other options does a supplier have? Relationships, surely relationships are an important factor. Think again! Remember high quality for the lowest cost? In that process, there is very little space for wonderful relationships. The days of giving a golden watch to your best client are over, they have not disappeared, but they are fading and certainly, they are for ethical reasons not acceptable. So much for the old way of Roman trading.

There are some other tools, like direct mailings and other traditional marketing tools like advertisements for example.

The boss of the procurement officer, mostly the financial director, has a target that needs to be reported at the end of the month. That target is a number and does not say anything about relationships, websites, materials, ads or how wonderful the product is for the guest, or easy to handle for the employee. So whatever the supplier tries, the impact on the final purchase is potentially minimal.

One last element that has to be mentioned is that the supplier has a cost, a large cost that is not hidden any longer. The cost of tendering or creating quotes is becoming larger and larger. This is as a result of mismanagement or lack of respect at hotel or property level, however, mostly not on corporate or centralized level. Because of the high costs of bidding, tendering and extremely low transaction ratio, suppliers are now charging this onto the hotels in the pricing offered. This results in an unbalanced and unfair pricing war, leaving hotels with a choice that is not in line with their core objective.

The role, the engine;

The internet has made way to long build relationships between suppliers and procurement officers, a sad happening. Or perhaps we should understand the role better and look forward, rather than what is behind us.

Procurement or product purchase is what keeps the hotel going, it is the face of the hotel, without goods the hotel cannot run. Roughly, the purchases can be split into the purchasing of products and goods that are part of the interior or exterior and operational or running costs. Thirdly, there is cost of the actual procurement department and the services that lies within that department, some direct like wages and others indirect like freight and custom costs.

The interior and exterior cost are those that are calculated in the capital plan and replacements are often a part of that, for example, a lamp that is broken, carpet that needs replacing or a television that is broken. They are part of the initial investment at a pre-opening, development or renovation. Those products are selected as part of an architectural design for example.

Examples are garden furniture, spa equipment, fitness equipment or a new kid's club.

Then there are the operational or running costs. This could be anything from food & beverage, to glassware, cleaning equipment, chemicals, stationary, technical equipment and much else that is needed by an employee to perform their duties. This is a very important part of the everyday running of the hotel. If anything fails, an employee or staff member will know and often has to deal with the issue directly, costing valuable time and resulting to dissatisfaction of the guest.

In addition, there is cost to run the department which includes freight, storage space, inventory and the cost of wages and benefits.

You see where I am going; the function looks quite different now when you take these three main elements into perspective. The role is large and it's sitting on an incredible amount of money that influences most employees in one way or the other. Even more so, the financial impact is immense, stock is expensive and purchases have to be made with a 50% prepayment from suppliers, nine times out of ten. This means an incredible impact on cash flow. This needs very secure management of every process and thorough education to those who are receiving and storing products from the procurement department, like the bar and the liquor, the housekeeping and their linen for example.

The power of procurement and the smell of roses;

Have I convinced you now that the role is of significant importance for the operation of the hotel? Not yet, well that's because I have so far described the role as it is applied in most hotels, pretty scary stuff.

I have always wondered, how do the guys in the basement know what is really required by the management? They have no idea, remember they are measured by costs and high quality. Amazingly, high quality has many numerous synonyms; perfection, greatness, merit, eminent, fineness and many more. So what is in the objective of the management? How should it be understood?

Here is a scenario, let's take a towel. The management want to purchase 3000 new towels, no lease, as they can do their own washing. The hotel has 200 rooms, 90% occupancy needs to have at least 2 towels per room and they are following the 1 clean, 1 dirty and 1 in the washing flow cleaning and storing process. The request, you guessed it, lowest cost highest quality and we need 3 suppliers to choose from. The last one is pretty much an industry standard, why? I have no idea, but apparently it's cool to compare.

After a couple of weeks of processing this in the order we discussed, the procurement officer comes back with a proposal and the management makes a choice. How does that feel?

You know where I am going right? How about information that is vital for the procurement officer, besides the star ranking? A few additional questions arise, besides thickness, size, brand, supplier, why are we actually in need of new towels? What is the target market? Is the hotel looking for a new market segment? Will there be more leisure travelers? More families? Are they aiming for generation X or are they turning the hotel into a more traditional one, so they can start charging higher prices. The thickness and size of the towel has impact on cleaning and handling costs, like washing capacity changes and use of chemicals. Was there a budget to begin with and if there was, what is that based on?

Convinced? My team recently created an offer for a hotel, outside furniture for a large beach and leisure area. We have a pretty decent relationship with this client. To be honest, I thought the deal would be ours; we even threw in some revenue increasing advice into the offer, at no extra cost. Our offer was substantial and was seriously considered. But we did not reach their goal, beside the fact that the procurement officer was told to get 15 different quotes, his goal was cost at the highest quality. Our relationship did not matter, our revenue view on the entire scenario was neglected, our 10 years relationship with the company we sourced from was of no importance and the presentation material was outstanding. We did not get a chance to revise the prices or come with alternatives where possible.

I am not sure they made the right selection and I am not sure this was the ultimate solution for the management and for the property in line with their goals. An opportunity lost? We will never know, but with 100% security, the process could have delivered a result which was much more focused on revenue increase, the process could have been fairer to the suppliers and above all, the procurement department would have gotten more out of the process with clear objectives and much more involvement in the entire procurement process.

Finance is changing, the circumstances are changing, but it remains the heart of the business. The power of data and communication will only increase over the years. It is the role of the Management to ensure that the finance department gets the resources needed to set the pillars of growth for any hotel operation.

In the next chapter, I will take on technology and how that will affect the business. Another boring subject? I don't believe so, it will drive the business in many ways, as long as the user is prepared for it!

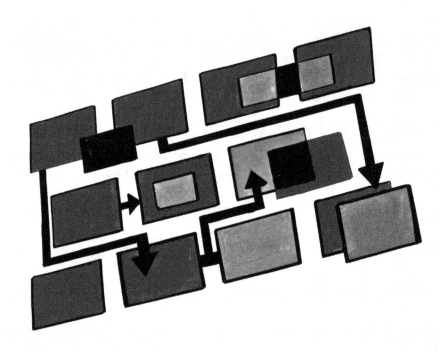

Chapter 9

Digitality
Why we need to know about
10 systems or more

In this chapter, I will write about going digital, technology, the use of it and mostly what digital really means to our industry.

Many executives are realizing that they need to fully adjust their company objectives and most certainly, the way they work. The digital revolution started in the 60's, following the mechanical and technical revolutions. Profitability is developing much speedier for commercial ventures that are adjusting to IT or Computer Technology, than for the individuals who don't.

It's enticing to search for basic definitions of digital, I believe digital is to be seen less as a thing and more like a method for doing things.

So what does this mean for the service industry like ours?

Will it increase productivity?

Will it allow us to be better connected with our customers and are we able to adapt to digitality quick enough?

The use of digital tools, systems and technology is so extremely personal and will vary from hotel to hotel, depending on location, size, market segment and many more factors. There is also a very little point to generalize, even though in this chapter I will try and explain some of the minimum requirements for success that every property and outlet needs to consider. I have asked for help on social media from a number of partners who are specialists on the main tools used by hotels namely Instagram, Facebook and Twitter.

Digitality for the service industry

In my opinion, our industry is taking steps to adjust to the high demand within the digital world. It is a slow process, a bit too scattered and without a clear vision from leadership and management. This is potentially due to the issue of locality, lack of innovation, non-clarity of the cost involved and the revenues generated as a result of implementation.

Locality

With the increasing demand for locality, for understanding culture and local reviews, the large companies are struggling to get the right data needed to attract the guest to book and book again. The information currently communicated to guests are generic. Just have a look at some of the sites and you can find information like distance to the airport, main sites to visit and internal information. Pre stay messages or post stay surveys are great for various reasons, like performance reviews, potential up sales and to start the connection with the guest. But then what? What more do we know about our guests? And how can we use that? I will answer this later.

Lack of innovation

On a recent trip I stayed in Athens in what would be considered a 5-star hotel. It felt like I was in a hotel from the 60's, apart from the pink carpets, green sofa's, there was no means of digital used. There was literally nothing in the hotel that was anywhere near innovation. The menus were old fashioned, it was all overpriced, the terrace outside were instable, iron tables, without any character. The wireless was still at cost, before you got to the TV channels, you had to browse passed movie offers and such. The lights had to be turned on with the main switch and the bed lights with a button, which kept falling under the bed. Considering the fact that I was actually in Athens to speak at a F&B conference about innovation and trends, I was amazed with how little this particular hotel has learned from trends, other industries and leave any sort of inspiration to the imagination!

Innovation is an opportunity for revenue and for creating a connection with the guest. It has to be taken extremely seriously, as this is what drives the use by guests of digital tools once implemented.

The cost

Another issue is that, management often does not see the real value of digitalization and merely as a cost. This is understandable as initial investments can be significant. But I also see that management is adapting and understanding the true value for the company, namely productivity and the guest; loyalty.

The service industry has opportunity to turn the above points around quickly, by changing strategy and setting goals. Emma Diacono, who runs a company fully focused on creating added value to business, answered a number of questions with regards to digitality. Emma's company delivers outsourcing solutions focused on marketing, communication and PR as an extension of an existing hotel team. Her replies clarify how digitality is a must for the service industry.

Interview with Emma Diacono
CEO Emmadiacono Ltd

1. Please tell us about the company objectives of your company?

Answer:

At Emma Diacono, we provide Perception Management services and consultancy. We specialize in strategic marketing, planning and implementation of integrated marketing and communications strategy. We provide our clients with access to a flexible and experienced marketing team and work with our clients to put forward a strategy that fits with the company's goals and objectives, whilst staying true to the brand and brand values. Our role is to allow management to continue to focus on their core business, whilst we take on responsibility for the brand and reputation management.

Perceptions are your stakeholders' way of seeing, understanding or interpreting your brand, your product or service, your message, your reputation. Stakeholder perceptions needs to be continually managed through proactive and sensitive communications, active listening, continued engagement and genuine relationships.

In traditional Marketing and PR practice, insufficient attention is given to the view from the external environment. PR and Communications campaigns often address the needs of the enterprise inside-out, one-way messaging initiatives. In reality, the success of any type of marketing is determined by the message perceived by the intended audience. It is essential to look at things with an 'outside-in' perspective. That is the only way marketing can work!

2. You have a large variety of clients, what is different in your client strategy between a product and service industry?

Answer:

I believe the service industry involves much more investment in the client's relationship. The ability to understand each client, how they think, what they prefer, understand how they approach things and being able to adapt accordingly is essential.

Everyone does things differently, that does not mean that one way is better than the other. I believe the key to success in the service industry is to be able to identify these differences and then be able to steer your team to work towards the same common goal, whilst keeping in mind the particular approach or personal style of the client. It's all about people at the end of the day; people buy people and how you approach or tackle issues, how personable you are and the confidence you enthuse is key.

3. Hotels continue to focus on customer retention. How will the digital revolution continue to change customer behavior within Hospitality?

Answer:

The digital revolution has changed customer behavior across all industries. It has given a sense of urgency and replies or even simple acknowledgements that are expected almost immediately. Customers have more of a voice and the power of 'word of mouth' has never been stronger. This means that service levels and an understanding of brand value is even more important than it was prior to the digital revolution.

4. There always has been a lot of discussion about the use of digital tools. What are the key elements for Hotels to consider to be successful in using these tools?

Answer:

I believe the most important thing is not to lose sight that at end of the day, we are dealing with people. People skills are still the most important, even if there is a layer of technology in between. I believe communication and people skills are even more important with the infiltration of digital tools as the room for misinterpretation is much higher and can be very damaging, especially across borders and across cultures. Hotels need to ensure that they can still provide a personable feel, that people are still the center of what they do and that, they find ways to ensure that the human personal touch is not lost behind all this tech.

5. What are some recommendations you can make to the Marketing and Communications team with regards to digital behavior?

Answer:

Remember you are dealing with people. Take a minute to think things through before hitting away at those keys. The skill of artful communication is harder and not easier – it is easy to type out a sentence and hit a button, but getting the right message across is another story.

6. What other industries do you feel the Hospitality industry can learn from and why?

Answer:

As mad as it sounds, I believe there is a lesson to be learnt from the IT industry. A couple of decades back, when communication technology first set in, we saw IT firms relocating their development to lower cost countries – a great shift to offshore outsourcing. Whilst great in theory and a few years down the line, many of the processes where brought back onshore as the firms realized that processes where high levels of human interaction and involvement were critical, were simply not working. They lost sight of the importance of human interaction, the cultural differences and communication difficulties that arised by losing the human contact element of certain processes.

7. What can independent or small Hotel companies do to make an impact on gaining Loyal Customers?

Answer:

I believe it's all about trying to find some way or other to strike up some sort of 'personal' relationship with the clients. As much as today's market is characterized by digital proliferation, it is also a very individualistic market where people like to be recognized and treated as individuals. Something as simple as calling someone by their own name or remembering something small about them goes such a long way. Tweak your service or product ever so slightly, to accommodate someone's particular needs and you have a client for life.

8. Your skill is a very particular one and requires much experience. Apart from that, what are the skills needed for a team like yours?

Answer:

I believe a key skill to work in our space is the ability to understand people, the ability to put yourself in someone's shoes and walk in them to deliver the common goal. It is not always easy as people are intrinsically different, so this in essence means that, I need to put more effort into managing and supporting my team to allow them express their frustrations, whilst enabling them to visualize and take ownership of what we are doing in order to be in a position to deliver.

Requirements and advantages

Customers are always connected, that means that our industry rapidly has to adjust to that behavior. I often hear that guests require only one thing, great service. That is most certainly true, however, full service delivery is an expectation as soon as the guest books. The actual way of booking, the way they are communicated to before, during and after the stay has incredible opportunity to create loyalty and a bond between the hotel staff and guest. The service industry requires the same from the company as any other industry. The process is different as people will remain the greatest service factor, however, the delivery or path to get satisfaction is not certain!

Use of data as a base for service delivery

Not only is collecting data important for any industry with regards to customer communication, it is particularly the case for the Service industry. To be able to understand the customer, data has to be collected and service adjusted accordingly. Not only service of course, but also, the product offered can be created or adapted through data. There are many such systems available that will handle data collection and analysis for the hotel. Cendyn is a good example of a company collecting data, that will drive increased revenue and loyalty.

Digital process improvement

Hotels are all about streamlining costs, the industry is in fact very advanced at managing cost. Digital means it can however, streamline manual processes. An example is the housekeeping handling process, the order taking in the restaurant, or automatic billing in accounts. Focus on the guest experience, it's even more something many hotels are looking at. Ease of online booking, key less check in and online concierge services for example; ROOM8 is a company that has recently launched these type of services all available through an application. Another service industry which has started this recent development is the care taking industry, like hospitals and elderly homes. An industry which is mostly run in old fashioned ways, from a design, operational and also technology point of view. One of the biggest revenue opportunities I believe is the way groups are handled. The complications of double booking, optimal pricing and operational challenges can be diminished by the use of digital tools.

Market segmentation

A business hotel with empty rooms on the weekend, a resort hotel with pricing challenges in peak season; we are fully aware of these issues. Use of digital tools, will pave the way for much better market segmentation, understanding booking and spending behavior. This will then result in better contracting, improved room allocation and planning. Of course this is also the only way forward for the marketing team. They will be able to address the right customer for the right marketing messages.

Story telling

Digital data collection alone does not work, it needs to be analyzed and used in the right way. It is the base for creating a connection with your existing and potential guest. Story telling is not new, far from. We have always been intrigued by opinions, stories about culture or origin. Think, what drives the sales of books, and always has? It's reviews of journalists or listings of bestsellers. Unknown writers have a much harder task to get their books on the market, as the supply is extreme. Story telling for hotels is a great way to connect with the market segment. Story telling is not to be misunderstood, it has incredible impact on customer's loyalty if done right!

Knowledge and skill

The use of digital tools requires training and education. Initially, the actual tool like the web, the software, or hardware or the application needs to be taught. Not only how to use it, but also how to get the most useful information and how to apply it best. Creativity is important in this process, as there is no way everything can be taught, the only way to get the most out of the systems is practice and continually find new ways. Hotels have to create a way to make the use, the education and the time available.

Food & Beverage and technology
On my recent trip to Athens where I spoke about Innovation within Food & Beverage at the Food & Beverage Conference 2016, a department which in general has incredible opportunity for improvement, I asked Adeline Barphe;

How do you think technology will impact your area of responsibility the most in the future? Adelina is the Vice President of the Food & Beverage Management Association in Greece and is known worldwide for her skill, creativity and mindset. The reason for highlighting Food & Beverage in this chapter is because it seems to be the department that is last in line with regards to innovation and digitality.

Adelina responded as follows: "Technology is a continually changing science and it will naturally continue to have tremendous impacts on almost everything in the future and not just the F&B industry.

Living already in the middle of a digital reality, it is evident that technological advancements have brought so many changes in so many areas of human activity and behavior and that has significantly affected our way of thinking, creating, communicating, travelling, having fun and much more.

The business environment has also changed dramatically. The traditional way of doing business has gone long ago. The digital technology has penetrated into operations and processes in such extensive degree that the increasing use of technology in the future restaurant development is rather a fundamental necessity and no longer a trend.

Nevertheless, the primary differentiation today and in the future would not be about new tech advancements anymore, but the way we use them. The new generation of internet users steadily follows the upward trends of socially oriented technologies. The web has gradually evolved into a major worldwide social networking, real-time information platform. These new communications and social trends are creating huge opportunities of course, but also considerable challenges for the F&B industry. Specifically, the future tech trends and impacts will be seen mostly in interactive dining and customer experience, as well as the escalation of mobile applications and social media.

What we are counting on most is data. Data was always king, but now more than ever, the leverage of information systems will have a tremendous impact and will absolutely determine the quality and the development of strategic competitive advantage within the industry.

Historically, the F&B sector at international level seems to have a very slow adoption rate to tech trends, mainly due to the high cost involved, but also due to a lack of technical knowledge. In the last years though, it has shown a considerable improvement in implementing new technological advancements as devices and software has become significantly cheaper and user-friendly.

From a managerial perspective, we have seen a spectacular increase in new and sophisticated features in all aspects of operations and also new ways of procurement and supply chain management. Naturally, POS, online reservations, table management system, back office software like inventory management, purchasing, and cost control are constantly upgrading their interfaces by adopting more effective and innovative solutions.

Since mobile technology has taken the industry by the storm, restaurants are already experimenting with smart apps and smart menu integration. Lately, we have seen a rapid growth in a variety of digital menus, which in most of the case includes small tablet menus for sit-down restaurants in fast food chains like McDonalds, Pizza Hut, Applebee's, we mostly see big wall and table-mounted devices. Additionally, we have seen many examples in the dining of the future where menus are entirely integrated into tables' surfaces, transforming them into smart tables. Such kind of interactive restaurants is Inamo in London, Mojo cuisine in Taiwan, Ebony in Dubai and an increasing number of restaurants in high-tech countries.

Despite the different devices and use of these digital menus, they all share similar features. Diners can browse through a digital food and beverage menu, choose and place orders, see multiple photos and description of a dish, find wine pairing suggestions, specialties, sold outs, calories and nutritional info, payment systems, multiple language interfaces and so on.

Interactive dining on the other side has been adding more entertainment and real-time interactions to the dining experience. The smart surfaces and tables have all kind of features and things that we normally do on our laptops and phones such as surf the internet, watching videos, social media interaction, listen to music, play games, find local attractions and events, transportation, etc.

Actually, anything you can do on your computer is now available right in front of you. The features that could be integrated or projected on these tables' surfaces are in fact unlimited.

Apart from the ability to easily and continuously update the menu and pricing, these integrations would bring a number of benefits and changes in internal operations as well. Moreover, cost related to servers and POS would be eventually eliminated, as electronic wallets and direct digital payments via smartphone apps have made the transaction process much faster and more efficient.

Many traditional sit-down restaurants debate about following these changes. Traditional paper menus indeed have a magic feeling, like an old postal cart, but the truth is that things do not stay still. That is the real magic.

Leaving the science fiction aside for now, the constant effort for digital engagement in food and beverage operation by adding fun and entertainment to a customer that finds and receives value in a similar way without a doubt, minimizes the risk of being left behind. The integration of high technology into the food and beverage environment and dining experience will allow restaurant management to be fully harmonized with the needs and wants of the customers, while being more efficient and profitable.

Social networks today facilitate the exchange of knowledge and information in real time and allows deep interaction with the customers. The restaurants that will open up to these interactions inside and outside the four walls of the restaurant have a better chance of surviving. Digital feedback and online interaction have also created an underlying demand for a smart feedback strategy. Feedback in a digital environment is considerably easier and faster. Rating the restaurant service, dishes, pricing, presentation, design, music and atmosphere is easy, with only 3-4 clicks on the feedback application, restaurants have real data instantly. Beyond that, we also have a substantial data flow through the information systems and applications, online reservations, social media, records of POS, labor, menu engineering, and others.

The use of data will literally be a goldmine for tracking down everything, menu items, popularity, sales analysis in real time, meal duration and all kinds of tools can be applied that will help us to understand how the customers think and act. This data will be a tremendous source of information for identifying patterns, demographics shifts and societal trends; How things are changing and how fast, what are the driving force, the emerging attitudes, limitations, intriguing variances and so forth.

Altogether, this is an incredibly fascinating field, especially for a person with a marketing background like myself, understanding and interpreting data does not come cheap. This will be a primary restriction on future growth, especially for independent restaurants. So a major challenge in the trend driving will be the ability to recognize all these implications involved and generate insight about the key influence factors that would be impacting the growth and the decision-making capabilities of a business.

Naturally, from a strategic planning perspective, knowing the impacts and influences of technology and how they are related to the broad environmental factors will facilitate the extraction of conclusions for concepts and locations, highlighting strength and weakness, identifying trouble spots and finally, will help in building a sustainable customer-oriented direction.

As I already have pointed out, technology will continue to forge forward exciting features and offer excellent opportunities in the F&B industry and obviously, there will be a continuous need to keep up with this primary tech-driven trends. Apparently, following tech trends is so much more than having an online presence and a social media account. It is crucial to understand the importance of digital technology in strategy, operation, marketing, promotion and online brand awareness. Otherwise it will be nearly impossible for a business to build a competitive advantage in the future. Finally, keeping track of these exciting innovations in technology, restaurant developers can and will continue to deliver a fresh, cutting-edge experience for diners, collect feedback, increase visibility and profitability.

Social Media

Hotels, restaurants, bars and cafés are reaching out to social media means to advertise their products and promotions. In my research, and experience with clients, there are so many different approaches to how to handle social media. For smaller independent companies, the role of addressing social media is often a shared role, or a position that is not full time. The resources available are clearly not sufficient to be able to afford a full time position for many of the smaller establishments. So consideration of outsourcing would clearly be an option. We have all been overwhelmed with social media campaigns, photos by bloggers and naturally all the independent traveler's worldwide9. Creating a strategy around social media is therefore essential. It is a way to communicate effectively and efficiently with our guests and potential guests. Rather than writing much more about theories, I have asked a number of professionals who occupy themselves on a daily basis with social media, on the best way to apply the main 3 tools used in hospitality to date; Facebook, Instagram and Twitter.

Facebook
Article Paolo Di Terlizzi – Internet Consultant – Refresh Creative Ltd
Effectively use Facebook for marketing your hotel

The goal of this article is to give you some power-starter strategies for Facebook and your small to medium hotel. You don't want to waste your life away on Facebook (easily done!). You want tactics that give you a measurable engagement, for minimum ongoing effort.

So if you haven't already created a Facebook page for your hotel, what are you waiting for?! Go here. Add a description, your location and a few pics. You will then at the least, have another placeholder about you for customers and Google to reference.

Okay lets put this in its place:

How much effort you should put into your Facebook page depends on how much of a destination your venue is, the typical age of your customers and the affinity that is possible to you.

How much of a destination are you?

Is your hotel a weekend escape or a city break place? Are you a Sunday lunch place? Do you have an epic location? Do you have a spa where people come to relax? Do you have 70's themed nights? Is your bar the after-work place people want to be seen at, or a live music venue? Are you a holiday hotel? Is your customer service end-of-earth amazing? – These are all compelling reasons that makes your place a destination, unique and totally Facebook marketable.

If a stay at your hotel is only a teeny tiny part of why the person is staying in the area (think business hotel or interchangeable basic hotel), then don't waste too much time on Facebook. Create a page, update it occasionally. Done.

Do you use Facebook yourself?

If not, you need to either start using it personally, or rope in a 20 or 30-something member of staff/family that lives on this platform. Understanding the grammar of this platform is essential to gaining traction.

The basic strategy is to post regularly, with reality.

The feeling that you want to get across on your page is, "this is the REAL hotel," not too salesy; your website is your official space on the web, whereas your Facebook is your more relaxed home.

So post regularly, several times a week with things like:

- New seasonal menu, the thought behind what went into that dish, words from the chef
- Mothers day gift package plus a mother/daughter pic
- The refurb of your big suite and what a happy couple said about their stay
- New historical attraction nearby, here's what we thought
- Words for a happy couple getting married tomorrow
- Reception staff thoughts on the 5 day weather forecast
- Always tie in with seasonal stuff like time for a summer town stroll and a beer in the sun
- That cheese festival that's happening next weekend
- Won any awards? Say so!

- Why your new Barman thinks a Long Island Iced Tea is still underrated
- And yes, when you have availability or offers put them here

These kind of posts will all show your place has personality and a vibe. The right mix would be around 80% content, and 20% salesy stuff.

Why not take a look at some hotels that are doing it right on Facebook for inspiration:
https://www.facebook.com/OvoloHotels/ https://www.facebook.com/theploughrhosmaen
https://www.facebook.com/BrownsHotel
https://www.facebook.com/NapaHotel

A picture for every post

Make it a habit to take picture or find a picture for nearly every post. Don't just have the 5 day forecast; take a pic of the sun rising. Don't just say Mark our barman has created a new cocktail; show a pic (or vid!) of Mark spinning the cocktail. Don't just have a post about Father's day offer; have a fantastic father/son pic.

And update your cover photo regularly. This gives instant freshness to your page.

Get the Facebook page mobile app

Make your life easier and post pics to your page from your phone, without the fuss of having to login to your page on a PC, by getting the Facebook Page Mobile App Manager (iPhone | Android), so that you post as you go about your daily hotel life. Simple.

Have you got a short username & check-in location?

If your Facebook page address has loads of numbers after it, you can shrink it down to something more memorable. Go to your page > edit settings >basic information and give yourself a shorty name.

Similarly, does your page have a geographical location? If so, you will see a "432 people were here" (or similar) in your page header:

Facebook-marketing-location

If not go to your page > edit settings >basic information and put a pin on the map!

Side note: this sometimes takes 30 goes to get it to accept, as you have to get the right address/postcode combination that Facebook likes. This also has some proven search engine benefit.

But wait! This all sounds like hard work.

It's good you stopped me there, because I've just increased your workload creating this "real" Facebook page presence. Let's dip straight in and see how it can plug in to social networks and get results.

The Basic Facebook power strategy is to work with the guests that you have.

1. Get people excited about staying at your place

In your booking confirmation (or pre-arrival email), add "Why not check us out on Facebook <link> to see the real <hotel name> and what Chris the Chef has conjured up in our delicious Summer menu".

By having a real-life statement about what is going on at your hotel or area, then people looking at your Facebook page before they've even set foot in your place should get a warm glow towards you and what's like being in a customer service industry.

2. Engage them afterwards

Similarly, in your thank you for staying email, you can use this as a hook for asking for engagement: "Enjoyed your stay, why not post a picture from your stay in <city> or in our hotel?"

I would suggest you alternate this with your "If you enjoyed your stay, why not say so on Trip Advisor <link here>?" statement, as you don't want to be asking for two favors in one email.

Side note: if you have booking software, you can usually automate these pre-arrival and thank you emails. If not, start doing them anyway; they should be an important part of your engagement strategy (more another time).

3. Integrate with your website

Integrate Facebook with your website, have a "like us on Facebook" button (make sure your web developer makes it, so that you get likes in your hotel and not your website!)

4. Respond to people if they post

If someone posts to your page for whatever reason, write a quick response! Even if it's just thanking them for their post and you hope to see them soon. It makes peoples hearts and social networks tingle when you re-engage with them.

Again if you have the Facebook Pages Mobile Manager app, then you (or your staff) can message instantly right from your smartphone, saving time.

5. Share to your page's Timeline when someone posts

As a page admin, you can then share their post to your page's timeline (click on it and press "Share") to elevate its presence on your page; from being in a small box amongst others, it can be a news item in its own. Doing this infiltrates more of that guest's network and makes your page inherently more social.

6. Ask questions

This works well once you have a few people looking at your page, you can then leverage them. "Should we have a Robbie Williams tribute act? or

Abba!? Let us know" or "What's your fav item from our breakfast?" Of course, if it's one-way and you get zero response, ditch this strategy until you have engagement.

7. Get familiar with Facebook Insights

Just like you check your website analytics to get a feel of where website visitors come from and what the quality of visitors are like, you can and should do this with your Facebook stats too. It's easy once you grasp the difference between "People talking about this" and "weekly reach". And what a 7 day moving average means.

Facebook-marketing-hotels

The list immediately below the graph shows you what content you had and which has had the best reach. Pay attention to this, it can make you hone what you post to your page and when.

Anything that you do on Facebook should be looked at from a campaign perspective; so that you can try something, see its uptake and if it works, keep it, if not move on.

8. Incentivize Check-ins, Likes and Shares

Offering a free cup of coffee for people that Like or check-in on Facebook is a low cost way to show that you are a place-to-be-at and get into a new friendship networks.

Be wary, in its most straight forward way, this is against Facebook terms and conditions. The way to do it is to make it a two-step process: So only people that Like you or have checked in can enter. The reality is that loads of small businesses are doing this and feigning ignorance as: what's the worst that Facebook will do? Also, as with any competition/prize draw, is subject to the laws of your land.

If you have a restaurant and want to be the place-to-be-seen-to-be-at for ladies that lunch, attach a flyer to your menu with a "check in on Facebook with a pic, to win a meal for 4"

You could run a" share this to win a night stay for two" promotion. This can get fantastic results, see below this place got 700 shares for their competition.

If you had a nail bar in your hotel, the act of female beautification is so social/one-up/sharing, you absolutely should do a check-in and share your completed nails for a free eyebrow threading promotion or similar.

If you have an arrangement with a forest pony trekking company and set up an excursion for a weekend bread couple, you've shown both an amazing customer service and given them an experience – experiences are so powerful. You absolutely can capitalize on this and ask them to engage/like and post a pic to your page.

Facebook-hotel-marketing-example

I also love Purple's Wi-Fi-in-a-box that has a Like Gate that people have to pass to gain access to your Wi-Fi. (Also helps covers your legal responsibilities around running a wireless hotspot). Costs £100 off then a monthly fee.

9. Encourage other staff

You can make other staff admin (on your page: edit page / admin roles) and then encourage staff to post as them, rather than as your hotel, this shows the people behind the page. Note: they have to Like you to be able to add them.

OK! Now, so here are some more ideas for what you can do to make a stronger presence and increase your outreach:

Integrate online booking

If you have an online booking system, this is usually super doper simple to integrate as they would have done the hard work and you can drop a widget into your page by following their instructions (e.g. FreetoBook's is here).

And you can also get a widget from your Trip Advisor Management Console which will show your reviews in the page.

However, don't expect too many booking from this source, as…

…The Timeline is where it's at

With the last major upgrade to Facebook, they elevated the importance of the Timeline (your news etc.), rather than your other subpages (or apps) on your page. This is significant. And just reiterates why a content and reach out strategy is really the way to do it.

Post to your page often with images.

Pimp your local business network

Engage with other local businesses, ask them to post a promotion and your post to their page reciprocally. These could be attraction or activity places or restaurants and shops. Consider offering the joint discounts with you.

This cunning plan works best if you have spoken or emailed the other page owner prior to posting to their page. This way you have a real relationship. Again, if you post an image (one that has crossover appeal to their customers too) it will have better results. And make sure they know how to "share" your post to elevate it to their timeline.

Events

Use the events tool within the Facebook page to list your themed nights, music events and send out invites to people that "like" your place. You can back this up with a photo of your flyer posted to your Timeline.

Worth a check!

Here are some things that may be holding you back:

Do you have multiple listings? Start typing your business name if you have more than 1 page, you can request them to be merged. https://www.facebook.com/help/249601088403018

And majorly, are you a person or a page? If you have "friends" not "Likes" then you need to change to a page! Read more: https://www.facebook.com/help/175644189234902/

Next level stuff

Doing some of this stuff already? Time for Advanced Hotel marketing on Facebook.

How Facebook Offers work – watch this video

Facebook has two kinds of advertising that you might need to be aware of: offers and ads. Being a bit broad here; offers are the right way to advertise for a hotel. Be cautious, you can raise money fast on Facebook! Of course you can set a budget and monitor results. Watch this video:

https://www.facebook.com/video/video.php?v=10152803965285125

Facebook advertising is a big enough topic for a post another day.

Conclusion: Facebook can soak up a lot of time. You now have some tricks to work with the guests and resources, encourage engagement and make it a space for your "real hotel" to shine through.

Instagram
Article
Katja Presnal
Chief Editor Skimbaco

Every week I send out a prompt email when the Instagram Travel Thursday linky post is up (subscribe it here) and I started adding a small tips for bloggers who read the newsletter. Today, I wanted to write an entire post about the importance of Instagram itself to travel brands, for travel bloggers and for travel industry brands and destinations.

Around a year ago, I realized that I was intuitively using Instagram not just for travel inspiration, but to get actual travel tips, where to stay or which neighborhoods to visit, where to eat and what to see on our trips. I was using Instagram as a travel guide! I realized that the travel community on Instagram is open to sharing tips and when I travel, it's common that my Instagram friends leave me travel tips. For example, when I was thinking about going to the movies on my trip to Texas last week, I received comments "go to an Alamo Draft House theater. You can drink alcohol and they have menu with real food!" and "Yes, Alamo for sure!! Loved the porter shake!"

This may come as a surprise to you; not all the people giving me travel tips the past year are not known "travel experts," they are not from tourism boards, nor promoting their businesses, they are travelers, or locals who know their neighborhoods. I wrote an eBook Instagram as your Guide to the World – How, What and Who to Search and Follow on Instagram, to Help You Travel the World and to help everyone easily use Instagram in that matter. How to connect with other travelers and find photos from specific locations and how to save the information for later use.

In my book, I also recommend over 50 Instagram accounts to follow, including travel experts and travel destinations and brands. I did extensive research on travel bloggers and travel brands on Instagram this spring and yes, found out amazing people and brands, also that many travel bloggers were not fully utilizing Instagram to brand themselves as travel experts, or they are not being travel experts there and not helping others to get more out of their travels. You might argue that you travel and write about it for yourself and maybe some do, but for most of us travel blogging is a way to serve others and help them to plan their travels. Instagram is an excellent place to show your expertise and help people in real time! And no, not by sending links to your blog posts, but actually by talking with people.

I admit, one thing that Instagram lacks is clickable links and many bloggers think it can't be used to fully benefit you, for example, driving traffic to your site. I actually think this plays in my benefit! I'm not being the self-promotional douchebag who only posts links to her site for people to come and check out the latest blog post (ha, I've got Twitter for that) and I am actually engaging! Last year, I realized Instagram travelers is one of the fastest growing audience on my blog though. How did I realize this? By the increasing number of people googling "skimbaco" around the world and what they read after finding the site, (travel posts) my Instagram name and the name of my site are both Skimbaco and I had no other explanation for the sudden increase. And by noticing I get direct traffic from Instagram, from the link in the profile. And by noticing my Instagram friends had started getting my site subscription (hello there Instagram friend!), liked my Facebook page or followed me on Twitter. It was pretty easy to notice, since these were the people whose names I'd recognize anywhere, since we had had numerous talks about travel destinations. Oh, and if you like stats, the Instagram audience on my site also spends 122.34% longer time on the site reading and the page views are 66.13% more than average, just to give you a few stats.

The photos "sell" the destination, your travel story and your engagement on Instagram sells you.

To summarize… Top 5 reasons why Instagram matters for travel bloggers and brands

1. Showcase yourself as an expert.

2. Engage with travel community.

3. Drive traffic to your website and ultimately sales, whether you are "selling" content or actual trips or destinations.

4. Showcase travel destination via images giving people the reason why to visit.

5. Make connections in the travel industry and form partnership with each other.

Twitter
Hotels should use Twitter for customer service, not marketing.
Article by Nancy Huang, Marketing Manager at Travel tripper.

About Travel Tripper

Travel Tripper is a full-service hospitality technology provider and strategic partner in helping hotels worldwide to generate demand, optimize conversions, and maximize revenue. Known in the industry for its constant innovation and exceptional expertise, Travel Tripper provides a comprehensive suite of solutions that empowers hotels from search to stay, including hotel distribution, website and booking and digital marketing. For more information, visit www.traveltripper.com.

Instagram has become the "hot" social media network for hospitality brands due to its highly visual platform and large engagement. But what of its predecessor, Twitter? Is it still useful for hotel marketers?

If a hotel brand is using Twitter the same way it utilizes Instagram and Facebook, then the answer is "no." When it comes to sharing content, Twitter is less effective than other social media platforms. But with more than 284 million monthly users who are hash tagging and utilizing the mentions/replies system, Twitter still reigns as the platform for listening, conversing, and starting real-time buzz.

Therefore, Twitter is most useful for customer service, not marketing.

The industry's poor track record

Research shows hotels are pretty bad at using Twitter for customer service. Hospitality brands have been overwhelmed by the volume of inquiries and complaints delivered via social media. A 2014 study indicates on average, hotels take more than seven hours to respond via Twitter, with less than 20% of @ mentions receiving replies.

While a prompt response demonstrates that a company is listening, extended silences implies the opposite. Part of the problem is that, there are more messages to sift through on social media than traditional phone or email channels. Hotel staff may not possess the necessary skills to respond since replying to tweets differs from in-person customer service.

Going above and beyond

While the industry as a whole might lag in using Twitter as a customer service tool, certain hospitality brands are doing it better than competitors. Some hotel groups have dedicated social media teams, while others integrate social channels within larger customer service departments.

Starwood has received a great deal of praise for its social media efforts. The brand's 33-minute average response time on Twitter is approximately 42x faster than the industry average. It's made possible with 3,000 customer service representatives in 10 offices across the globe. Starwood's staff replies quickly and they keep their eyes peeled to "surprise and delight" new and returning guests, remembering that even small, personalized gestures leave positive lasting impressions.

Hilton also impresses with prompt response times, aiming to reply within an hour and resolve within a day. The global brand has expanded from providing mere response management to proactively offering recommendations in 120 cities. Managed by a decentralized team to offer the best local travel tips, the hotel group launched the @HiltonSuggests handle to provide valuable, authentic information. Users, whether they are current customers or not, can reach out to the account for personalized expert advice.

One final noteworthy brand is Hyatt, which takes the platform's listening function to a whole new level. The brand recently hosted the "world's largest focus group" on Twitter to receive feedback on guest experience and used the findings to implement on-site improvements.

Proactive customer service

Hotels can use Twitter for proactive customer service. This strategy involves listening to travel issues of people in the area, complaints about competitors and reacting accordingly. For example, if a traveler tweets "X hotel overbooked and doesn't have a room for me now" or "help, we're stranded in Boston because of travel delays," a hotel brand can jump in and assist.

Proactive customer service presents massive opportunity for hotels to gain loyal new customers. Follow these tips to develop a proactive Twitter strategy:

Set up custom Twitter feeds to follow mentions of your competitors + certain keywords, like "frustrated" or "disappointed." If you see an opportunity to respond, reply directly to the tweet.

Set up custom feeds to monitor stranded travelers who might be in need of a room. Use combinations of words such as "flight + canceled + stranded + (your city)."

Monitoring combinations of hotel names + "I" or "I am" or "I'm" will reveal tweets expressing personal sentiment.

Not everything has to be about complaints. Similar to @HiltonSuggests, you can delight first time visitors to your city. Look for combinations like "first + time + travel + (your city)."

Tweet your way to success

Ultimately, it's clear Twitter is more effective for listening and conversing versus broadcasting. Take a page out of some of the global hotel brands' books and go a step beyond basic response management. Implementing preemptive tactics on Twitter could be the key to publicly demonstrating outstanding customer service, bringing in more business and nurturing a valuable new generation of social-savvy brand loyalists.

Hotels Getting Personal

The digital conferences for hospitality started popping up more than a decade ago. Digitalbuzz a blog to get inspiration about what's going on in the digital world, explains values of the digital world, the transparency of travelers and highlights that, technology will be driving guest loyalty and guest satisfaction in the future.

That really is not a surprise with the fabulous movement that we currently experience in particular with introduction of online check in, for example the Aloft hotel chain by Starwood Hotels & Resorts. Guests have many expectations, for example why can you order seats online before your flight, pay an invoice on your phone with an image or code and in hotels you still have to check in at the desk and physically pay your bill when you leave. According to Terence Ronson, there are 4 technology trends we clearly need to envisage as our challenge.

1. Mobility – the simple desire to work life with a tablet or phone
2. Connectivity – no more summer holiday destinations without Wi-Fi and it better be a fast connection too
3. User Experience – overall voice and touch are the norm of the future
4. Work/life balance – remote work, communication with friends is shaping and makes this balance a let's say, an interesting one

The passion for hotels is to deliver an amazing experience to the guest. We want them to come back. The many years I have worked with Six Sigma, a process driven way to improve your business, we looked at the correlation between loyalty and guest satisfaction. Obviously, one might assume, but much more complex than you might think and certainly it does not have a clear conclusion. What is however clear is that, there are a number of questions that arise when finding loyalty drivers. In research of top performing companies, I found out that leaders are obsessed with asking and answering these questions:

• What do customers in our target market really value?

- Which issues make our customers unhappy and cause them to leave?
- What pleases customers and causes them to recommend us to others?
- How can we turn customers into true advocates for our business?

According to The Management Study Guide, the answers find themselves in the attitude, the product & service, the technology, the human resources and the supplier's culture. Lifting the one we can influence well is technology.

The Technology according to Hospitality leadership
'Technology: The technological aspects of product manufactured by the supplier plays a vital role in customer loyalty. The more products are technologically sound, more is the loyalty'; says MSG. The subject can be spoken about in extreme lengths and I would love to share more information with you, clearly I am not the only one interested in what the future will bring. Reading up on what's needed in our hotel industry has intrigued me for many years. Just now I am really understanding what the different generation feel about technology, like the generation Y compared to the Baby boomers. But I still like to rely on what our leaders are saying too, they are the decision makers on what expectations can be met from our guests. Accenture held a survey amongst Key industry executives around mobility, here is what the result was:

1. Do you have a strategy for implementing mobile websites for existing Web-based (desktop) applications?
   - Main work has been done around providing accessibility to Web content via mobile websites.
   - For those lodging companies that have or are considering mobile applications the main focus is around
   - Planning functionality – hotel/room search
   - Reservation/booking functionality
   - Loyalty functions

2. Where do you see the biggest application of mobility in your organization?
   - Most important is guest-facing – The complete life cycle
   - Prior – Search for hotels and book room
   - In-house – On-property services
   - Post-stay – Marketing feeds

3. Do you see a demand from your guest population to enable additional on-property functions via mobile devices? If so, what are the top three?

   The following are the top on-property functions:
   1. Advance check-in functionality and bypass the front desk and use mobile device as digital key
   2. Check-out functionality
   3. Location-based services – Send guest messages based on where they are in the hotel
   4. Recognize guest arrived at the hotel
   5. Interactive offers based on guest location (e.g., spa service while at gym, offers for drinks while at pool/bar, etc.)
   6. Self-service concierge services
   7. Order room service
   8. Order food/drinks at the pool
   9. Set up wake-up calls
   10. Request parking valet service
   11. Information about the hotel, local attractions, local restaurants, etc.

Additional on-property functions raised:

- Using guest mobile devices for entertainment/ Download own movies and music to in-room devices
- Electronic/digital currency – Purchase of services and products using mobile devices
- What are the key issues that you focus on as you seek to develop and implement your mobility road map?

- Developing something that is platform independent with changing technology
- Choosing platforms to develop (e.g., Android, Apple, BlackBerry, etc.), choosing between smartphone, tablets and gaining biggest market share
- User interaction variations per device
- Security around PCI compliance and capturing credit card payments
- Integration – Enabling legacy systems to work with the mobile devices in a secure and structured way
- Investing in features that are going to be the most valuable to the guest
- Speed to market to ensure that by the time a function is deployed, it is not obsolete demand
- Guests now brings multiple mobile devices and want to interact with on-property devices (e.g., TV, stereo system, etc.)
- When outsource service to phone company now have security issues and data sharing on carrier side on top of bandwidth issues

Digitality will continue to develop and leadership will take a key role in developing and communicating the strategy that will affect the way the business is run operationally and from a sales and marketing perspective. Communicating with our guests has never been so complex, yet with incredible opportunity when handled well!

In the next chapter, I will talk more about the wellness industry that is impacting hospitality tremendously.

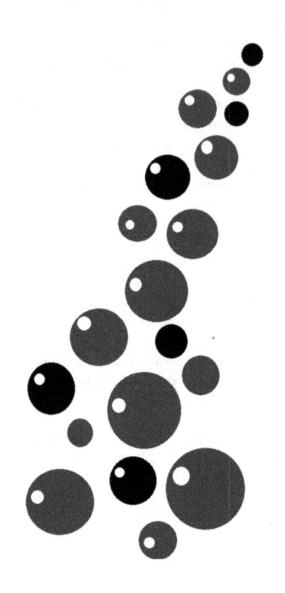

Chapter 10

Taking wellness seriously
Run fast

Have you ever wondered what the chocolate on your pillow in the evening is for? Me too, but I have never found the one answer. Sure it is part of the turn down service, an evening service where housekeeping comes in, gives you clean towels, closes your curtains and opens your bed, so you can jump between the sheets as soon as you return in the evening. Traditionally, the chocolate was put there to show that the hotel cares and wants to give you a little extra. Since chocolate is clearly not something you should eat before you sleep and most of them ends up in your suitcase or in a melted version together with you between the sheets, I wonder how serious hotels take the real need that can actually make a difference to the guest. In that search of exceeding guest expectation and looking for value, I found out that hotels have started taking the gym and spa business seriously. Healthy food and snack options are appearing on menus, organic materials are used for bedlinen and bathroom amenities, and additionally, Hotels are adding Spa to their brand name. The gym has always been there as a must have in whatever shape or form, but hotels are taking more steps to create a serious difference. In that path, there is a lot be learned and much opportunity to be implemented.

Why taking care of Hotel guests is a necessity!
The research within the hospitality industry with regards to increased
Spa and Wellness trends is numerous. All mayor hotel chains are already
engaged in increased Fitness and Spa offerings.

The education is continuous worldwide, with an increasing popularity,
the knowledge of guest's increases and more so from those who deliver.
The fitness and Spa are purchased by those travelers who are choosing
accommodation, personal consultation, a good Fitness center, a selection
of spa treatments that include meals, drinks and a range of activities.

The objective of the visit is to feel better, to get something out of the visit
that creates personal wellness. That can be in combination with work,
it can be in the city, in the desert or at the sea; the objective remains.
These guests are different and they require more attention as they are
actively seeking health. The size of the room becomes secondary, and the
atmosphere, quality of the bed (sleep), surroundings, access to music and
healthy choice of meals becomes of much higher importance.

There is need to feel educated and bring home what has been learned
or used during the stay, so the journey to well-being can continue. This
concept takes this trend to the actual bedroom. One may wonder why
the room is such an important element. Some interesting details about
guests to take into consideration when planning or considering health
and wellness:

1. The bedroom is a safe haven and should welcome the guest to
   stay there
2. Increased female business travelers with a continued wish to
   exercise or eat in the room, rather than public areas
3. Personalized products improves a calm mind and better sleep
4. Good sleep results in improved strength and alertness
5. Nutrition is the base for a healthy lifestyle, resulting in alertness
   and a deep sleep resulting in energy
6. The room will improve mental activity over other areas in or
   outside the hotel

7. The environment and use of lighting results to calmness and energy
8. The end result and the heart of wellness of the guest will deliver increased loyalty, in room sales, product sales and potential additional yield opportunity.
9. Market share improvement as a result of solid marketing efforts.

The above points are to be taken very seriously if a hotel seeks to deliver what the guest is really looking for. If done right, this also creates great marketing opportunity and social media will shine!

The Elements of wellness for the hotel guest
The biggest opportunity for development within hotels is understanding the customer. As mentioned before, collecting data about the guest and tracking guest behavior will set the way for innovation and change. With regards to wellness and health, the employees needs to adjust even more to each guest, as each person has different needs with regards to health and wellness. Take for example a nutritionist who prescribes a certain eating pattern based on a very personal analysis. That shows there's a need for the hotel staff to understand the guest, and offer a service or product that follows that analysis or data. In hotels, it remains hard to please everybody just because everybody is different, but to generalize these, there are some main elements to consider:

Social Behavior – Hotels recognizing the need for interaction between people

Mind & Mental activity – Stimulation of brain activity will assist in better brain functions and efficiency

Health, Nutrition and Diet – Personalized food and beverage solutions are key to well being

Relaxation, Rest & Meditation – Offering great sleep and rest areas for kids and adults are the foundation of well being

Environment – The design, the light, the sound are all factors that contribute to our nerves and well controlled

Body Fitness, Body & Care – Exercise & motion and personal care are a part of life, live with it every day and stimulate all senses

Wellness & Self Responsibility – The core of wellness influenced by external factors, as mentioned above

#Fitness #health #wellness #food #drink #hotels #traveler; what do these hashtags have in common and what can Hotels do to create a synergy?

Article published by 4Hoteliers.com – Jeroen Gulickx

Fitness and Business travel

Ever returned home from a trip, energy reduced, feeling an unhealthy week had passed? A successful week within business is often likely to be a struggle for the body. Unhealthy eating habits, lack of exercise, time changes, different sleeping patterns, different temperatures and many other factors contribute to lack of energy. According to the World Health Organization, these are just very few of the main factors that influence your health while traveling. The WHO also discussed travel related risk and many other factors, but I will focus on the elements that Hotels can influence.

The power of wellness remains with the traveler, there is no discussion about that. But many hotel companies now make an effort to assist in that process. It's all part of the promise to offer the best service to the guest. From own experience, it is highly tempting to go away from normal eating or sleeping routines and habits, a bit more work before you sleep, a glass of beer with the dinner, nicer to be at the pool and catch some fun than to sweat in the gym, recognize it? You have a choice and so does #hotels to make the choice of feeling energetic, healthy and rested more easy for the guest. In recent years, there clearly is a trend for #wellness which you can see in hotel brands popping up like Even hotels by IHG. That clearly is a large step in the right direction.

People are caught into making many decisions during a trip, the easy and most straightforward ones are those often chosen. And that is one of the roles of the hospitality industry, to make decisions easier.

#Food & #Drink

Sure, making decisions easier can be done by offering the obvious, a burger and a beer at reduced price before 7pm. Choice made pretty easy and you can see a match at the same time. But what about a salad and a smoothie at discount after a Massage in the spa, or a few laps in the pool. You can combine exercise with a healthy food option resulting in better sleep, improved nutrition that eventually creates relaxation and increased energy levels.

The breakfast is another example, more #hotels are now offering biological options, healthier granola's, fresh fruits and smaller portions. Again, I am not scared away from a good portion of bacon one morning, but stay away from it four days in a row.

Hotel Management needs to make decisions mostly based on the cost/value issue. However increasingly, the guest or consumer influences the decision. We see for example many Spas popping up in existing hotels. Main reason is that, it's a more complete offering for the guest, in the hope they will choose that hotel over others. I am not convinced this is the case, research surely shows that over 66% of travelers now select a hotel that offers a gym or fitness facility, whether they use it or not is another matter.

For the marketer, this is the opportunity that clearly plays a large role in convincing the decision maker. The Spa also offers that opportunity but still, too many fitness or Spa's disappoint, creating dissatisfaction, resulting in decreased loyalty or no return and negative word of mouth. There is a cost for all this that can be significant, so the trick for management and their strategy is to find the guest who is willing to pay for the 'luxury'. That is where many hotels are seriously challenged.

One of my Marketing teachers told me once "there are so many ideas, there are just a few people who know how to implement it". My company lives by that, everything we create or sell needs to have an angle, a difference that can be marketed in the right way and above all, to the right market segment. The statements above really do not have to mean a big change in the hotel, other than small adjustments in operations, keeping in mind that services will only be used if the guests are aware and even better, if they have chosen the hotel for that reason. Some examples are introducing training times by staff for guests, a city running map, a changed menu with healthier items, a more streamlined breakfast, different minibar items, advice on sleeping habits and many more.

There are more serious changes that can be made by management, playing into the new trends. Investments into hotels deliver great value long term, with regards to property value, and there are also small investments that can be taken out of the normal running costs and P&L. Here, the risk of failure is larger if the investment is not thought through properly.

Together with Casall, my company created the 1Sq Meter Gym for hotel rooms. This innovative concept trains all parts of the body and there is no more need to bring gym clothes. The guest can exercise in the room and the hotel has a great marketing tool and an opportunity to upsell to this room type, 'The smallest gym in the world, and guests love it'

The Fitness room or Gym
An example is an investment in a new or renovation of a fitness room. Some recent data tells us that, over 80% of the traveler using the fitness room cannot find the right machine in there, or it is occupied as most people will go to the gym between 5-7pm, losing the purpose of the investment totally. Also, the investment is often made without prior research, leaving opportunities untouched. Clearly, hotel management has more opportunity going forward to meet the needs of the healthy traveler. It needs to seek the value of this market segment in their existing guest portfolio, as well as attract a new potential guest. There are solutions, simple and complicated ones. My company has been dealing with many of those and we can happily confirm that the healthy traveler is taken seriously.

Hotel companies are taking significant steps to meet the requirements. Travelling will continue to change, it's the hotel management's role to stay ahead or even more, to set an example when taking responsibility of people and their well-being.

Wellness and Medical Spa's a service or amenity?

The Spa market is clearly a growing one, you notice it simply by walking the streets of every city, but also, it follows the trend of feeling better and looking after yourself. In fact, according to the Horwath statistics by the end of 2015, the global wellness tourism economy grew till 438.6 Billion USD worldwide, with a growth of 9% compared to the previous year. Naturally, these numbers really represent the destination spas. That's where tracking becomes hard and the definition between the delivery and service vague.

I would like to refresh the memory on what actually started the Spa concept and more so, what the industry needs to do to maintain the incredible growth, hold on to roots and to stay on the right path to wellness and health.

Spa defined

The actual definition of the Spa is very misunderstood. Dr Puczko of Xellum states that, the Spa in mainly Europe is often seen as a few massaging and pool area, and has become a 'catch all' or bastardized name. Really that is far from what it should be and makes it a product of price and popularity. Both the business and the consumer needs to understand and appreciate the difference. Wellness seems to be the word that's just added to give it that little extra marketing.

Traveling is already an experience and originally, together with a treatment that is actually recommended by the doctor created the need for a destination. That destination should be a pleasurable one, keeping well-being as the key delivery. There, we have the start of the association between travel or tourism and the Spa. Some say that it was only in the 1940's, when the evolution of the Spa started, with the Rancho La Puerta, a dedicated destination spa, wellness retreat and health resort. Over the years, the Spa's have developed, also because of clear public recognition and awareness of bad eating and exercise habits, signs of allergies, increased number of diseases, the need for health growth and it kept growing. It was only at the turn of the century, the shift to a holistic and more medical approach within the Spa destinations became apparent. That trend continues to grow till date and some serious places attracted much more attention and created a path for an entirely new market segment within the Spa destination tourism. A few examples of game changers are Chiva Som in Thailand, Palace Merano in Italy, Ananda in India and the SHA Wellness in Spain. Many activities which are now common came out of that, like Yoga, Ayurvedic medicine and the inclusion of a personal analysis.

Finding Wellness

The education continues worldwide, with an increasing popularity, the knowledge of guest's increases and more so, from those who deliver. The destination Spa are purchased by those travelers who are choosing accommodation, personal consultation, a selection of spa treatments that includes meals, drinks and a range of activities. The objective of the visit is to feel better, to get something out of the visit that creates personal wellness. That can be in combination with work, it can be in the city, in the deserts or at the sea; the objective remains. These guests are different, they require more attention as they are actively seeking health. The size of the room becomes secondary and the atmosphere, quality of the bed (sleep), surroundings, access to music, and a healthy choice of meals becomes of much higher importance.

There is need to feel educated and bring home what has been learned or used during the stay, so the journey to well-being can continue. Destination Spa's are clearly seeing a longer length of stay than usual, mostly between 3-7 days, a 60% higher spend from the guest inside the premises, than the usual guest and a 40% higher chance of loyalty.

Spa Management

Apart from creating the most beautiful design, peaceful surroundings and all physical efforts, it looks like there is much more to it to deliver the result our guests are really looking for.

I perceive a requirement for an adjustment in management, an adjustment in learning and aptitude and correspondence that begins inside the organization. Education and marketing that is not targeting the right market segment are some of the main reasons for failure of success within the wellness industry.

The marketing challenge is also where we need to differentiate the wellness travel and the medical travel. The wellness traveler is the returning guest, the medical travel which could be a rehab, hip replacement or a clinical surgery often goes once or twice and are less like to travel for a long time. It is important to get a good mix of offerings that suits a wide variety but decisive potential guest.

There also is the pricing element, again within the marketing of the destination Spa. You can wonder whether there is space or a gap that can be filled for a less expensive option than many Spa's are currently offering. As acknowledged before, you can start small, throw in one healthy dish on the menu, use thinner towels, which use less energy and water to clean etc. Intercontinental hotels launched Even Hotels, all based around fitness, Westin Hotels, with bringing green elements into the public spaces. Environment and sustainability factors will also continue to play a key role in the development of new Spa's.

The Spa of the future

The future of the Spa is somewhat unknown, but according to Susie Ellis, president of Spa Finder in New York says it looks like this, 'by 2020 the health issues of travelers will be even more extreme than they are today. Stress, chronic disease and obesity will be at an all-time high and hotels and spas will have to accommodate even more over-worked guest. No longer will things like fitness centers and spas be considered "amenities," said Ellis. 'They'll be necessities.'

I agree with Ellis. Generations to come will be more conscious about wellbeing and health and more educated, leaving the Spa's with only one option; to start taking the business very seriously. Focus on reaching the guest objectives; through delivering the best within wellness and medical care. It starts with the analysis of the guest, of the actual and potential deliveries. Understanding the markets, differentiating between Wellness and medical stays, adjusting packages, pricing and other marketing elements accordingly, will be the platform for any Spa. It is not a side business, it is a serious business. Training and education of the management and team members in specific treatments and service to these conscious, particular and rewarding guests are essential. I am convinced many of the authentic and antique methods and remedies will continue to keep a very strong place in the future development of the destination Spa and there are many to be uncovered.

It is not a trend, it is not an amenity, it's an evolution that will comfortably keep its place and play a significant role in the overall development of Hotel & Resorts.

Interview, Anna Bjurstam
Managing Partner, Raison d'Etre Spas
Your quote on the Future of Spa & Wellness:

Exponential growth potential in all areas of hospitality.

1. Please tell us about the company strategies and objectives of your company Raison D'Etre?

    Answer: With the incredible growth in wellness, we have seen in the past 3 years that our strategy is to continue to lead the development of wellness in the hospitality industry. We also see that our offerings might expand to both the built environment as well as work place wellness. The trend is that wellness should be evident in the room products, with not only a pillow menu, but a much more comprehensive sleep offering and sleep environment components. Further enhanced wellness food and beverage products, biophelic design, spaces for mindfulness and so forth to expand outside the four walls of the spa.

We are working with leading doctors as well as Harvard Medical School to have a scientific and result oriented approach to our wellness offering and be able to offer solutions that will lead the market.

As we are experts in building brands, with brands such as Kempinsi, Resense, Six Senses, LivNordic and so forth, it is an important strategy to build this into the brand pillars of each of the future's confidential brands we are currently and will be working on.

2. You have many years of experience in Spa & Wellness. What are the 3 biggest changes you have experienced in recent years?

    Answer: 1. How wellness has grown in all areas in our world and that it is now over a US$ 3.4 trillion business and continues to grow at an exponential rate. The "un-wellness" of the world is part of the reason why increasing number of people are turning to wellness. 2. The inclusion of wellness outside the four walls of the spa and fitness in a hotel to be included in other areas, weather it is fitness/yoga/mindfulness designed hotel rooms, healthy food and beverage options or focused wellness advice in a turn down letter. The rise of Even Hotels as well as Equinox Hotels supports this growth. 3. The governmental institutions all over the world embracing wellness, such as Bhutan's GNH (Growth National Happiness Index) to measure their success instead of GDP, The United Arab Emirates just recently appointed "Minster of State for Happiness" as well as the rise of Wellness Tourism as a focus for many countries.

3. What are the principles of creating a successful Spa within Hotel surroundings?

    Answer: People are today expecting results and gimmicks are not well received, as we have seen several examples of the past years. Thus, when including fitness, mindfulness, sleep, food and beverage wellness offerings, it needs to a) be scientific b) result oriented c) tailored to the guest of the specific hotel and finally d) tailored to the hotel and its local surrounding. Guests do not want to have a Swedish Massage or Swedish Meatballs in India, they want to have an Indian experience.

4. What type of Hotel Spa do you feel are setting the standard for guest experience?

Answer: What we are developing in Six Senses is certainly pioneering in the wellness hospitality industry. Being a hotel chain with brand pillars of being sustainable, rooted in wellness, in tune with the local fabric and use nature in design as well as experience. Including wellness in lighting, air, sleep, food and beverage as well as personalized scientific integrated wellness programs in the spa are setting new standards in the industry.

5. You are a frequent traveler yourself, what do you feel hotels are gaining with offering the Spa experience?

Answer: For me it is important to sleep well, to be able to eat well, have good functional training offering as well as qualified spa treatments to help alleviate any travel stress such as jet-lag, bad neck or stiffness. I chose hotels that can offer this when I travel and preferably, with a sustainable commitment as well.

6. New Spa brands are being created to attract new market segments. How do you continue to innovate and where do you get your inspiration from?

Answer: We are working right with wellness in over 40 countries and wherever we go, we discover more about native wellness secrets and we constantly read and study as well as being invited to speak at most wellness/spa conferences in the world. Then, at Raison d'Etre, we are built around being trend maker and having the ability to invent and be creative and we have done so successfully in the past 20 years. There is no limit to the source of wellness inspiration, we just have the ability to make that into practical business models that both makes money and are able to improve people's lives.

7. You develop Spa concepts as well as manage them. What are some of the biggest learnings you can pass on to hotels who wish to manage the Spa themselves?

    Answer: Unless you have a very comprehensive understanding of wellness from top management down to General Manager level to start with, it is difficult to successfully run spas. The second step is to have a developed spa division with trainers, technical services, HR etc. that has focused expertise in operating spas, then quality will falter and it is better to bring in experts to run spas. If one desires to run one's own spa, the above need to be in place. For example in Six Senses, there is over 15 dedicated corporate spa members operating the 40 spas worldwide.

8. The Spa industry has moved on from the original Wellness concept, but is now returning to its roots. What impact will this trend have in the future?

    Answer: I am not sure that it has moved away from the original wellness concept, it has constantly evolved and what we see in our crystal ball is that, it will embrace more parts of wellness truly involving therapies for a healthy mind and more inside out wellness, treatments for cancer as well as treatments to enhance libido are both up and coming. To be more local and tuning in with local healing traditions, herbs and products is another trend and most importantly, being much more result oriented and holistic than it has been before.

9. The Spa is much more than a service to hotel guests. Education is a large element in the delivery. How do you ensure that the service is aligned with guest expectation?

Answer: We work with a number of quality management systems including LQA, Richi, monthly mystery shopper, our audit system as well as guest feedback and when we consolidate these sources of feedback, we get a very clear picture of where we need to focus. We then work with both management, training and general development of concept to improve and it is done through a very structured system and works well.

However, spa is the only place where you have an hour one to one interaction between a member of the staff and a guest and with one party not having much clothes on and therefore, QMS for spa are more complex than any other department of a hotel.

10. The Spa & Wellness industry has incredible potential to grow further. What do you believe are considerations for property owners who are looking to invest into newly built Spa's?

Answer: First of all, the spa is not an isolated profit center, the incremental revenue in terms of average length of stay, double occupancy and also average daily rate is proven and should be taken into consideration. For example, just this week we had a guest in one of the Six Senses resorts who did an integrative wellness screening towards the end of their stay and were so motivated to go on one of our programs that they lengthened their stay with 10 days in the Maldives. Therefore, investments proforma and underwritings should include both spa operation as well as incremental revenue.

If I was a hotel investor about to invest, I would make sure that I look not only to the spa, but the whole hotel and how to incorporate wellness. Then make sure that target market and guest logistic analysis is understood, to have accurate guest load in each area such as locker, pool etc. understand the needs and wants of the particular guest of that hotel and then, design the spa around that to get maximum ROI. Too often, this is only considered after the spa is designed.

It is comparable with a restaurant, before you design it, you have decided if it is to be Italian or Chinese, for example, and how many guests it will be able to cater for and what that means in supporting areas. The same logic goes for a spa, yet we still see examples where this is not the case today. In a nutshell, first, now, What, Who and then look at the How.

Defined: The Spa delivery for Luxury Hotels

The Spa is not a trend, it is eternal. Sanus per Aquam means "health through water," something that is only recently getting attention of hotels, whereas 15-20 years ago, hotels did not pay any attention to this industry. Initially, spas were created only as a service and a well-appreciated one, but not really with the full understanding of the actual delivery for the guest or patient it is intended for.

The recent developments in the last 4-5 years show a changing trend for hoteliers. Also for online booking sites, like Mr and Mrs Smith that have breaks & pamper section, or some travel companies are even fully focused on this particular travel, like Sanctuary Spa holidays, offering tailor made trips. With the development of the wellness Industry, management of hotels understands the marketable difference between a hotel with or without the wellness facilities. Note that within the wellness department of the hotel, we also include the gym. The gym being a much spoken about service element, which out of recent surveys from the Hotel Association shows a need for every hotel, in fact 78% of the business traveler want a gym in the hotel.

Within the Mocinno Spa client base and consulting requests, we can see a clear difference in Spa profits, in line with the attention that is given to the department by the management. Guests want a choice, as stated by the Stanford Business School, they want to be given options, make and stand behind the final decision. In today's hectic lifestyle of megacities, Spa is an oasis of appeasement, where you can get away from the daily hassle, from stress, to make up the energy and find new strength. The guest when given a choice will choose the hotel that has a Spa. That was the reason for the beginning of the recent Spa Boom.

In addition to the Spa being a service, there is a growing demand by guests for improvement of health, which was what the Spa really was intended for in the old days. Development of the Spa and Marketing it at the hotel is now one of the leading trends in modern hospitality industry. A recent showcase of the Leading Hotels of the World show almost all leisure hotels featuring a solid Spa concept.

Interaction of the hotel and spa is becoming very dynamic and helps the hotel to increase occupancy and profitability. Senior Management is engaged in offering a range of treatments in combination with an F&B and hotel room offering.

The spa is no longer a service, but is becoming an additional revenue stream as well as adding to the bottom line of the Room division.

Hotel management that understands this trend is gaining business from new market segments as well as retaining those who have been and experienced the service. Perhaps even gaining an entirely new generation to the hotel.

In the struggle to get the most out of hotel stock at the right pricing, combined with the increasing online bookings, the management needs to get ready for the next level of Spa business. Education and learning from competing industries like fitness or treatments centers as well as clinics is the platform for the next generation Spas. Only when that is understood and the customer is defined can the hotel start with the design and product selection process. When aligned with the hotel strategy, the Spa can become a very successful addition to the complete offering of the business.

The final delivery is one of yielding, sales, marketing, managing budgets, inventory, design and HR. Only if all assets are managed well and like a business element should, can and will the spa be a successful addition to the hotel?

The organization and management of the spa area has become one of the most important and expensive investments within the conventional hospitality industry. Architects, designers, spa consultants solve problems posed by the hotels owners. When all done and implemented with passion and strategy, correctly accompanied by a professional sales & marketing team, one can count on media and finally gets to buy the amazing combination of travel and wellness. The Spa delivery within the hospitality industry may have different formats, but each must represent the richest variety of services needed for health, recovery, improvement of appearance and a comfortable communicating and leisure of guests. For the industry, it simply needs to show a healthy balance sheet and an educated team that innovates and understands Spa management more than ever before!

In the next chapter, I will focus on Marketing. I have kept that part of the book for later stage, as I feel everything that I have written so far needs a handle. Taking all innovation, food & beverage, technology and wellness to the market requires the hospitality industry to make a considerable change in the market space!

Chapter 11

The end of the 4 p's
Data as source for sales & marketing

This chapter is split up into Sales and Marketing. I will start with Marketing as I would like to highlight the importance of what Marketing can do with regards to the use of data and all the opportunities that comes with Marketing. Marketing within hotels is a department within the back of house operation. Typically, it consists of a marketing manager, an online marketer, a PR agent, reporting to the Director of Sales & Marketing. The online marketer is a role that is often centralized, which I will come back to later. PR is often outsourced to an agency on a retainer or ad hoc, some of the larger hotels have their own employee to do this. Hotel chains benefit from marketing that comes out of the head office. They decide the colors, use of logo, in fact the entire brand book, to ensure that guidelines are followed in line with the hotel brand. Allocation of financial resources for the marketing department at the head office often is a percentage of the room revenue or total revenue. This set fee is quite a burden for many hotels that have a strong local marketing team and need the resources to operate that and for sure, a point of discussion at every owners meeting. The fees at the head office are used mainly for branding purposes as well as loyalty and campaigns.

Is this the right set up to get the most out of marketing? It's certainly traditional, which can be a good thing, however, it's missing some of the basics of marketing and one in particular which is to understand your customer or guest and ensuring the marketing strategy matches and exceeds that. Hotels and in particular, chains describe their typical guest which is often very similar to their similar 4 or 5 star competitor and leaves little or no space for localization or serious change in the marketing. An example is a hotel in Dublin that has an amazing old bank hall inside the building, which would be a perfect wedding location. The materials and brand standards gave strong direction from the head office in another continent. The team suggested a change in the materials that was used for the presentation of costs and possibilities for future wedding couples; the standard, a typical of what you would call banquet folder in the industry. When I personally took the fight with the head office, that we should create material that is more like a typical wedding brochure with table settings, flowers, the local church, ribbons, you name it, I was told that it was the way to traditional for the brand. Traditionally, if there is one event that is traditional, it surely is the wedding. I did not win the battle and it is very simple example of not listening to the customer, but rather to blindly follow a standard.

So let's start with some data and perhaps a different way of categorizing the hotel guests. There is a lot of talk about generations, it certainly is a trendy way of looking at the customer and when I started digging deep, I started finding a lot of information that is extremely useful for marketers when I understood it can be applied to every part of the organization, internally and externally. I will describe the generation, their travel behavior and a short simple toolkit, that can be useful for implementation within hotel marketing.

Understanding your guest

**Understanding the 'Generations' of Travel – Part 1:
The Post War Cohort.**

In recent month, I have tried to make every effort to understand how well we actually know people and their behavior with reasons to make certain choices and in particular, leisure travel. The reason for the research and data collection is to understand the characteristics and needs based on their age. The management team who has to make important marketing or branding decisions, can optimize the decision process by using this information. And develop an understanding of how they travel and how we can market and steer the hospitality services best towards these generations.

The reason age is so interesting is because, so much is happening decade by decade that causes every generation to have a completely different view on life, on work and above all, what gives most pleasure in life, like travel. Is travel still fun or are some happy with the images that pop up on Instagram and the CNN news notifications on the phone. And what do leisure travelers look for to make a trip a memorable one.

Boston Consulting concludes that all ages have a great impact on the overall economy with regards to travel. 'Young and old travelers are prioritizing life-enhancing experiences over stuff, driving the continued growth of the travel market.' What the reasons are for this trend or statement are yet to be understood, but in the next 5 articles, I will explain what categories we can put travelers with regards to General Characteristics, Travel, and suggest a Generation toolbox.

I will dig deeper into the generations that are known as, The Post War Cohort, The Baby Boomers, the Generation Jones, Generation X and the Millennial, or often called Generation Y. This article will mostly be about The Baby Boomers, but before I start there, I would like to touch on a generation that was born before them called the Post-war Cohort. They travel a lot less nowadays, simply because their age limits flexibility and mobility. It's an admirable generation, as they have set example for much of what's considered industry or innovation nowadays, or Post-war Cohort.

Characteristics
Post-war Cohort Born

1928-1942

Key words: security, comfort, familiar, known activities and environments

Wars and financial crashes

These guys know their stuff, they are well educated and have a wide knowledge due to the many years of affection to media like radio, television and newspapers. They use their existing environment as a source of information and trust. They rely on them, not on technology or advanced systems. Even though the banks have changed opening hours and closed branches everywhere, the Post Cohorts are the ones that want to feel comfort in the personal clerk.

Yes, the postcard does very well and the radio continues to be a source of reliable information, every hour of the day. They have been through contradictive times in their lives. Imagine the threat of nuclear weapons, the Second World War, the Vietnam War and the numerous civil wars. As well as a large number of economical crashes like the Wall Street crash in 1929, savings and loan crisis in 1990 and the more recent banking crisis in 2008 that left great impact on spending, security is their game, they are resourceful and have built up a great financial platform for themselves and the entire economy. They have money in the bank and have saved up for a pension. They had kids earlier than any other generation.

Travel

The Post war Cohort is a loyal traveler. They have built trust booking through the same agent they booked through for years. They are not afraid to try new things, but prefer to have the tips from trusted sources like friends. They don't travel as much anymore, but when they do, they are likely to do that with family or to family. They would have set money aside to live in different places for longer periods in the year to avoid the cold. They travel in style and luxury and appreciate the great things in life. The have the need to feel 'lucky', so upgrades, welcome cocktails and airport transfers work really well! We love the Post war Cohort. They are kind, pleasant and easy to associate with. Treat them well, as they set example for many generations to come.

The toolkit

Clearly your Instagram campaign won't work here, Use 50's pictures and personalities. Create personal effect. Make them feel comfortable and

242

commit them to future travel. They travel with class and prefer to travel less with rather good and solid airlines and hotels rather than the last minute charter. Preferred media is traditionally advertising through papers and travel brochures. What's next "the amount of travel for the Post war Cohort will continue to decrease clearly, because of age". That's also why I will pay more attention to the next generation; the Baby Boomers, which you will find in the following article;

Understanding the 'Generations' of travel – Part 2: The Baby Boomers. In the previous article you have been able to read and understand more about the Post War Cohort; the reliable traveler, who loves to travel the world and has the disposable income to do so. In this article, I will focus on the more recent generation, the Baby Boomers, while I have been doing the research and some of the traveling myself.

I have seen and understood much of what is awaiting us, our families and our children. In fact, a very interesting app to download is called urban world, developed and updated by McKinsey & Company.

It helps you travel in time and understand what countries are developing and also where you and your business should keep your focus. Some of the smaller cities in the BRIC countries are taking over the entire countries in Europe in Gross National Product. The app will take you through time and estimates growth in population and much more. Even more reason to continue to analyze the traveler's behavior if we want to, will continuously adjust our service levels to match or exceed! In this chapter, I will write about the Baby Boomers, a very interesting generation, which has seen and experienced, war, financial collapses, extreme national and international cultural clashes and the invasion of 'low cost' concepts.

The Baby Boomers
Characteristics

Born 1943-1956

Key words: Good economy, experience, optimistic, good jobs, growth

That dedication.

The post second world war Baby boomers are a generation which keeps surprising. In the digital research which is one of the main drivers of social behavior these days, I was surprised to see the rapid way the Baby boomers are still adjusting to all new technology. Sure, there are exceptions, but the latest Deloitte report on digital behavior tells us how experimental this generation are and how easily they will adapt to what's the now. Actually, this generation was the one that embraced the credit card, the plastic device for good and bad. The credit card still and always will be some kind of concern and potentially, the only thing that will keep this generation from booking online.

They have seen the fraud and also the complications credit card on travel could give. The security we see now leaves little to be scared about. Still strange when you are expected to fax over a copy of your credit card as guarantee. This generation is also the one that started to introduce the personal computer to household. Formal and face to face meetings are preferred, confrontation is ok and team meetings are key to solutions.

They travel, yes the Baby Boomers have the gold card and stay at luxury and comfortable hotels. They are used to flying business class in the working spheres and using the points for private travel with their families.

The Baby Boomers are hard workers and also make the most trustworthy employees. The Baby Boomers have the biggest impact on our economy still, they are the work force. They will work overtime and can be trusted, however, they are ready to confront the boss and peers, as their experience and age allows them too. One characteristic that is highly important is that they need privacy, at work or at home. They care about their own space and need to feel at home. Recognition plays an important role in the decision to return to the same airline or hotel or any retail venue. Samples of Baby Boomers are everywhere we look, the top CEO's of corporate institutions like IBM, Microsoft, presenters of TV shows and some of the top sports people; a few names are Bill Gates, Madonna, Michael Jordon, Al Goore, Obama, Steven Spielberg, Tom Hanks just to name a few. They influence us in many ways, we see them and we follow them. Again the impact on how we see the world, is highly influenced by the Baby Boomer.

Independent Travel

The Baby Boomers have seen and traveled many destinations. They are very knowledgeable and have a high disposable income or at least, ensures that the spending of money on the holidays is of extreme importance. They will take every opportunity to travel. It creates increased knowledge of cultures and stimulates independence; the independence and privacy that they require. They have been to places that are less accessible nowadays, because of natural disasters or where civil wars have taken hold of the country's beauty and people. They take risks and don't mind trying new destinations, hotels or travel means. But discrepancy in expectation is harmful; it will trust and will take a while to establish that trust again.

The Baby Boomers have kids who have moved out of the house and are now ready to enjoy the travel on their own. Interesting long distance trips and destinations which have always been on the to-do list are actual. Loyalty is key, like the next generation, the Generation Jones, the Baby Boomers will be chasing loyalty points no matter what. The benefits are important; they decide what airline or hotel to choose. Low cost travel is not so interesting, good flight times, a reliable airport and service are more important.

The toolkit

Even though one might not think so, these guys are into Social Media, they will try every app and catch up with the next generations. More so, they actually seek understanding and reasoning. So be clever and understand your market segment really well. They travel in business and appreciate the high level rooms. They like to benefit from promotions before and during travel and having the opinion heard after is also key. Well educated commercials in traditional media are backed up by smart online campaigns, which is the key. A key client to get and keep, they will create further business for corporate and pleasure purposes! Travel in style and class. It's acceptable to show that you have worked and continue to work hard, resulting in more exclusive travel.

Understanding the 'Generations' of travel – Part 3: The Generation Jones.

The Baby Boomers, a very active and traveling generation you were able to read about in the previous article. Those with good economy, happy travelers, like to see the world and are counting on growth. Loyalty and respect play vital roles in the travel arrangements and marketing.

This article the third one in range, a more recent and also these days a more talked about generation, the Generation Jones.

Conde Nast traveler, a solid resource for travel, looks to remain just that. Even though there is an influx of new channels to subscribe to, Conde Nast remains comfortably right there on top. Some of the recommended sites for those with a serious interest are Skift, or Smartbrief, where you can select the specifics of your interest. It remains a serious task to describe the generations, as the behavior is directly related to Sociology. Sociologist Mannheim wrote in his script, that generations are an undervalued legacy and that it is hard to generalize. However, he recognizes that even though there is a long way to go, there are many characteristics and measurable theories.

The Generation Jones is often seen as part of Baby Boomers, but because they have undergone some significant social differences, I will mention them separately. Generation Jones is the cautious generation, they have seen masses of Layoffs, started getting introduced to yearly contracts with incentives, performance based salaries and pay conditions. Another typical behavior is power shopping and impulse buying. Working and social events are less calculated and the start of the credit era is reality.

Generation Jones
Born 1957-1966

Characteristics
Self-motivation, Competitive, Last minute buyers.

Key words: Outspoken, last minute, growth, money

Social and civil rights

Generation Jones, is a generation that was really first in becoming extremely active in political issues and discussion, they still are and they want to have their voice heard before agreeing to anything. They are often called the Jonesers, the people who have gained tremendous media attention over many years. Perhaps with the idea that all wanted to be some kind of journalist or reporter, or just because the previous Generation, the Baby boomers, were very similar but kept success or failure silent. Today, some very key figures are Jonesers, like Barack Obama, Jonathan Alter and David Brooks from the New York Times.

It leaves very little surprise that this generation also wants to learn and understand through travel and face-to-face meetings. However, saying that they remain a rather traditional generation, for example keeping the decision making at home in hands of the lady.

Seize the day

The Joneses want to try new things, everything they have done and seen before of off the table. Travel the world, a new destination every year. This is the generation that started buying online, spending on impulse and like it 'green'. They take every opportunity to drop one brand and try a new one, without leaving control over the bookings or decisions.

Even though the Jonesers are somewhat adventurous, they like to fall back on their original desires, which they understand and will develop well. Hence, the extreme interest in 'Green'. With Green I mean ecological environment friendly and ultimate standard with health & safety for the family, as well as, the surroundings. They need to be well informed which should be reflected at the time a booking is made or even before.

Product performance is key to the loyalty of generation Jones. Fail once and you have lost them, they are not the loyal type or like to test new things, experiences, hotels or airlines. Product performance needs to be on top and it all needs to be easy and straightforward to understand how, where and when. No complications, otherwise it will be made clear through verbal or nonverbal communications.

Since this generation is very keen to explore, they will compare. What better place is there to do this than the internet? They will review your website, in fact out of research by Boston Consulting, 87% of travelers review whatever they have booked online before they press the final purchase button. Clearly also, that your website needs to reflect your brand and should not promise things that cannot be kept. Even more so, all communications should reflect your brand exactly, you need to get the customers to 'feel' or test your product or service. Once convinced, they buy fast.

Lastly, nostalgia totally works. They love rock music, TV & film icons, the more the hotel relates back to those feelings, the greater the chance to get loyalty and happy Jonesers.

The toolkit
Social media is the way to start communicating, even though they might not be too into it, they will follow it and most certainly, read and understand reviews and opinions.

They need to feel comfortable, associate them with ease and hassle free solutions.

Price is important but most certainly not the decision maker, its feeling and emotion that counts.

They travel in business or like to feel upgraded and important. Commercials, ads or promotional materials need to reflect their era.

Branding is important, making them feel that they need the service, you.

Understanding the 'Generations' of travel – Part 4:
The Generation X
You are probably excited to read about Generation X, after having read about the Generation Jones. They are the feisty ones, quick decision makers, without paying too much attention to the budget. And where the hospitality has serious challenges convincing them to choose just their brand over others and even more to keep them loyal.

The Generation X is the tolerant but skeptical generation. The generation is perhaps the first generation that caused many journalists, writers, and researchers to look into all the generations in the first place. This article, the fourth one in range is about a generation which has experienced an incredible amount of significant, historic, social and cultural events in their teen years. Just to name a few, the mobile phone was developed, as well as the Sony Walkman, CNN was launched, AIDS was discovered and the first artificial heart was implanted. They were also not kept from wars like Iran & Iraq or the terrorist attack on Pan Am.

All in all you can say that the Generation X grew up in a time of uncertainty, perhaps too many inventions and discoveries took place whilst social freedom was key. This social and mental freedom, resulting in a steep increase in divorces, insecure jobs, redundancies started to be the power word for stockholders and high educated and expensive employees are being replaced by inexperienced youngsters, for financial reasons mainly. The introduction of the Laptop by IBM, made work also possible on business trips and stimulated work at home and in the evening, leaving this generation with considerably less time to socialize.

Ownership is important for this generation, they have a need for self-esteem, much more so, than the previous generations, but also they need the security. This mostly results in a clear shift in the working situation at home, where now both partners need to work to generate the incomes associated with home owning. Deloitte takes Generation X a step further and defines the in's. The in's are defined as worthy and respect, facts, do it because it makes sense, streamlined and efficient.

Within hospitality, the Generation X are considered learners, and the educated ones; they go the extra mile to get the best value for money, the highest quality. Travel should be affordable, yet fashionable. They have an amazing ability to take in a lot of information in a short time and read all information available about the place they are visiting, the trip they are booking or the details of the executive suite. They feel opportunity.

Jeroen Gulickx

Generation X
Born 1966-1980

Characteristics

Independent, Self-going, Cautious, Family, Today

Key words: Educated, Skeptical, Experienced, Informal

The .com and MTV generation
They like a challenge, several projects at the same time, not an issue. As opposed to the previous generation, generation Jones, they are not so outspoken, as they are exact; they need to have analysis before opinion.

Technology is key in this generation, they really are the drivers of technology and have an amazing understanding of a wide variety of machines, programs and applications that have been developed and launched in these years.

It is the first generation that was educated at school with computers and started sharing video games with friends after school, producing a clear shift from exercise and play to the explosion of information and visuals available from TV and games.

MTV is another significant movement that is currently fading away or rather being replaced. There was no household that would not play music through the TV station, letting opinions, social behavior and song texts, travel freely through the living rooms. Just like technology, paving the way for open and indirect communication, breakdown of authority and welcoming flexible gender roles. Not in the least keeping 'the me' in key consideration.

The Generation X has focus on results and they rely on their own abilities. They have seen the incredible downsizing and mergers of corporations, leaving many in the cold. They have experienced cutbacks in social programs, seen the collapse of the Soviet Union, have respect for their work and the work/leisure relationship.

Defining Life

The independent generation X wants to be in the driver seat, they want to control the trip they book, the hotel they choose and don't mind sharing the experiences within the family and friend surroundings. They are proud of what they reached and have an educated opinion about what others present to them. They are extremely technology savvy, being able to control and book according to the many standards that have been created and the goals they have set themselves.

Flexibility is key in the lives of this generation, for the right amount of money and social value; for example a trip might as well go to Miami, as to Rome. This they reflect at work as well, they want to enjoy, feel appreciated, get results immediately and get the job done. Since the balance family and work is high on the calendar as well as education, home owning and sports, they tend to watch more carefully than the previous generations what they spend their money on. Often leaving them with less international trips with the family, but still being amongst the biggest business traveler's worldwide and the ones to watch when they spend well.

They love design, the hottest, the newest and the technology has to be ever changing. Fall behind and you lose this customer. At home they redecorate constantly or fill the house with new gadgets. They follow the latest trends with online buying and set the tone for what's coming next. They are catalysts.

Since this generation is assessing life, gets married later and is extremely playful and intelligent, they make a great customer you can test opinion with, learn from and develop solid and lasting relationships.

Generation X are the quick thinkers, sensible and put emphasis on practical experience. The latter is the platform for many to admire, as there is a well-defined difference between experiencing something for real or just reading or seeing about it.

The toolkit

Quality, longevity and reliability are the key communicators, in any campaign. They need to be combined with high technical resources but also advantages, like Wi-Fi or free phone calls.

They make decisions based on social or physical value and need immediate results, the best view, the non-stop flight and the executive floor.

High style is importantly combined with modern trendy, yet traditionally values. Marketing programs are important and will drive the client back to the same place.

They like to travel and need options when they choose to feel comfortable and in power of the best experience to come.

Respect and recognition are important, but when they need it, they will ask for it and they will only ask the reliable hotel or airline they chose to travel with in the first place.

Understanding the 'Generations' of travel: The Generation Y / Millennials – Part 5.

Much written about and also the most recent Generation, Generation Y or also referred to as the Millennials. Understand them, tweet it, when you see them, Instagram it as fast as possible! This group is the most tech savvy, they are on the internet all the time and have nonstop access to information. You are probably wondering why I am writing about this Generation and why this Generation is of such importance for the travel industry.

The Generation Y is the one with the least loyalty and therefore, also the one that is hardest to catch as a client. They are constantly on the lookout for something better, cheaper, faster and can access and read about all they want online, instantly, as they are always online.

This article is the fifth one in this range about Generations. The purpose of writing these is to get a clear view of how and what the Generations are trending, their buying behavior, how you can influence them and get them to become your client. Naturally, this is also the customer of the future.

Generation Y has been growing up in a very insecure society with layoffs, globalization, endless media and social communication. They continue to see and understand the immense growth of India, Russia, Brazil and China, and there with, the influence, takeovers, corporate mergers and influx of travel from these countries. They have experienced some mayor events like 9-11, the war in Iraq and the crashes of Enron and WorldCom.

They are the Generation that can be least trusted according to the ethics resource center and make the least loyal and dedicated employees. This in line with Generation X, which is a lot about the social and mental freedom. The challenge is that opinion is spread freely and not always according to ethical standards. Talking bad about the company they work for, and tweet about the sour boss is a regular occurrence. Some could say opinion is and should be in line with freedom and democracy, but clearly, there are limits that make the social environment function, as other stakeholders are becoming the victim. Blogging and tweeting are two activities directly reflecting trends within this Generation. In fact, there are now many travel blogs and you can find anything you want on twitter, about a destination, a trip, a hotel or airline. Whether you find the sources trustworthy is up to the reader, but statistically, one can wonder who to follow and what to trust. Within the hospitality business, important roles are dedicated to social media and entertaining to supplying this Generation with feeds, information and updates on the business and beyond.

Learning and paring with experienced or known brands is highly important, not that it might necessarily increase loyalty, but for sure you will get the attention and get a chance to get the impulse or instant purchase of your service. The Generation Y is highly flexible and extremely good at breaking down issues. They see opportunities and most certainly, they are willing to test without knowing too much in advance.

Within the hospitality, Generation Y are considered one to test, a Generation that is not well defined as they rule their own lives and therewith their expectations. The world is but a click away and they have virtual experience rather than first hand through their computer or hand device.

Generation Y
Born 1980 – 2000

Characteristics:
Diverse, global, entrepreneurial

Key words: Independent, Objectives, tech savvy, Determined and self-confident

Online, always
The Generation Y or Millennial has never lived without a computer, they are connected, everywhere. This is one of the most important ways to voice their opinion, have themself heard. They are heroes, they know what their goals are and will not rest until that has been reached. They use the phone or IPad as the biggest source of information and are dependent on other opinions. They make great team members as they are tolerant and diverse.

Innovation
Technology is key in this Generation and also, innovation. They like to be the ones who find out about new products or services, and communicate that to their friends or colleagues. They are also known as being streamlined and efficient. They are known to find new opportunities and solutions in old problems. The Generation Y has focus on passing and gaining respect. They want to know and tell it how it is. They create their own path and it is more difficult to define the marketing plans around them. However, they like things structured, are great listeners, they want to be influenced and are open to new communication and messages.

Marketing
This Generation is independent, smart, well informed and know that they are marketed to. They understand media and messages. They actually like to be the center of the marketing effort and feel that the product of service has been created just for them. They are highly educated and career minded. They take cash and income serious and consider every penny.

Their spending pattern is ad hoc, but savings online and offline are one of the platforms of their economy. The Generation Y is extremely well connected and can be a great source for any business. They use technology and social media to support themselves in their decision and creation of opinion.

Sophistication

Even when luxury is not affordable, this Generation most certainly knows all about the services or products and has a goal to get it at some point in the future. More so, they already at an early age want to be part of the club, learn and communicate about the fancy car or a good glass of red. The brand has to keep the promise that is given through messages. This calls for correct and strong communication that leaves to be a sophisticated one. Relevance is so important because, they want to be understood and will drop a brand like lead if they are sending the wrong message. Like the Generation X, the Generation Y also wants to be in the driver seat and take control, but cares more about what can be communicated socially as part of any effort that has been made before or during the purchase of a product or service.

The toolkit

Shaping the future is the key for successful communication within the hospitality, sales and marketing efforts for Generation Y. There is a need to be treated equally and yet, individual understanding is of essence. This Generation loves to be in the limelight with great outside events that can be communicated with the use of social media.

Social mentors are of great help to any campaign; associations with great brands or people create great number of followers. Brands and products needs to help them reach their ambitions and make that visual by letting them be a part of a larger team.

Decision-making is no longer an individual effort, it has become a group effort and nobody is afraid to share this.

They travel when they want and will find the best value and price, yet clinging to names and brands. Respect is of great importance and being able to share the greatness is of extreme value. They don't like to be fooled, so hidden charges and decreased leg space are extremely dangerous for business.

They want to be educated and are highly responsive to new efforts.

A great Generation to work with and clearly, a game changer for most traditional marketing efforts.

The Marketing roles redefined

Hotels have departments, each with their own head. Recently, I stayed at the "Good Hotel" in Amsterdam, where they seriously challenge this set up. My thought and potential misunderstanding has through the years been; this is the way it is, or supposed to be. It functions, so why change it right?

You know how large IT companies like IBM runs their departments differently, they use units, in which each manage their product or service. They need to make sure that that product or service is sold internally or externally, in the perfect scenario and in their own financial, sales and leadership set up. This works, it makes it easy for leadership to understand what works, what needs change or what needs adjusting. When the product or service sees a drop in revenue, it simply becomes of no value; it becomes known that there is a problem that needs immediate attention. The functionalities within the department need to back up their actions and thoughts. This set up makes it straight forward for management to see where the problem and also opportunity lies.

Hotel teams are very creative and innovative; mainly because they are in front of guests and communicate with them daily. Simple conversation with the guest can give the most amazing ideas for innovation. The trick is to make a note of that and even more so, use it and implement it. This data needs to be collected by the marketer, to create opportunities based on facts. In reality, this does not happen, or at least very limited. The idea box in the canteen does not exist any longer, and if it does, the HR department is the one that will open and read it. They have no knowledge or skill to evaluate the comments made and I have hardly ever seen some type of reward for a good idea. Apart from that, where does this message go?

An example is, one small project I had which actually came from the personnel in the bar. They asked if I could convince management to purchase a small dishwasher for the bar. The reason was that, they had peak hours with high turnover of glasses. Sounds simple and uncomplicated right? Rather than just taking the idea to the management, I created a project description which was almost binned, but I got it through. I started with interviewing a few of the bar staff, asking them about the peak hours, how that functions and highlights their pain! Apart from the usual feedback, we don't have enough staff, the actual glass issue came up a number of times. Turns out that the staff has to take the glass wares to a different floor, via a stair case or very slow staff elevator. So they collected glasses on a trolley and once in a while they brought this to second floor, where the pot wash would do the rest. At times 2 or 3 trollies were filled up, waiting for one poor sole to balance this through the hallways and elevator to pot wash. The project became larger and larger, as it turned out that there was enormous breakage in the process, the staff cleaning the dishes had to stay behind just to clean glasses (overtime) and after 12 at night, were always able to go home by taxi, as public transport was unreliable after that hour.

The new dishwasher in the bar was installed within a week, resulting in large cost savings, improved staff satisfaction and more time with the guest, being able to sell more or simply more in front of the guest. It was one simple idea or pain, which became a best practice project for many hotels and bars. This example is one of thousands, which would have been solved directly if the bar had functioned as a unit. Financial opportunity would have been a source of data that would have resulted in immediate change.

Back to marketing and a further look at this unit concept. Again, there is no right or wrong, I am analyzing opportunities that I do not find in most of the current marketing set up. The role of a marketing manager on property is often an estimated 60% occupied by implementing rules and standards coming from the head office. Fully understand standards, nothing is more important than ensuring that the target market has been defined, standards and procedures that create guest loyalty! However, this leaves little time for making an effort for communicating with the guest you have or should have. Hotels that are part of a hotel chain benefit hugely from loyalty systems, traveler are hunters for points, which they can use much later for an upgrade or a holiday with the family; which is also why these standards are so important. A traveler in Georgia staying in Zurich for business wants to know that the Hotel is of certain standard and is willing to pay a premium for that. So, is this the role of the Marketing manager? I am highlighting again the need for units, their own management, a knowledgeable marketer that can make a difference by creating an attachment to a hotel, build a relationship with the guest and in that way, attracting new potential guests. The media will do the rest, if that is managed correctly.

The marketing manager

I want to start with the hotel budget. The allocation of financial resources for 'the marketing team' is allocated on an annual basis. When you look further into the department, there is no way or there's only small opportunity of tracking success, apart from maybe a campaign, a weekend package (boring) or a special event. The nature of a good marketer is to make a difference to be measured on success, it gives energy and an emotional incentive to do more and better. A good description of a marketing manager is of course a need, but should be potentially one of the most flexible ones in the entire hotel operation. They should look for opportunities based on internal and external data, readily available by listening to colleagues, following great success from outside and inside the industry. Social media has become and will be a larger part year after year of the activity. Guests look and understand much more than ever and want to be challenged. Over 90% of people check out the hotel website before booking it, many of those look at the comments on Trip advisor, images online and other social media channels. A hotel team can learn so much from this.

A brand is no longer built in a little office, it is an open forum that a marketer needs to manage and needs to manage with care and involvement of colleagues, guests and where possible, with third party objective assistance. Hotels slowly understand this need and are making changes accordingly, however, all too often with too little support and certainly too little understanding. There are numerous books, online videos and newsletters about how to improve the marketing effort. It's right there, the challenge is to implement it in the right way.

The role has changed, and will continue to do so. There is enormous opportunity and each unit within the hotel should take its responsibility. Will this become a reality soon? Only time will tell, but the business is so traditional in many ways that action should not be too far away, as there are competitors or entirely new concepts out there who are winning, big.

The online marketer

Recently, I was asked to give my thought on online marketing, its growing importance, visibility and trends within the hotel industry and within online marketing. This role is so extremely important, it calls for strategy in line with the leadership roles. It is a key role that will develop to be much more important than the traditional Key account manager in the hotel. There is much discussion about how this role should be defined, as online marketing is becoming a vast and complicated role that needs buy in, support, data, strategy and a thorough implementation plan. Question is, what part of this huge market should and can be managed by one person. An example is affiliate marketing, is that a role that can be managed by one person? Again, much of this is organized from a head office in the typical hotel chain. Reality is that, this role is replacing a sales manager or account manager's role slowly. The smart teams are already realizing that and understands that, face to face calls with key accounts can be dramatically reduced by offering an IPad to the client with daily updates and statistics on travel, travel costs, contracts and such. Should that be a lively excel sheet or should this be the new communication channel, directly integrating with social media? Will there be funding for this role or will this remain a grey area in many hotel teams?

Article: 4 Reasons why centralizing online marketing by hotel companies is a bad idea!

Published by the International Luxury Hotel Association

By Jeroen Gulickx

There are endless titles for jobs that have been created in the last decade to form a role that signifies the ever growing business levels and importance of online representation. These job titles are now stabilizing themselves, but clearly the roles are not. The positive development is that the role has become more senior over the last years, nowadays these guys are part of the revenue meetings, part of the budgeting process and a permanent member of the internal sales meetings.

That of course is only the case when the employee and colleague is actually based on property, sure the title says it, online, but does that mean the role, is the actual position online too? In the last 10 years, on many visits in several geographical areas, as well as numerous independent large established hotel brands, we have seen incredible marketing opportunity vanish, through many notable decisions, one of the largest being the centralization of the online marketing role.

The following will tell you why so much financial opportunity is lost and why it takes significant time to get the role up to speed with the one hotel or property.

1. Going local: Sure, corporate online guidelines and the brand book are of extreme importance, there give the company direction, a strategy to grow, expand and deliver to stakeholders like shareholders. More so, they should be used to educate and motivate employees to become a part of the company's culture. Question asked, is the material that supports every hotel valuable locally, for one or two properties?

Sure, we need those guidelines, but a centralized set up will not promote any local development. In fact, it will do quite the opposite, local knowledge is of extreme importance. Not only following that ever growing trend of "the need to be and experience local", but the actual physical need of a person being there to understand the market segmentation, pricing, packaging, efforts of the outlets like restaurant or spa, knowledge of what's going on in the city to be able to plan ahead with co-sponsors or partners and yes, they require meetings, time and valid local input to create successful campaigns. One rule definitely does not fit all within online marketing.

2. Physical attendance: As mentioned before, the online marketer needs to have a key position in the management team. Not only because online travel is soon or already surpassing 30% of the room revenues for many hotels, but also because decisions in room management, yield management, inventory, corporate and leisure contracting is still in many cases a local decision.

An example is, a recent client contracting with one of the largest Japanese electronics companies, bidding for about 4000 room nights. The sales calls went smooth, the RFP was approved and much was done with the local travel manager in London. There was one challenge, the company wanted to make use of their intranet, with full support of the hotels, last minute promotions, monthly local updates and much more. In fact, they are fully open to opportunities like special weekends for the employees, Spa packages, last minute upgrade opportunities and much more. Clearly this requires someone who know what's going on, knows what gaps there are in the future and also, builds a personal (not virtual) relationship with that client. In this case, the client was not only lost, but the opportunity to create or build an additional revenue stream and marketing opportunity for the brand too.

Understanding the property or hotel is vital, it's that local knowledge and skill that should be communicated, worldwide!

3. Cost or revenue. The large corporates are continuously showing the trend of centralizing, clearly with many financial benefits, streamlining in efficiency and creating effective processes. Our team has been a part of many of those, both with Six Sigma as well as Lean activities and implementations. Main results are not only cost saving results but even more, removal of non-value added steps in the process for particularly

the guest. Defending roles to the management in marketing have always presented themselves with challenges; how do you calculate success? Many companies have come with resourceful calculations and other efforts to show results of campaigns, PR activities and events. Yet, there is not one that is widely accepted, particularly not when it comes to leadership or management decisions and definitely not within the hospitality industry.

Besides the role description as described before being an issue, the wage is also a hot potato within the management team. Can and will the hotel be able to afford the online marketing position? All too often do we come across the function being filled by happy, creative but unskilled people who do not only fill a position that can create an entirely wrong profile with the simple touch of a button, but also, are not strategic, do not communicate with the revenue department, or show only basic skills within marketing. This leads to an incredible potential revenue displacement.

Tools available online; booking codes, virtual or physical codes can help show results of marketing efforts, but the biggest result by far making the position worth every penny on property and it's marginal revenue growth and bottom line profits through upselling or yielding.

4. Instant results and seasonal efforts: In my many years of consulting, but also in analyzing business and business performance, we have come across something which is rather sensitive in our hospitality industry called low seasons. An industry jargon, which is baked into the way business levels are viewed over a certain period. We predict the business and base pricing and sales strategies around that.

All too often, we find out that the online marketing role is used mainly for last minute campaigns or to filter through standing promotions, like the typical Romantic weekend.

The focus is on existing contracts, corporate, leisure or group contracts. The online marketing role is too often seen as 'last minute' fill up solutions. They are even account managers for Booking, Expedia and as such, highlighting exactly that. Sure, that role together with the revenue director is of great importance, but long term strategies for all low seasons are so extremely important, as we know that with existing contracts and the chance to get those filled are minimal. Early planning and campaigning can be a great solution and offer brilliant opportunity by thinking outside the box. With support of the entire executive team, great financial efforts can indeed make a difference to the somewhat old fashioned way of addressing these low seasons.

Finally, a few more words on the online marketing role. The above list is by far nonexclusive, there are many other pros and cons to centralizing or decentralizing the role. However, the trend is affecting business levels and makes many companies in the hotel industry more of a slow corporate monster than is needed. And that really makes the industry very unsexy to attract the best people in the market and also create a competitive environment, which all comes down to one thing, pricing; putting a hold to incremental growth, creativity, innovation and people development!

The Public Relations manager
When I started in the industry, all my colleagues wanted to have this role. The PR manager has such a glamorous job, so many amazing parties and always dressed up in a smart suit or dress. The role in hotels is often disappearing or outsourced. Old style, but the role was a sexy one, one of glamour, one of mostly external importance. The role is moving around mainly external communication and should reflect the hotel's positive image and reputation. The role is important in crisis management too. In fact, all external communication should be channeled through the PR manager. Also, press related issues and a lot of writing and creativity also rests with the PR manager.

So let's first understand the outsourcing strategy of hotels. Cheaper is often the first argument, second is the lack of good people who have the skillset, third is specialization and fourth the network. PR companies are often on retainers, meaning a monthly fee to handle basic communication. Existing information gets funneled from the hotel to the outsourcee. That information can come from many levels in the hotel, General Managers are getting more involved and more often, take on this role than ever before, otherwise the responsibility lies with the Director of Sales. A retainer is cheaper than a full time person, particularly in Europe with the high social service costs and taxes. The skillset is another challenge. The PR Manager should have an ability to write and communicate with many different levels of stakeholders and still keep the message in line with the brand. Not an easy task for many, as it also requires them to work flexible hours and nighttime. Naturally, specialization and network are the third and fourth reasons for outsourcing. Clearly true that, a company existing of a team with only that target and vision, can firstly offer more focus and most likely, has a large network based on history and size.

I have learned much from outsourcing, one rule of thumb is not to lose control, I write about that in the Housekeeping chapter too! This is most often the problem also within PR, as soon as this is outsourced, there is not necessarily a strong drive or rather push from the hotel any longer, resulting in unfocused PR and even unneeded costs. Clear messages and goals have to be delivered on a constant bases, otherwise the outsourcee will lose interest and your communication will no longer be standing out, or be aligned with your goals.

The proper PR role is so much more than organizing a party. The role is key to success to bring out innovation, ideas within the hotel team, bring out the amazing brand standards, values and much more to a large network of people that can seriously influence the occupancy of the hotel. That network is extremely important. I have been to many parties or events and found out that, people attending are totally uninterested in collected news or a message.

Staying in touch with the news and updating the management is another role that is extremely important. This way, the team can make strategy changes, react and actively promote opportunity that arises from the local area or even worldly events. This is directly related to maintaining relationships with the press. The press is such a vital element as it will deliver news from within.

The role of PR is not to be underestimated; there is benefit in working with an external company on this, as long as there is control, regular updates and full involvement from key team members within the hotel. PR is a role that should be part of an executive team as they collect and deliver the most important messages externally, as well delivering important information to base executive decisions.

Interview with Marie Garreau
Marie runs her established PR Company in Paris and has clients from all over the world.

Your Quote on the Future of Public Relations and Events
Please write here:
Stay human and passionate about what you do

The Questions

1. Please tell us about the objectives of your company CHERIE CHERI?

   Answer: my main objective is to gather people who want to have fun, to create synergy and good vibes between people and make them dream.

   My priority is to create synergies between the people who come to my events to connect with a brand and find themselves there, entertain them and to distract them from their everyday life and obviously, offer a unique and warm experience moment with a real sincerity.

   Like a good puzzle that is being assembled, planned to the millimeter for everybody involved. To anticipate possible surprise without an ace would be no more special event management, well to surround itself is for me, the key to success.

2. The importance of Public Relations within Hotels is often not a large part of the Marketing budget, unlike example fashion. How do you think they are wrong?

Answer:

I think that it is necessary to fine tune the visibility in the press and to look for ambassadors. Anything with social media and online sites like trip advisor and others, will continue to have huge impact in hotel business.

The reputation is created and established, thanks to the customers.

3. What is the core of having a successful event and is Paris any different in that than any other city?

Answer:

The Passion, a good networking, personalized contact with people, try to understand what they expect and want the most, always stay close to them.

Paris is a wonderful city where you can find beautiful places, full energy, always in evolution, but keeps the French touch that you can't find anywhere else.

4. How do you and your company continue to innovate and come with new ideas to expand the network for your clients?

Answer:

I am a good listener and stay alert to all that is happening in around the hotel industry, to ensure to stay ahead of time.

Inquire about all the new places and the trends, it's the basis for the creativity that people look for, to be able to stand out and to bring them novelty regularly, which will make the business continue.

5. You have a very interesting and fun way to engage your clients to your Brand, through the use of sunglasses. What are some important aspects of keeping your Clients loyal?

Answer:

Everything is a question of the development of customer's loyalty, everything stays around the good mood, it is a community work, people play the game and the party is a space of freedom for everybody! Photos with glasses almost went round the world.

6. What Social Media channels are important for you and your company, and how do you believe that compares with Hotels?

Answer:

I work regularly with the daily and female press, some radios to spread and broadcast the information in the largest number.

7. What are important aspects for you in choosing establishments for your events and what are the reasons for using Hotels as a venue?

Hotels and luxury hotels have knowledge in the quality of the service, which is close to their customers, therefore, a big asset or trump card to organize a quality event.

8. What industries do you feel Hotels can learn from with regards to Public Relations and why?

Answer:

I think that the trust and faith of the customers is essential in this job and business.

There is a lot of competition, thus it is necessary to protect the network with surprises and sponsors from other industries that can inspire.

9. Public Relations and the Event business is a vibrant one, particularly in Paris. It is also highly associated with personality, like you.

How do you motivate your personnel and partners to reflect their personalities and yet, keep to the objectives set?

Answer:

I am working very closely with all my partners because we communicate on daily basis, setting the objective has to be clear, accepted and respected.

Good and strong relations are kept best when working towards that one goal. We are all different and I try to bring to the foreground the best of each.

10. What does the future of the Public Relations industry look like and how are you adjusting to that?

Answer:

Always the same the work, remain diligent. The perseverance, the respect for the customer combined with affordable prices, even in the luxury segment, will create a loyal client. They will always return with the biggest of pleasures.

The end of the 4 P's

I remember the first marketing class at the Hotel Management School, to my surprise at that time, we talked a great deal about data and statistics. After a career in Sales & Marketing in Belgium, the UK and France, I decided to take an offer from Starwood Hotels to re-school me with Six Sigma. Six Sigma is a methodology that can be applied in all industries and reduces or removes non-value added steps, creates opportunities and strategies that is fully aligned with the target group, based on data and facts as well as analysis. I have learned a great deal about data, how to analyze it and how to stop making decisions based on opinions, but rather use facts, research and piloting before finally implementing something. The company Mocinno International that I run, goes with the credo, 'Don't make a change, create a difference'.

The Hotel Management school taught me more, that I find useful within marketing these days, things like process driven learning, a way of learning or applying methods in different teams to promote learning from others and working towards one solution. Already, there was one thing clear to me, people around me do not communicate like me, they have different opinions and yet we can come to one solution that works for all of us.

That's the biggest learning for what is going on now within marketing and what will continue to be the focus for many of not all hotel companies. Some have not understood yet, but most are working that way, it's called content marketing.

Content marketing

Does content marketing kick out all the old traditional ways of doing marketing? There is a full value in analyzing and using the old 4 p's in marketing, Place Promotion, Price and Product, or at least elements of those. I will not go into too much detail with regards to the traditional way of marketing. But one thing to point out is that, the old ways used to work with limited availability of media. That is the biggest change with today's marketing. There are numerous ways of communicating these days with tools that were never available before; social media, online video channels, blogs and newsletters to name some of the most used ones at this point. With one press of the button, you can reach millions of people, so you need to figure out what media to use before and spend large amounts of cash on an ad on TV or a magazine. Again, advertising is not dead, will never be, but there are now other ways that hotels or in fact, any industry can implement it, which are strategic and are easily accessible.

Content marketing is a strategic marketing approach whereby content, which is relevant, valuable, is distributed through the tools mentioned before to attract a new customers or guest or an already defined customer. The data available these days is unique, just think about what your credit card company knows about you, or the data you provide when you check in or when you browse the internet for information about a hotel, just to mention a few. That information is of such great value for the marketer who needs to create content that is interesting for exactly that target market that it requires to generate the revenues needed.

David Meerman Scott, a well-known marketer has taught me a great deal about content marketing, in fact, he gave me a story that he published on one of his hotel experiences. Most interesting in there is the buyer persona, the ultimate guest according to this hotel, called Nobis in Stockholm, Sweden.

> From the blog of David Meerman Scott
> Persona based content marketing at the Nobis hotel

Have you noticed that nearly all hotel websites are exactly the same?

There's the photo of the property on the front, the "reserve a room" widget usually in the top left and a bunch of boring, superlative language. Basically, the sites are interchangeable. I just booked a hotel in California for later this month and the three hotels I considered looked like they had all been designed by the same agency.

Oliver

Several months ago I stayed at the Nobis Hotel in Stockholm. I made the choice myself based on - you guessed it - the site. This hotel website seemed different.

That difference continued as my wife Yukari Watanabe Scott and I checked in and explored the property. It seemed so perfect that we had to find out why. So we met with Ana Maria Nordgren and Oliver Geldner to learn more.

Persona based content marketing at the Nobis Hotel

The persona of the Nobis Hotel

The most fascinating story that Oliver told us about Nobis Hotel marketing was the persona they used when they communicate for the hotel on social networks like Facebook. This is what Oliver told me about the Nobis persona he uses on social networks:

"The Nobis Hotel is a grand old lady who lives in a vast apartment in Stockholm. She's a dame of means. She has a cocktail party starting every day at 11:00 am and is slightly tipsy by 5:00 pm and that is when she is communicating to you via social networks as a friend.

The Nobis is a Swedish hotel, but she insists on communicating in English even though the majority of guests are Swedish.

She has a sense of humor and has interesting things to say. She wants to be relevant, have a sense of humor and not take herself too seriously.

*** WOW!! How cool is this description??!! ***

Storytelling at the Nobis

Here are a few short stories I pulled out from the Nobis Hotel Facebook page. I can see the slightly tipsy grand old dame writing them:

"Animal question of the week: 'I am travelling with a duck and would need a room with a tub'. I can't wait to see the cleaning ladies' face when she comes in to make up the room! Well, at least today we got nice weather, for ducks..."

And this:

"Note to all parents of 3-old boys: there is a subtle but very distinct difference between peeing in the steam room and peeing into the steam room. The first can be the sign of an emergency, the latter is a signal you might have a hooligan on your hands...."

Isn't this fantastic! Can you imagine a big chain hotel communicating like this on social networks? Not a chance!

Amazing the way Nobis looks for words and phrases that are important for their business.

Oliver told me that he does a semantic analysis of the Nobis Hotel listings on travel review sites such as Trip Advisor to find out what words and phrases visitors use in their reviews. These are then used in Nobis marketing.

So rather than make up their SEO terms, they actually use terms like the "beautiful modern hotel in Stockholm" that people use in social networks as their SEO phrases.

Love it!

Offline content marketing at the Nobis.

Amazingly, the Nobis Hotel published a book! There is a copy in each room and in the common areas. I thought it was so cool that I purchased a copy.

The hardcover book explores how they created the hotel all the way down to fine points like the typefaces of the written communications and the furniture and fabrics used throughout.

There is a section of the book talking about the original building which was a bank made famous by the robbery and hostage taking that came to be known as The Stockholm Syndrome.

Oliver told us it was not conceived as a marketing book but rather, a way to tell stories about the choices of what materials and designs were chosen and why. They did not create what Oliver would call "an artificial brand" but instead, focused on the actual stories of how the hotel was built and the book shows all of that to guests like us.

As a marketer and author, I found the book fascinating and had never seen anything quite like it.

Content marketing even offline!

Source: www.webinknow.com

This is a great example of content marketing for hotels indeed. A resource dedicated to creating a wonderful buzz for the company. They mainly use Facebook as their Social media channel.

Social media is clearly a way to communicate globally with your potential and existing clients. I remember hotel 1888 in Sydney, who offered a free stay for instagrammers with more than 30k followers, as long as they mentioned and spoke about the hotel. Clearly, the brand was created in no time, the word was out and everybody wanted to stay there, a new hotel on the map, just like that. I have read numerous books on Instagram, Pinterest, Vimeo, YouTube and Twitter to name those mentioned and used most. Each has their own target and by selecting the one that you find most appropriate based on the persona using it, you will get a message out in a way that can have incredible speed. That in combination with Content marketing, you might just really create a difference.

Sell Sell Sell

The corporate structure of companies is dictating an advanced structure in the sales and marketing department of hotels. The sales structure is one of the extreme hierarchy divided into geographical area or industry type. It starts with the director of sales and marketing at the top. This position is leading a team that is divided into corporate sales, leisure sales, event sales, yielding and a variety of marketing roles. Yield management was introduced around the year 2001. The director of sales and marketing is part of the executive team. There lies great responsibility in the role, responsible for all revenue stream within the hotel. These revenue streams include rooms, food & beverage, spa and other areas. Traditional focus is on the rooms department, since the margin and the volume there is highest. That also makes sense as that is the area which can be contracted with clients together, also contracting with the group department that takes event and meeting bookings as well as larger groups.

The sales department is a department where it takes time to grow the ladder. The roles are well established starting with the sales executive followed by account management, sales management and finally, either an assistant director of sales and marketing or director of sales of marketing. The sales executive is normally charged with finding new accounts, again each responsible for a designated market. The sales executive role is a tough one, it involves cold calling, much traveling and entertaining at night time. Accepting this role is a big decision for employees, even though the sales department is a very popular department to work for. It also sets many up for a career that is not necessarily just within the industry, as opposed to most other roles within the hotel. Below, I will describe some of the key roles in the sales department.

Covering those costs

The sales department is considered an expensive department because of the structure and also because of the skills required to work here. The sales staff have to have many skills like negotiation, listening and persuasive skills that can close a deal for the entire hotel. However, it should most definitely not be seen as a cost center, quite the opposite is true. The sales department has a huge responsibility to make sure that there is cash flow in the property. Many hotels are suffering what is so called "low seasons". They can be very painful to the organization as employees have to continually be paid, stock needs to be kept for sudden changes, often, energy costs and such are the same or almost the same.

This means that there is a need for the much disliked customer, namely the volume account, like a corporate company that pays low rate and does not spend any money in the other departments other than rooms or an airline crew with its weird arrival and departure times. Same goes for the events department, who are doing everything they can to get boardroom meetings, conferences or incentives to the hotel. Again, that is great business with great margins for the hotel. I have seen many hotels who suffer in many months of the year and find no other solutions than to lay off staff in these periods. This leads to recruitment and training costs that are not taken in consideration when layoffs occur.

Another phenomenon is all the third party booking channels like Expedia, last minute, hotels.com etc. they are sitting on an incredible database of travelers that every hotel wants. It is a business that is incredibly important for hotels. Not just because this business can be turned on and off whenever it's needed, but also gives guaranteed business outlook to ensure opportunity for yielding the rooms. Nowadays these big third party agents want guaranteed rooms and rate com parity. This means to have availability of a minimum number of rooms as well as the lowest rates available. This means that, leading traffic to your own booking system is crucial. And did I mention these lovely giants take 25% commission on room sales? Something to think about when signing contracts with your alternative clients or potential clients. More on third party later, but for now lots of decisions to be made in the sales department to ensure the continuation of the hotel.

The internal client

The sales department is complex as it's involved with many stakeholders. Even when I was on sales executive level, I was invited to meetings with the owner or with the head office representative of the company. They are the spider in a large web needing to bring clients and hotel employees and services together. Even more so, they are torn between all revenue generating departments. The restaurant, the conference center or the spa, they are all dependent on the sales skills of the sales and marketing department. The sales department is normally mostly focused on the room sales, which is logical as this is usually the department that generates most revenue at the best margin. That seems to function best, at least when you look at the existing operation.

Looking at the functionality of this current sales set up, I am personally not convinced that this delivers what it should to the departments other than rooms. Take a stand-alone Restaurant for example, do they normally have sales? Probably not, however, their personnel has full focus on selling their restaurant best, with help from a website, guest reviews, word of mouth and social media. They do not have a person going out selling, signing contracts for the lunch for example, but they can rely on a focused team of employees with only one vision and a few objectives. In operations, the employees can focus on selling the right dishes in line with stock levels of products in the kitchen, as well as up selling beverages. Direct sales is not that common and yet, part of a hotel's responsibility of sales and even marketing is left in the hands of the hotel sales and marketing team. Note that, I also don't believe many stand-alone restaurants get it right, as there is too much focus on the product and not enough on the story or atmosphere they are trying to create, resulting to very monotonous ways of communicating through social media for example.

Below I will describe some of roles and requirements for the sales and marketing team to get the best out of the entire hotel team:

Vision and objectives

The vision of the hotel often is not specific enough to describe every department, and it should not either, however, every department can create their own vision that come with a set of objectives. The objectives can and should be adapted, when there is sudden change in marketplace, or consumer behavior changes. They can be both short and long term goals. The sales team needs to be a part of this process, they need to ask and be fully aware of what the objectives are, so they can act accordingly. The management of the outlet in their turn should be ready to present changes in objectives and keep the sales team updated.

Communication

All too often within the hotel, communication flows through the virtual means only. It is important to share the success of a new client, losing a client, the sales strategy for the next six months and much more. These matters affect the daily business directly and will raise many questions that should be answered in an open forum. Regular updates and also joining departmental meetings to ensure that information and feedback is shared.

Visibility

The reputation of the sales department is of glamour, sales and marketing employees only tend to appear when there is a lunch, presentation or such. Ensuring the employees to join meetings and do regular visits will improve knowledge, focus and relationships.

Education

As described before, part of inter departmental communication is knowledge, knowledge of what is going on, how business objectives are developing and also, knowledge about how the departments actually functions. Many hotels have developed cross training programs to elevate the processes that are making it all happen. Even better, would be to start educational sessions to understand how a restaurant functions, how sales get to a contract or how the front desk manages the rooms.

Attitude

A positive attitude will spark energy throughout the company, it will elevate trust and openness paving way to generating ideas and cooperation in last minute needs from operations, in-hotel activities, site inspections and much more. Since the sales and marketing team is also the face of the hotel to the clients outside, attitude reflects the overall experience that can be expected from the hotel.

Knowledgeable

The sales and marketing team is required to understand market segmentation, economic circumstances and all kinds of other external factors that might influence the business levels at any point. They are required to communicate these internally. The information or data from sources like clients, events or fair are extremely relevant for the operations of the hotel. It can and will influence decisions made, affect the business objectives or suggest a need for a sudden change in strategy.

Flexible

Just like operations is supporting sales and marketing, the opposite should also be expected. As operations is often managing extreme rushes or exceptional events, the team has great opportunity to show their involvement and dedication to the success of the hotel. Clearly this should be an exception and not a daily event.

Social Media impacting sales

The sales department is complex, as its involved with many stakeholders. Even when I was on sales executive level, I was invited to meetings with the owner or with the head office representative of the company. They are the spider in a large web, needing to bring clients and hotel employees and services together. The communication with all the digital tools available has become more straightforward and is also changing rapidly. It opens up for new opportunities but also creates new challenges. A recent article by Social Media specialist within hospitality explains this better.

Article by Are Morch, specialist in Social Media Management

Let's start with the definition- what is social selling? It is leveraging your professional brand to fill your pipeline with the right people, insights, and relationships.

For the Hotels Sales department, transaction processes are changing. Customers are no longer coming in at the top of the hotel's sales funnel, where they seek general information and awareness of the brand. Previously, both parties anticipated someone from the Sales Team would guide them through the sales process, but now the situation is flipped and customers are defining the buying process.

Customers utilize social media for research, comparison and community input. Hoteliers need to understand that, by the time customers end up on their property's website, they are almost in the end of the buying process. They did all their research, narrowed down their options and in many cases, they already have an established relationship with the hotel brand.

In this process, the customer is so close, but in many cases, so far from making a direct booking. Here is why, and what your hotel can do to fix this.

Why is the social customer NOT making a direct booking on your hotel's website?

One part of the reason is that many hotels simply misunderstand social selling. Many in hotel marketing and sales departments believes that this process requires implementation of a whole new sales process, but nothing could be further from reality. Services like Airbnb and UBER have not replaced other already existing services, they are just providing alternatives that take advantage of new marketing mechanisms.

From a hotel's perspective, our job is to use the same marketing mechanisms to create new awareness and focus on alternatives that will add new value for customers.

Customers are a creature of habit. The hotel options available have to meet their basic needs- location, amenities, price, and availability all in one place.

Customers also prefers information that will add value to their experience. This is also one reason why many customers will check hotel reviews before a booking decision is made.

Sites like Airbnb and Home Away have been able to identify new intriguing trigger points that appeal to customers when it comes to their booking patterns. Two key factors are:

- Identity
- Personalization

Learn to understand your customers' identity and where they belong. What does this mean you might ask? Customers today identify themselves with their communities.

Social communities today are the real drivers that influence the customer's decision process. They build a foundation around listening, awareness, trust and culture.

Tony Hsieh, CEO and founder of Zappos, understood these principles. Zappos implemented games so that when employees logged into their computer, the face of a fellow employee would pop up. They were then asked to put in the name of this employee. If the answer was wrong, a correct bio and profile of this person would populate on the screen.

Zappos also had a four-week training program for all new employees. At the end of the first week, everyone was offered $2,000 to quit.

My personal favorite was that every employee at Zappos was challenged to make at least one improvement every week, which better reflected Zappos core values.

One interesting point is that, Tony Hsieh believes that the telephone is one of the best branding devices out there.

What can hotels do to meet this challenge?

Social media today is very disruptive and noisy. Rumors tend to amplify things in ways that cause many social marketers to jump. We hear Twitter is dead, Millennials don't use Facebook and Snapchat is the new thing. Yeah, the sky is falling.

Zappos built their foundation around culture, happiness and their core values. They focused on building their communities, having employees that supported the customer experience. If a customer had a concern, it was handled swiftly and efficiently and the company did not question the customer's honesty. This action supported the culture, happiness and core values, which in turn laid a solid foundation for a unique social community.

Communities are similar to social networks, where people with similar skills and interests gather to discuss and exchange ideas, or participate in events of joint interest.

If your hotel is experiencing challenges where you see a drop in customers, a drop in inquiries, a drop in guest satisfaction or high employee turn-over, social media will not fix this.

You have to start within the hotel to build a new foundation around culture, happiness and your hotel's core values. Make sure you include listening, awareness, trust and relationship strategies.

Many might believe what Zappos did is a bit extreme. A four-week training program for new employees? $2,000 to quit?

Can you really put a price on employee happiness? We know happy employees are more productive. Some of Zappos core values include: be humble, do more with less, be passionate, determined, create fun and a little weirdness.

In your training programs, if you embrace new technology and new marketing mechanisms together with listening, awareness, trust and relationship strategies, you have a foundation to communicate with your social community.

If you take a deeper look at Zappos, there is nothing unique with their products. The uniqueness was in the culture, employee's happiness and their social communities. Their mission was to value their customer's experience and as a result, the Zappos social community became their best social media ambassadors. Zappos did not sell their products, they exchanged experiences.

Are Morch explains the change in sales well, with all the disruption hotel sales and marketing teams are facing. It will continue to change and the impact of social media, content marketing and other online tools will lead the way business is done in the future.

The Sales roles

Traditionally, the sales roles were fully focused on sales, yes that's right, going out there, finding new clients, having meeting goals of at least 14 face to face calls a week. Those were the days. They have changed, already in the early 2000's, I found out that every time I met with a Director of Sales, their biggest worry was the overflow of data input. Revenue systems, registering sales calls, budgeting, employee reviews and numerous other things were disrupting the normal sales working days. Whether that was an excuse to stay behind the computer or simply reality, we will never know. I believe a good Director of Sales needs to plan according to priority and well in advance. I will go into a bit more details of some of the roles that will remain essential in the hotel industry.

Director of Sales

The role of the Director of Sales is to represent the team in the best possible way internally and externally. It is a very demanding role as much of what the Director of Sales does these days in analytics, people management and client management. They are also the ones who take care of the meeting & events team. The role is ever changing, which is fun but also challenging. It is difficult to see where this role is going in the future, so rather than describing the job description, I'd rather focus on some of the key skills this person needs to have to be able to function well.

People skills – Dealing with people is one of the key skills needed for a Director of Sales. They will sit with people from all levels within the company as well as externally. They normally handle some of the biggest accounts for the hotel and needs to be able to read people. Goal setting and career handling for the employees requires people skills.

Negotiation skills – Clients negotiation has become harder than ever with all the external tools and media that reflects the performance of the hotel. Increased competition and decreased potential to exceed customer service levels are influencing the way negotiations should be done. There are fewer resources available compared to the competition, like room size, amenities etc. that in the earlier days, were great tools to negotiate contracts with.

Analytical skills – Since pricing, budgeting and setting financial goals is much more vital than it ever was, the Director of Sales needs these skills to set strategies for the entire hotel.

Sociable – Most likely not a skill that can be taught so easily, but certainly one that everybody in the sales department needs to have. The way the department behaves is important to reflect the positive attitude that is needed to communicate, get new and confirm existing accounts.

Communication skills – Communication is a big word with many meanings. The Director of Sales is a communicator, and has to make all efforts to be understood, be a careful listener as well as a great speaker.

Team player – The Director of Sales is part of the management team, runs the sales department and should be a visible player to the rest of the hotel.

Account Director

The account director or account manager is most likely the one that will change soonest, even though you can't really see that yet. This person takes care of the most important accounts that drive the business for the hotel. In time, I believe this role will mostly be taken over by technology. Technology that can show the client details on the account production, spent and much more. I am not saying this role will disappear, far from it, but it will certainly change dramatically.

Sales Executive

This role will also always remain of extreme importance. Based on data received from competitors, from the front office and many more sources, the sales executive is in charge of finding new accounts. Not an easy role at all, it involves cold calling and requires a strong personality who is not giving up!

In this chapter, I have tried to make clear what Sales & Marketing means to the hospitality industry and their impact to the entire hotel organization. The team and roles will continue to change all the time. The data, trends and sources of information will continue to be the best source for decision making and hotel representation. The department has a key role in the success of the organization and will take that responsibility online and offline.

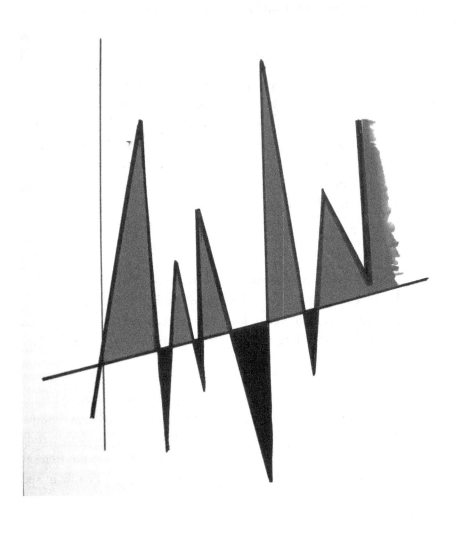

Chapter 12

The final challenge
Implementation and people

In this book, you would have read about innovation, ideas, trends, ways to improve guest satisfaction, streamlining of cost and drive revenues. Together with all the people who have contributed to the book, we continue to strive to keep the hospitality industry the most energetic and fun. The challenge remains with attracting people to and keeping people in our industry who can build on history, knowledge and tradition. Hotels are struggling, keeping the salaries at levels of competitive industries due to the character of many of the roles, but also entry level of many of functionalities. Yet, guests expect service of highest level and we have to keep trying to exceed those expectations. When purchasing a water cooker, one can pay anything from 20€ to 150€, perhaps one machine saves energy, the other is better looking at and the third heats the water up quickly; still, the final delivery is the same. With service delivery, the expectations are also more or less the same depending on the department naturally, but a check in is a check in, even if it is a 3 or 5 star hotel. Hotels are more challenged since employees cannot possibly know each individual's expectation. That is changing, now that we know so much more about our guests, through data collection, CRM and social media, we have a much better idea of what the process to final delivery actually should be.

It requires specialists in each field, in each department, to align décor, music, concept, branding, marketing, design or the menu to name but a few, to align the delivery and the process to get there. Change is good, change is needed and just like any other industry, leadership needs to drive implementation through a people strategy that is transparent and visionary.

Leading Change

On a continuous basis, we identify changes in trends, in customer needs, in opportunity and much more. Either through learning from other industries, using and analyzing data or using techniques like innovations and blue ocean strategies can make a hotel team adjust to fast and even more so, plan in advance. This key is not only a survival, but also a way to stand out and ensure that business is growing and expanding the way it's planned to be.

There is no doubt that management needs to see the change needed and that they need to fully buy into it. Even though most of the time there will be resistance amongst some of the team members, good leadership will ensure that they will follow the vision long term.

Leading change means communicating change within the organization in time to ensure that employees understand what is coming. In this book, I am talking a lot about people and their behavior, their need to feel a part of a team and be incentivized accordingly. Change rarely happens fast, it takes time to get the big results, however small successes in the process to get to the vision motivates to get to the final. Recognition of people involved in this process is therefore vital for success. Finally, as stipulated in the book on many occasions, involving people from the start, and making sure that change is supported by data and facts will drive the process from idea to implementation.

Motivating people to innovate

Just by looking around, understanding trends and mostly by tracking people's behavior is and should be a daily task for all of the people in the

Hospitality industry. There is no secret to innovation, as it should be an accessible technique available to all.

As designers are facing more challenges to create a bathroom with a spa feeling, guest rooms with all kinds of digital tools, yet staying practical, the service remains the main element of loyalty for guests. Service is a requirement for great success and as people interact as much as they do, they need to be given the opportunity to be heard, to be part of an innovative process and incentivize accordingly. This is what will keep people building their self-esteem and career. The value of innovation is not to be underestimated, as it will impact margins, revenues, costs and eventually, expansion and growth.

In an interview with Arnie Weismann, Arnie explains more about communication, what keeps customers loyal, the customer value and the future of people within our industry.

Interview
Arnie Weissmann
Chief Editor - Travel Weekly
Editorial director of Northstar Travel Media's Travel Group

1. Please tell us about the objectives of your company the Travel Weekly?

    Answer: Travel Weekly's objective is to provide people within the travel industry with the critical information that they need to make the best business decisions.

    We do this through print, digitally, face to face events and other Media.

2. You have lengthy experience in the Hospitality industry, Travel trade, Technology, Hotels, Consultants, Airlines and many more. What are the elements that all these industries have in common and what can they learn most from each other?

Answer: The travel industry is a very complex industry with various vertical segments, like hospitality, aviation, cruise, tour operators, retail travel agents and digital travel agents. They all interact together and in different ways. The standards which they all can learn from, hospitality is one area that is most critical that others can learn from. One main factor is guest satisfaction. An example is the cruise industry, which has a hotel manager who typically delivers all standards one can find in a hotel. If you take the entire experience from a guest from when they leave home until they return home, the most likely part they remember is the hotel. The airline industry is also creating more and more value to the customer's experience based on what the hotels are already delivering.

3. Over the many years of travel related content, you have built an incredible loyalty in readers, subscribers and continue to build trust in and outside the industry. What do you think the hotel industry can learn from your industry, with regards to loyalty and engagement?

Answer: Our business is media, the one word that is critical is trust, same as the hospitality industry. Loyalty is clearly an element that will continue to drive our business when you have lost your value. To a large extent, we both need factual information, we need quotes and data to be correct. It is a clearly cut a matter to ensure the information is correct. With hotels, a complaint for example is more delicate than in media when it comes to customer's satisfaction, as it is more subjective. Ultimately, trust is the foundation, whether it is a large hotel brand or single hotel and that starts when the guest walks into the hotel. From the moment there is that trust, there is also more engagement leading to loyalty.

4. You are clearly committed to managing content that delivers value and variety. What can Hotels improve to keep their company varied, interesting and yet maintain consistency?

Answer: Do you follow your customers or do you lead the customers, that really is the main question. In media, we are not necessarily reactive, we look for trends for things that are happening, much more than just the news of the moment. The news of the moment does provides intelligence that clears the path to variation and significant change. For hotels that is more complicated, an example is that, you can't renovate every year or even couple of years. The model and structure is very different, the numerous guest surveys are about what they want and what has been their experience. In hospitality there is a lot to be learned from value creation by leading through change. If Henry Ford would have listened to his customers, he would have had faster horses.

5. What are the core principles of creating a good story that inspires travel, and motivated people to come back and read more?

   Answer: I got some great advice from one visiting writing instructor at college. The reader should act on what they are reading. The reader has no obligation to go from one sentence to the next unless you give them that motivation. Parallel to hospitality is the attention to details, to keep the guest engaged from when they walk into the door and every time they walk back into the hotel. It has to be refreshing, interesting, whether that is the design of the lobby or the bedroom. There has to be continued attention to detail.

6. Communicating internally as well as externally is the key driver for change. With Hotels targeting new generation, how will that affect the way we have to communicate?

   Answer: Within media, communication is what we are all about. Within hospitality, there is internal and external as well as third party communication. The biggest change in this generation is the loss of messages; that is, you no longer fully control the soul of the brand. The key advantage of losing this control however, is that you can enter an entirely new range of market segments. If you look at twitter for example, when your brand has a follower, which means you are entering into an entirely new potential market as your followers have followers who for example, retweet your message. You are reaching broadly this way. The audience is not as targeted as the brand director might want them to be, but that also can lead to new opportunities.

7. You are a contributor to the PBS Television show 'The Travel Detective', what are some of the main takeaways from the show for the Hotel Industry?

Answer: The Travel Detective's objective is to make travelers become smarter travelers. We do that by focusing on things that travelers are doing, to be able to understand their behavior. Also, we follow what suppliers to the travelers, like airlines or hotels are doing to understand what they should or shouldn't be doing that will have a big impact on the traveler to make the best travel decisions. An example is how cruise liners used to charge more for people who wanted to travel on their own. That clearly was not a very inviting proposition, to which a Norwegian cruise liner reacted first by offering special deals and particularly small cabins and meeting areas for single travelers.

8. The Hotel industry is focusing on the ever-rising need for technology. This trend is affecting Hotel operations in many ways. Can you give some suggestions to Senior Management on how to strategize this?

Answer: Technology is indeed changing the way we travel, with regards to media. It can recommend a rule of thumb that is really important with regards to the value of technology; it could be to look for what will improve the costumer's experience and simultaneously save me money and clearly also, what delivers increase in revenues. A great example is RF ID (Radio Frequency Identification) which is used by Disney. They manage a visit that starts online, motivates the customer to stay in their hotels, it manages the flow of the attractions and it ultimately improves the customer experience. I can see hotels can use this to their advantage in many ways.

9. We see an incredible demand for Wellness and Spa solutions in the company. How is your company participating in this trend and how do you communicate the true value of Wellness travel for both hotels as well as end consumers?

Answer: Wellness Spa and medical tourism is growing tremendously. People have it in mind, there is no need to really sell it. The question is, what percentage of the traveler's time is to be dedicated to this element of travel. There is medical tourism for example, like cosmetic surgery where travelers choose a location that is more economical, or simply just a place away from home. Or you are just a business traveler, who is looking for relaxing during a stressful travel. Information in advance is extremely important as the traveler needs to be given opportunity to choose exactly what they expect or rather, need on their trip. Giving clear and straightforward information keeps hotels ahead of the game.

10. The Travel industry is and will remain vibrant, fun and energizing. How do we ensure we keep attracting skilled, educated and motivated individuals to join our industry?

Answer: Recruitment within hospitality is facing challenges. Accessibility to travel today is much greater than it ever was, for example 30 years ago, hotel companies attracted a great number of people by offering them incentive to stay in sister hotels worldwide, or travel agents with special deals, or as a flight attendant to be able to see the world. Today, with globalization there is any number of careers available to be able to see the world. These incentives have now eroded somewhat. The upside of this is that when somebody is going to pursue a career in the travel industry, it is the area they are especially passionate about in the industry. And if you are going to be in hospitality unit and be able to offer that to for example your family, there is a significant element of inspiration in there. I believe we will continue to see future generations that have this travel experience to pursue that passion for culture and inspiration into a career.

Comparing the hospitality with media is perhaps not the most straightforward, but as Arnie states, there are many similarities and both have a clear vision to not only please, but also keep customers loyal and drive revenues.

Motivating people to innovate has a lot to do with recruiting the right people like Arnie states too and it certainly feels like we are doing enough to attract people to this industry. Since the glamour is gone, the paycheck is not great, the working hours are very different compared to those of 'normal' positions and the initial motivator to the hospitality industry is not significant. Innovation is one of those aspects that will attract new people, as well as keep those who are passionate within the industry or organization. The company should therefore, do anything in their power to ensure that people with ideas for process change, for new markets, or implementation should be rewarded and preferably publically, via Social Media for example. A business that rewards will get great mouth to mouth marketing and also attract the right people who really have the passion to make a difference in the product or service.

Operational Excellence
Operational excellence is defined as the way tools, systems and a variety of principles can or perhaps should be used to deliver key performance metrics. Developing a company culture that strives to work with people and use tools best is challenging. Leadership is faced with a number of aspects that influence our business greatly. New hotels and hotel chains are entering the market, as hotel business is one of the continuous cash flow, new investors are entering the market space, as well as existing hotel companies or owners expanding. More hotels lead to bigger supply and in certain locations, lower occupancies or average rates. Standards and strength of company, service, culture and products are leading loyalty. With

increased expectations, guests are getting used to higher standards and hotels are finding it harder to meet those. Furthermore, payroll continues to be not only the largest cost, but it will remain on the increase. This means that leadership will have to put more and more focus on operational excellence, with all the techniques available like Lean or Six Sigma and making optimal use of Best Practices.

Employees are the center of this exercise, the way they are involved will create a constant reminder to keep the flow of all processes. This means they need to be educated to be able to work–out the steps needed, and also to monitor. Tracking or monitoring any work process has to be introduced to notice any type of change or variation, so that employees can react immediately. Even more so, employees who are the closest to any process will also see the greatest opportunities for change to drive revenues, reduce costs and create guest satisfaction.

Companies Driven by People

Hotel companies are doing everything to differentiate themselves. This can be through innovation, creation of new brands and launching an entirely new concept. I will give you examples of hotels or hotel chains that are making every effort to understand their client well, and change their operation, communication or design accordingly; they get the most out of their people, by a number of companies who follow much of what I have written about in the book.

Soho House & Co

Soho House is a creative membership concept for the posh traveler. Soho House was founded in 1995 as a home from home, for people working in the creative industries. It has since grown into a community of like-minded individuals with Houses all over the world. The outlets and affiliates are carefully selected to deliver to the vision of the company. Nick Jones, the founder of Soho House, aims to deliver 'the good life', with large beds, easy access bathrooms, by creating popular yet basic themes, to ensure a parallel between normal life and travel. The design of the hotel is robust, stylish, with good sofa's and comfortable features can be seen everywhere.

And again, you can only stay when you are a member of the Soho house company.

Ovolo Hotels

I came across this company a while ago, when 1888 started to get attention through incredible Instagram campaigns, offering free stays to those with a minimum number of active followers.

The vision of Ovolo Hotels is 'shiny happy people'. You can feel that directly, even when you visit them online. They want to deliver something extra to their guests, yet understanding the need for a work place, good sleep and great relaxing areas. They call it effortless living.

Ovolo Hotels is based in Hong Kong, and they own and operate a collection of individually designed lifestyle hotels and serviced apartments. The company keeps in touch with the modern traveler through award-winning interiors, detail-driven comforts, focused all-inclusive services and cutting-edge en-suite technology, all done in a signature style. It was founded by Girish Jhunjhnuwala in 2002. Ovolo is now taking the brand to a larger, international audience and giving more shiny happy people a chance to enjoy their bright rooms and ideas.

Outsite

A genius hotel company targeting entrepreneurs and busy business travelers.

Outsite is a collection of unique work+play accommodations that cater to the growing community of entrepreneurs, business travelers and digital nomads who are looking for alternatives to uninspired hotels and conference halls.

The Outside team offers a combination of hotel, solid workspace and the ability to surf famous waves, Ski Mountains, climb walls or just bike around town between working sessions. Outsite offers a place to stay with creative co-working spaces and a growing list of innovative "New Networking" activities, designed to spur meaningful and creative collaborations.

Each Outsite location is conveniently accessible from urban centers. The aim of Outsite is to find inspiration, new friends, fresh air, communal classes and dinners and of course, do fantastic business!

Soneva Hotels

The pioneer of back to nature luxury accommodation and experience. Soneva Hotels offer breathtaking 'remote but accessible' natural locations, effortlessly chic accommodation, incredible food, truly memorable activities, an inspiring ethos of sustainability and service that is uncannily intuitive.

When Eva and Sonu Shivdasani built Soneva Fushi as well as their home on the deserted island of Kunfunadhoo in the Maldives in 1995, they started and had no idea that their intensely personal vision of a locally crafted villa and environmentally responsible lifestyle would form the basis of a successful collection of world-class hotels, resorts and spas.

In our busy lives, a luxury experience like this can really make a difference, and with regards to people and environment, Soneva hotels is a company of the future.

25Hours Hotels

I came across this magnificent hotel concept, when I first stayed in the 25hrs Hotel Bikini Berlin. I was intrigued by the design, by the way I was greeted and treated. The innovative hotel company lives by their vision, fun, pleasure and relaxation. Bruno Marti has created this brand with passion since 2006 in the role as chief brand officer. Together with CEO, Michael End, they have created a true experience.

25hours Hotels are sexy, cheeky, bold, innovative, cosmopolitan, unique, charismatic, a little crazy, and locally connected. They stand out in their respective market. With all the creativity and trendiness, our hotel rooms offers both clarity and functionality. We use technology to simplify, not to complicate life.

25hours Hotels are not showrooms. They are for loving, living and lounging around. A crucial part is played by the public areas, which caters for the need of our guests according to the time of the day. These form the heart of the hotel, a workplace for urban nomads, a marketplace for commodities and a starting point for expeditions into the city.

These are some examples of hotel companies who clearly have understood the guest of the future and chosen to work with people who can really make this happen! I am intrigued with the entrepreneurship and skill of attracting knowledge, skill and experience, to deliver something refreshingly different to guests.

Recruiting for the future

In this final part of the book, I want to highlight a few elements that you have already read about earlier in the book. The hospitality has lots to learn from and also to teach to other industries. You have read many examples in this book.

Creating or vitalizing a brand in hospitality does not start with the employees, it starts with leadership. Investing in leadership is the primary reason people will apply to a company and most certainly stay in the company. With the right leadership and management, the company will become a breeding ground for skilled staff.

Clearly all the tools have to be in place to do proper training on company standards, core values and skills that are needed to carry out the jobs that need to be done. Hotels are good at that, they take the job description serious, even before recruitment, however, we should not over complicate it. We hear we hire attitude a lot. I believe over complicating the hiring process with endless forms and interviews actually does quite the opposite. Instead of focusing too much on technical skills, we should focus on emotional intelligence, motivation and energy. You can see that in all the brands that I have mentioned in the book, and in this chapter. The energy and motivation of the people translates directly to the delivery of customer's expectations. The final opportunity lies within keeping people, good people, by promoting them and incentivizing them. All too often, companies are looking into recruiting from outside, while there are lots of opportunities to promote or recruit within the organization. Important is for management and leadership to ensure annual appraisals, which includes questions about the individual's wishes for the future, his or her personal goals and vision, so the company can match this, and educate or re-educate accordingly.

In this book, you have read about how you can be part of keeping our industry the most exciting industry in the world. The book is written to inspire investors, to make leadership think differently, to get people excited to join the industry and to keep magnificent employees in the industry. I aim to educate in an encouraging way, leading to change and development of our exciting hospitality industry.

Acknowledgements

My intentions with the book are to inspire people within and outside the hospitality industry. I have many reasons for writing the book, that are personal and professional. The support of my close family, friends and colleagues have lead me to believe there is so much more to give and share than we sometimes care to. But when we do, we privilege others, like the learnings and experiences I have been given by so many, over all the years in the industry. I can't name all who have inspired me, taught me, supported me, but you know who you are, and I know your favourite drink! Below a list of passionate, innovative, successful and knowledgeable colleagues and partners who have contributed directly to the completion of the book. Thank you!

Adelina Barphe	Vice President – International Food & Beverage Association, Senior Partner Mocinno International
Alexandra Sarantidi	Artist and art curator
Anna Bjurstam	Managing Partner, Raison d'Etre Spas
Are Morch	Social Media Manager, Hotel Blogger
Arnie Weissmann	Chief Editor - Travel Weekly, Editorial director of Northstar Travel Media's Travel Group
Barak Hirschowitz	President of the International Luxury Hotel Association

David Meerman Scott	Online Marketing Strategist
Doug Lansky	Doug Lansky, Tourism Advisor and Keynote Speaker for Destinations around the World
Emma Diacono	CEO Emmadiacono Ltd
Erica Nicole	Founder and CEO, YFS Magazine
Erik Jonsson	CEO Grupo Cappuccino
Frank Braun	Process Management & Optimization WMF AG
Hai Poh Cheong	President of the International Food & Beverage association, Chairman Hospitality Alliance Singapore
Juan Picornell	Owner Grupo Cappuccino
Juliana Cavalcanti De Andrea	Consultant Fashion Industry
Katja Presnal	Chief Editor Skimbaco
Lola Akinmade Äkerlind	Travel Writer & Photographer, Editor in Chief
Lori Katz	Strategic Advisor
Marie Garreau	Owner PR agent Garreau
Nancy Huang	Marketing Manager Travel Tripper
Natali Telichenko	Senior Partner, Mocinno International
Paolo Di Terlizzi	Internet Consultant
Pedro Do Carmo Costa	Director and Co-founder Exago
Rachel Pietersma	CEO Kids Party and Nanny service
Stefanie Patch	Managing Director – Patch Music
Stuart Birkwood	General Manager Le Meridien Abu Dhabi

Partners

| www.4hoteliers.com | Hotel, Travel & Hospitality News. |

| www.yfsmagazine.com | The definitive digital magazine for start-ups, small business and entrepreneurship culture. |
| www.alexandrasdesign.net | Design and drawings for the book |

Company websites
www.mocinno.com
www.designhotelsupplies.com

Social Media

Facebook	https://www.facebook.com/jeroen.gulickx
Instagram	https://www.instagram.com/ jeroen_gulickx/
Twitter	https://twitter.com/MocinnoIntl
Blog	http://www.jeroengulickx.com/
Google+	https://plus.google. com/u/0/+JeroenGulickx/posts
LinkedIn	https://www.linkedin.com/in/ jeroengulickx
YouTube	https://www.youtube.com/channel/ UCLHcZDJBvWo5bLHYPwHY2mQ
Pinterest	https://se.pinterest.com/jeroengulickx/
Facebook Company	https://www.facebook.com/pages/ MocinnoInternational/146004118781784? ref=hl
LinkedIn Company	https://www.linkedin.com/company/ 5320923?trk=tyah&trkInfo=tarId% 3A1409303311749%2Ctas%3Amocinno %2Cidx%3A1-1-1

Printed in the United States
By Bookmasters